VIGILANCE
and
VENGEANCE

ROBERT I. ROTBERG
Editor

VIGILANCE
and
VENGEANCE

*NGOs Preventing Ethnic Conflict
in Divided Societies*

BROOKINGS INSTITUTION PRESS
Washington, D.C.

THE WORLD PEACE FOUNDATION
Cambridge, Massachusetts

Library of Congress Cataloging-in-Publication data

Vigilance and vengeance : NGOs preventing ethnic conflict in divided
  societies / edited by Robert I. Rotberg.
    p. cm.
    Includes bibliographical references and index.
    ISBN 0-8157-7588-1. — ISBN 0-8157-7587-3 (pbk.)
    1. Ethnic relations. 2. Culture conflict—Prevention. 3. Social
  conflict—Prevention. 4. Non-governmental organizations.
  I. Rotberg, Robert I.
  GN496.V54 1996
  305.8—dc20   96-25349
                                                          CIP

                          9 8 7 6 5 4 3 2 1

The paper used in this publication meets the minimum requirements
of the American National Standard for Information Sciences—
Permanence of Paper for Printed Library Materials, ANSI Z39-48-1984.

                    Typeset in Times Roman

                Composition by Linda Humphrey
                      Arlington, Virginia

              Printed by R. R. Donnelley and Sons Co.
                    Harrisonburg, Virginia

Preface

THE GLOBE is awash with ethnic and religious conflict. Nearly 40 million persons have lost their lives in the maelstrom of intergroup bitterness since the end of World War II, at least 5 million since 1990. During the latter period there have been about 150 civil wars and warlike intrastate battles. The wars continue ceaselessly in Africa, Asia, Europe, and Latin America, and even in Oceania.

Ethnic, religious, and cultural fratricide remains a constant global theme. The end of the Cold War unleashed long-suppressed rivalries and hatreds. Now, about thirty civil wars and twenty complex humanitarian crises are active every year. About 50 million people have been forced to flee their homes during the past ten years, including 20 million refugees who fled across borders and 30 million people who have been displaced within their own countries.

Europeans continue to kill Europeans, Asians kill Asians, and Africans kill Africans. In some instances, early warning was timely, but no one listened. In others, however, preventive diplomacy has avoided, limited, or restrained internecine hostilities.

Not all of Europe, Asia, Africa, or Latin America is tense and inflamed by ethnic and religious animosity. In some situations non-governmental organizations (NGOs), local and international, have helped to bring conflicts back from one or more brinks. What lessons about early warning, early action, and preventive diplomacy have been learned?

Discerning those lessons and stanching continuing hostilities around the globe motivated an urgent project sponsored by the World Peace Foundation and the Program on Non-Governmental Organizations of the Harvard Institute for International Development. Could NGOs help peace break out? Could their efforts improve the world's ability to contain ethnic and religious violence through the exercise of preventive diplomacy? In particular, could NGOs contribute to the early warning of conflicts and thus to early action that would reduce their intensity and potentially diminish killings?

A meeting organized by the project's sponsors took place in Cambridge, Massachusetts, in April 1995. Convened exactly a year after the massacres in Rwanda, amid continuing troubles in Burundi and during the lull before the continuing storm in Sri Lanka, the meeting explored the role that NGOs had played and could play in reducing ethnic and religious conflict in troubled countries. Local and international NGOs had made and were making a difference in Burundi, Guatemala, Macedonia, Nigeria, Rwanda, Sri Lanka, and the Sudan—our case studies for this volume. But in each case the influence that local and international NGOs had exerted or were exerting depended on the level and immediacy of the battles in their particular locales. Intervening to reduce hostilities in the Sudan, or in Guatemala, demanded skills that were similar to but not exactly the same as the peacebuilding interventions in South Africa and Sri Lanka and the continuing pre-conflict attention that NGOs were giving to tensions in Macedonia and Nigeria.

The meeting in Cambridge was devoted to both theory and practice and to drawing out the lessons for preventive diplomacy and early warning derived from the cases. The participants in the discussions came from relief and human rights NGOs, both local and international; from diplomatic ranks; from the academy; from the press; and from foundations with interests abroad.

The participants discovered that preventive diplomacy represents a host of efforts on the part of both local and international NGOs, sometimes in concert, often not. Likewise, early warning embraces a kaleidoscope of early, not-so-early, and belated bellringings. In Rwanda those signals were heeded only far too late. In Macedonia and Burundi, early warning has been ample, but killings continue anyway in Burundi. Early warning, however, has not always been followed by effective early action—certainly not in Rwanda or Burundi and perhaps not in the coming days and months in Nigeria.

Theoretical examinations of these concepts and a cautionary survey provided the framework for a discussion of the case studies. The cases represented a combination of failures and successes, of trials and errors, and of different and significant lessons for enhancing the effectiveness of early warning, early action, and preventive diplomacy.

This book includes chapters on preventive diplomacy and the country cases mentioned above. The chapters on preventive diplomacy, the Sudan, Burundi, and Rwanda were written especially for this book and were not presented to the meeting.

Martha A. Chen, director of the Program on Non-Governmental Organizations at the Harvard Institute for International Development, effectively cochaired and organized the April 1995 meeting and project that is the basis for this publication. Our project would not have reached fruition without her wise and intelligent leadership and contributions. Nor would our meeting have been held, a report produced, or this book prepared without the generous support of the United States Institute of Peace, the cooperative efforts of Catholic Relief Services, and the backing of the trustees of the World Peace Foundation.

Emily MacFarquhar was primarily responsible for the writing of the report of our meeting. The organizers were assisted in innumerable and important ways by Missy L. Allen, Carol J. Grodzins, Karen L. Hirschfeld, Moyna Mathias, Stephanie Rupp, and Elke Wisch. Their assistance, as well as the stimulating contributions of all of the participants in the April 1995 meeting, is greatly appreciated. The book was proofread by Carlotta Ribar, and the index was prepared by Julia Petrakis.

Particular recognition should be given to Ann Barger Hannum, who skillfully translated the prose of many of the authors into the readable chapters that follow. She was the primary organizer of the meeting, designed and helped edit the Report, and assisted in the editing of this volume.

R.I.R.
1 June 1996

Contents

Macedonia

Sri Lanka

Nigeria

The Sudan

Rwanda

Burundi

NGOs, Early Action, and Preventive Diplomacy

INTERNATIONAL
PREVENTIVE ACTION

Introduction

Emily MacFarquhar, Robert I. Rotberg, and Martha A. Chen

PREVENTING ETHNIC STRIFE in divided societies is never certain and never easy. Would-be peacemakers, whether insiders or outsiders, governments or NGOs, need to understand fully the roots and political contexts of existing conflicts, as well as to define precisely the nature of challenges posed by particular conflicts, before attempting to intervene or to prescribe cures.

There are two kinds of crises: those likely to blow over and those likely to blow up. The first kind includes quiet, chronic disturbances that do not normally attract international notice and that local communities and indigenous NGOs manage every day. The second encompasses violent outbreaks that require diplomatic or military firefighting. Violent crises also range in intensity from street battles to genocide.

Preventive diplomacy is the concatenation of actions that might be taken to deter disputes from arising between parties, make it more difficult for disputes to escalate into warfare, and limit the spread of any ethnic or other conflicts that do develop into hostilities. As Kalypso Nicolaïdis defines preventive diplomacy in chapter 1 of this book, it is the instrument that "seeks to promote the peaceful settlement of disputes between nations or groups within nations." Preventive diplomacy is what governments do, together or alone, to keep disputes from escalating into warfare.

A similar way of approaching the notion of preventive diplomacy was

3

supplied by Raimo Väyrynen and Janie Leatherman in a paper that they produced for the large meeting out of which this book developed.[1] As described generally in their work, preventive diplomacy is the use of coercive or non-coercive means to avoid, deter, deflect, or reduce conflict. It takes three main forms:

— conflict prevention—averting disputes between states and other parties;

— conflict containment—preventing the horizontal and vertical escalation of hostilities;

— post-conflict conciliation—preventing the reemergence of disputes.

Nicolaïdis offers a similar categorization—the three stages of conflict prevention: early, late, and continuous (or what the United Nations calls post-conflict peacebuilding)—and the charts that accompany her chapter provide a graphic illustration of these differences. She further elaborates helpfully on the barriers against as well as the opportunities for prevention during each of these stages.

Techniques of preventive diplomacy, as elaborated by Nicolaïdis and Väyrynen and Leatherman, include:

— peacebuilding—the removal or reduction of conditions fostering violence between or among groups or states;

— preventive deployment—the interposition of military or observer forces between contending elements;

— mediation—the resolution of disputes before hostilities emerge, or afterward.

Early warning is sounding alarm bells at the right time and in a salutary and appropriate manner. At its most effective, it alerts local and international communities to the likely onset of violence between or among groups or states. It has at least three components: information (which must be accurate); analysis (which must be dispassionate); and communication (which must be accessible and clear). Even so, the concept of early warning is messy, fuzzy, and ambiguous. What if nobody is listening? Or what if people respond and the tocsin turns out to have been sounded prematurely or erroneously?

Early warning, at its most refined, is the apex of an array of indicators, each of which has been assessed, calibrated, and recalibrated. Detecting early warning indicators and weighing their importance require judgment and experience. As UN Secretary-General Boutros Boutros-Ghali has observed, vital indicators are often hidden within an immense volume of inconsequential material.

Yet, when early warning is reliable and persuasive, it can encourage decision-makers to take preventive measures in a timely fashion. Making warnings public increases the transparency of a crisis and creates public expectations and pressures that can encourage governments and international bodies to deter disasters. But publicity can also raise tensions and sometimes lead to the very outcomes that the warnings were intended to avert.

Early warning and conflict prevention are, above all, about politics. Reports of intra-national hostilities are invariably filtered by politicians seeking to manipulate them for partisan ends. NGOs can serve as valuable independent sources of facts. Yet the more tense the confrontation, the more likely it is that NGO efforts to gather information will be viewed as interference. Issuing early warnings can also compromise NGOs' service missions and put field workers at risk.

There are many ways that NGOs respond to early rumblings of conflict: They serve as silent witnesses, thus preserving their neutrality; they are annoying witnesses or bell ringers; and they are political witnesses with a mission to arouse an external response. Indigenous NGOs are the more capable of detecting early warning signs; international NGOs are best placed to encourage external intervention and to channel resources to local partners.

Human rights and famine monitoring provide two models of early warning. Human rights violations are often the first signs of abuse of power and the exacerbation of tensions. Thus calling attention to them is one way of sounding a warning about potential violent conflicts, refugee flows, and internal displacements. During famines, media reports of early indicators raise public expectations and put pressures on governments to act. The more open and the more democratic the state or region, the easier it is for early warnings to be raised, and the more likely that they will be heeded.

The relevance of famine, or even human rights–alerting mechanisms, to conflict warning is limited for two reasons: Famines and human rights abuses can be defined by well-established standards, whereas the work of identifying conflict indicators is just beginning; and, unlike human rights violations, which can be investigated by fact-finding missions, monitoring conflicts requires a long-term presence on the ground and a broad political mandate.

Conflict-prone societies can be identified by key background factors: unequal access to entitlements, social cleavages, and historical grievances. But the presence of one or more of these factors does not inevitably lead to violence. Social stresses are often tolerated as long as political institutions are seen to be legitimate and evenhanded. The breakdown of political legitimacy is both a necessary and a sufficient condition for the slide of a society into turmoil. That is why democracies do better than autocracies at containing conflict.

Assaults on democratic institutions such as a free press and an independent judiciary and on democratic freedoms such as free speech and unimpeded travel are also telltale signs of an incipient crisis. Although different communities have different breaking points, the intensification of intergroup hostility tends to follow certain patterns. Signal flares to watch for include: statements of extreme threat; ritual acts to promote group unity and to legitimize violence; dehumanization of opponents; and the redefinition of political divisions in emotionally charged ethnic, religious, or tribal terms. Accelerators like propaganda, misinformation, rumors, or symbolic violence intensify the impact of triggering events.

Hostilities may be precipitated by an individual who articulates or manipulates ethnic sentiment or by an event such as the assassination of a prominent leader. The start of a destructive spiral is indicated by breakdowns in communication; increasing rigidity of positions; rising levels of hostility; and portrayal of the conflict as a zero-sum game. Other indicators of escalation are fewer or shorter pauses between incidents; increasingly frequent demonstrations; the training or arming of fighting units; and empty streets.

Once negative mechanisms have been activated, the only viable way to prevent conflict may be to create a stalemate to buy time. For conflict management to work, there must at least be some open communications channels, some flexibility of positions, and some acceptance of a rival's legitimacy.

Field diplomacy, a new and untried form of intervention, may assist in the deescalation of conflict in the new era of hostilities.[2] Field diplomacy involves sending non-governmental teams to regions of antagonism for extended periods to stimulate and support local initiatives for peacebuilding and, if necessary, to provide early warning. The aim of field diplomacy is to create a network of trusted persons to monitor the ongoing conflict and to create a favorable climate for generating solutions.

Each conflict is unique. Nevertheless, there are categories of pre-conflict conditions into which NGO and other observers on the ground can sort indicators and precursors. Long lists of generalizable indicators are obviously useful; even more helpful are hierarchal rankings of those same indicators. What are the most reliable indicators of incipient crises? How should NGOs sort the several varieties of warning signs? What are the most sensitive and the most telling precursors, especially in potentially genocidal situations?

Representatives of NGOs, especially those focused primarily on relief but constantly thrust into conflict situations, thirst for such guidelines. This need for clear frameworks and for training was emphasized by a survey of international NGO operations in conflict situations across the globe. It concluded that international humanitarian NGOs had often performed poorly in conflict situations, sometimes inadvertently exacerbating hostilities that they were intent on ameliorating.

As grassroots workers, NGOs are in a position to spot warnings of disaster as well as signals of hope and deescalation. Positive and negative indicators often occur simultaneously. NGOs need to be alert to such complexity and to seek opportunities to accentuate positive developments by exploiting local stocks of social capital, such as local peacebuilders.

For local people to attempt to stem the tide of ethnic rivalry is difficult and dangerous. NGOs can provide support for independently minded individuals who feel silenced by political pressures but are nonetheless ready to take a stand. Local NGOs and international NGOs can both sound the early warning bells. In that way, and also by assisting local individuals working to bring about peace, they can contribute significantly to the deflection, if not the avoidance, of further hostilities. Empowering peacemaking forces is one of the ways in which NGOs can become peacemakers themselves.

This book examines seven humanitarian crises on four continents for lessons applicable to preventive diplomacy, early warning and early action, and peacemaking. Warning lights are on in Nigeria and Macedonia, where ethnic violence remains possible. In Sri Lanka, the Sudan, Guatemala, Rwanda, and Burundi, violence has been chronic for years; all five are studies of the failure of the international community to react in a timely manner, despite warnings issued both early and late. The Sri Lankan case also illustrates the need for, but not the sufficiency of, continuous preventive diplomacy to stop the recurrence of conflicts.

The cases of Liberia and Sierra Leone, which are not discussed in this book, provide contrasting examples. Late preventive diplomacy worked effectively in 1996 in the latter country but not in the former, where the efforts of outside governments, regional consortia, and international

NGOs lurched from failure to failure. In Sierra Leone, determined individual and local NGO activities finally stanched hostilities and even permitted a national election.

In five of the cases, NGOs operate actively and attempt to intervene effectively in zones of continuing ethnic civil insurgency. In the other two, NGOs are attempting to minimize or avoid the imminent outbreak or a renewal of hostilities between antagonistic rivals.

The record of NGO effectiveness in the seven conflict zones discussed in this book is mixed. Warnings were duly conveyed and reconciliation attempted. But nowhere did NGOs have the capacity to compel a response from internal powerholders or an intervention from outside. If issuing warnings without an assurance of action is not only futile but often dangerous, should it be attempted at all?

Rwanda

"We knew," said Alison Des Forges at our meeting in 1995. The problem in Rwanda in 1994 was not one of not knowing, but of not acting. Des Forges's chapter makes that point clearly. Human rights activists in Kigali alerted foreign partners days (even weeks) in advance that a catastrophe was coming, although not even on-site Cassandras could predict the precipitating event—the murder of the country's president in an air crash—or the scale of the killing that followed. What should have been more predictable was the disbelief and unresponsiveness exhibited by the rest of the world.

The cataclysm, in which up to 1 million people died and another 2 million were displaced, was the climax of more than four decades of Hutu-Tutsi hostility. When Rwanda became independent in 1962, minority rule by Tutsi chiefs gave way to Hutu majority governments. Many thousands of Tutsi went into exile in neighboring countries. An abortive Tutsi invasion in 1990 was followed by widespread arrests. In August 1993, an internationally mediated peace accord between the Hutu-led government and Tutsi rebels (attacking from Ugandan bases in the north) was signed and a tiny UN peacekeeping force dispatched.

When Hutu extremists began their killing spree in April 1994, Tutsi exiles invaded again. This time they succeeded in seizing power, setting off a massive flight of Hutu refugees and one of the world's largest, messiest, and most controversial relief operations.

Before Rwanda became synonymous with genocide, it had been a favored child of international development agencies for at least a decade. When repression intensified after the 1990 invasion, local human rights groups started up and collaborated with international NGOs. Relations became close and were based on mutual trust and credibility: "It was like crying on the shoulders of friends," said Monique Mujyawamariya, a Kigali-based local NGO leader who participated in the 1995 meeting. She chose seven foreign partners as the most reliable outlets for her disaster warnings, dropping several dozen others whom she regarded as less than fully committed to her crusade.

Mujyawamariya and her NGO colleagues investigated and publicized atrocities committed by government forces and escorted foreign ambassadors to massacre sites. Sometimes, with the help of humane policemen, she managed to warn prospective victims and save them. Most of the time before April 1994, the aim of her human rights monitoring was to pressure foreign governments into restraining the Rwandan (Hutu-run) regime.

But there was no reaction, as Des Forges's chapter details, until an international commission produced a report on human rights abuses in March 1993. Then the United States redirected its financial aid away from government agencies, channeling it instead through NGOs; Belgium withdrew its ambassador. (The killings stopped when the commission arrived in Kigali and resumed within hours of its departure.)

Diplomatic pressure helped to bring about the Arusha agreement in August 1993 between the Hutu-led government and the Tutsi rebel army, but that concord was quickly repudiated by extremists. The assassination of the Burundian president in October 1993 and the massacre of 50,000 Tutsi that followed evoked no international intervention.

That failure to act sent a message to Rwanda's Hutu militants. They began preparing for a further bloodbath: training militia; distributing arms; and broadcasting hate propaganda. They adjusted their tactics in response to foreign pressures, shifting from using state radio to using a private station for their propaganda and from using the army to using the militia for their killing instruments. They tested international reactions with political killings in early 1994. Again, there was no perceptible response.

The UN Human Rights Commission, presented with a report on Rwandan atrocities, told Human Rights Watch/Africa that it already had too many African countries on its agenda; come back next year, it said.

In March 1994, Mujyawamariya knew that the apocalypse was at hand. She sent her children out of Kigali and warned friends and colleagues to leave. (Three later died with air tickets in their pockets.) Although she was aware that preparations were being made, she still had trouble herself coming to terms with the unimaginable reality of impending genocide. On 24 March 1994, she dictated a three-page fax on the impending catastrophe to Africa Watch, then held it for two days because she worried that it was too alarmist. When the Human Rights Watch director for Africa telephoned on 28 March, again Mujyawamariya had second thoughts: "We all fear looking ridiculous; if hysterical fear is heard with skepticism, it is difficult to cope."[3] Africa Watch took Mujyawamariya's message to Washington, the latest of many that winter. On 7 April, it was the turn of Africa Watch to feel distraught at not having recognized a true prophecy of doom.

About 2,500 UN troops were in place when the killings began. But they were used only to supervise the evacuation of foreign nationals, including international NGO workers. Then the UN, lacking a Security Council mandate, withdrew the troops themselves. Troop commanders later said that it would have taken no more than 200 men to have saved at least the orphans of Kigali.

African NGOs pleaded with the Organization of African Unity (OAU) and with African governments to intervene. The United States promised logistical support, but for three months the Department of Defense and the State Department haggled over how much the logistical items would cost and who would pay for them.

Africa Watch bombarded the Security Council with warnings and pleas. Eventually, it was invited to brief members privately. The Council then voted to send UN troops back to Rwanda, but it was months before they were actually dispatched.

Africa Watch now regrets that it did not try harder to rally public opinion. Sympathetic U.S. officials told them: "Make more noise; we're not feeling the heat."[4]

Rwanda is a dream laboratory to study the pathology of NGOs, said Christian Hennemeyer of Catholic Relief Services (CRS) in Rwanda, who was at the 1995 meeting: "All that knowledge, hard work, and goodwill counted for exactly nothing." The point, he continued, is that "information does not equal action." But neither did it equal preparedness for disaster. Hennemeyer said that in April 1994 there had been "an atmosphere of tempered optimism" among the fifteen international NGOs on the ground, all of them providing relief services or doing development work with local partners.[5]

In 1995 and 1996, the government of Rwanda eased the United Nations and many NGOs out of its country. Reconstruction has proceeded slowly, and reconciliation, in part dependent on the meting out of justice, is more talked about than achieved. The repatriation of Hutu refugees and their reintegration into Rwandan society has occurred only hesitantly and at the margin. NGOs have not managed to play a significant role in continuous peacebuilding despite their critical activity before 1994 and as providers of humanitarian relief.

Burundi

In mid-1996, Burundi is another Rwanda waiting to happen. Burundi lies next door to Rwanda and has a similar ethnic mix. It experienced a forerunner of the Rwandan massacres in the autumn of 1993, when the first Hutu president was murdered and vengeance killings by both Tutsi and Hutu left 50,000 to 100,000 dead. The assassination and its timing were not anticipated, but ethnic strife and violence had been a feature of Burundian life for decades. A massacre in 1972 had claimed 100,000 to 200,000 victims and decimated the Hutu elite.

Since the bloody autumn of 1993, tensions have remained high, punctuated by frequent outbreaks of murderous violence and the displacement of many thousands of people. In 1996, a coalition government barely functions and exerts little control over the Tutsi-dominated army, as Richard Sollom and Darren Kew's chapter makes evident.

A dozen international NGOs, some long-time veterans of Burundi like CRS, and some quick-response groups like Médecins Sans Frontières, have concentrated on emergency relief. The UN High Commissioner for Refugees (UNHCR), UNICEF, the World Food Program, and WHO are also active in Burundi. The indigenous NGO sector is weak, although Caritas Burundi and the Burundian chapter of the Red Cross have been active. Coordination, division of labor, and information sharing among NGOs and UN agencies has been good.

The volatile political situation has been monitored by a UN special representative, an OAU observer mission, a delegate from the European Union, and diplomats from the United States, France, and Belgium. In the expectation of another cataclysm, the international press has watched Burundi closely; violent incidents are widely reported.

International NGOs are not actively involved in ethnic reconciliation or conflict prevention in Burundi except as a byproduct of their human-itarian work. They have no influence on the army or the warring militias who are responsible for most civilian casualties. But, along with the rest of the international community, they have acted as "annoying witnesses," calling attention to a continuing crisis.

The Office of the Special UN Representative has taken the lead in pro-moting negotiations among Burundian politicians. But the church has also been active in urging talks between the majority coalition and the opposition; two Catholic bishops, one Hutu and one Tutsi, serve on a mediating forum that helped to put the interim government in place in late 1994.

Continuing mediation and negotiation have been required to hold this fragile mechanism together. Extremists have remained outside the polit-ical process and are often the cause of breakdowns and killings.

Burundi is an example of a sudden-onset emergency followed by an ongoing crisis or mature emergency. It is in need of continuous response and monitoring. Many of the people who were displaced by the 1993 spasm have been helped to resume normal lives, but, with Hutu killing Tutsi and Tutsi slaughtering Hutu, there are constantly new victims. Fear is pervasive.

The central questions in Burundi are whether there will be genocidal violence and, if so, whether the outside world will intervene. In mid-1996 Burundi remained a subject of intense anxiety. African parliamen-tarians were working with Washington's National Democratic Institute and other NGOs to avert disaster. International NGOs and others were participating in the Washington-based Burundi Policy Forum that func-tioned as an alerting mechanism. An international working group on Burundi was also active in London. Spurred by the United States, a UN task force was also preparing for a possible interposition, whatever the government of Burundi might say.

The Sudan

Civil war has convulsed the Sudan, Africa's largest state, for most of the past four decades. The African Christian peoples of the south, claim-ing forty years of discrimination, seek autonomy or independence from the Sudan's Arab and fundamentalist Muslim government. More than 1 million southerners have died, and 1 million have been displaced in the bitter conflict. The southern way of life has largely been destroyed, and malnutrition and famine have become commonplace.

By 1991, after a struggle renewed in 1983, the rebel movement controlled most of the Southern Sudan. But then the Southern People's Liberation Movement (SPLM) split along ethnic lines, and another destructive conflict erupted. In 1994 and 1995, the Sudanese army took advantage of battles between the southern Dinka and Nuer factions of the SPLM to regain large swaths of territory once held by the united rebel army.

For NGOs, the Sudan represents a chronic and complex humanitarian emergency as well as the conflict resolution crisis discussed in Francis Deng's chapter in this book. Occasional months of relative stability have been followed by longer periods of acute turmoil. Throughout the period, Western NGOs have rushed in to deal with food crises, beginning in 1984, when the northern government could not and would not cope. International NGOs took over the relief effort and set up an early warning system to detect signs of starvation. Spearheaded by church-based groups, NGO efforts then expanded into conflict-torn areas of the South, where they became conduits for information about the progress and destruction of the war.

Fighting escalated sharply in 1987, when northern tribal militia were inducted to fight for the government and were armed with AK-47s. A brief interval of civilian rule ended in 1989, when the Islamic extremist ruler, General Omar al-Bashir, took power as a result of a Libyan-financed coup. Bashir's junta is responsive to the guidance of Hassan al-Turabi, a cleric of deep fundamentalist fervor.

Since 1989, international NGOs and UN agencies have worked in the Southern Sudan under the authority of Operation Lifeline Sudan (OLS) and, more recently, the Nairobi-based Operation Lifeline Sudan, Southern Sector, both of which provide famine relief and attempt to guarantee access to needy civilians. International NGOs have tended to operate in an emergency relief mode, although in recent years a larger share of their funds has been devoted to supporting local food production, promoting barter trade, and rebuilding the Southern Sudan's infrastructure.

Indigenous NGOs were created only after 1991, and their agenda is to assist the shift from relief to development. Both the Sudan Relief and Rehabilitation Association (SRRA), the mainstream SPLM's humanitarian agency, and the Relief Association of Southern Sudan (RASS), of the SPLA-United, were identified by the OLS as the principal bodies charged with coordinating and facilitating aid in southern Sudan. Both are still structurally weak, partisan, and vulnerable to local pressures.

The few international NGOs working in the Southern Sudan before 1991 knew that the rebel Sudan People's Liberation Movement (SPLM) was a ruthless, autocratical movement that was sowing discontent among local people. They did not, however, foresee the violent internecine struggle that ensued. After the split that year, some southerners blamed relief agencies for having provoked it by linking Dr. John Garang, the American-educated leader of the SPLM, to Mengistu Haile Mariam, Ethiopia's ousted Marxist dictator. Others accused NGOs of offending the dignity of the northern Sudanese by eroding their sovereignty. Yet the presence of foreigners in the south may well have prevented an extermination campaign.

Among nonpolitical groups in the Southern Sudan, Roman Catholic and Anglican churches have the best ties to the two insurgency movements, although the ethnic divide between Dinka and Nuer is also reflected in the church. Local churchmen have quietly sought to bring the warring factions together.

Most NGOs and churches still participate in coordination forums at the local level and also cooperate with the humanitarian wings of both southern fighting factions to promote reconciliation. The SPLM, the larger rebel group, manages camps for the displaced and, until recently, controlled much of the humanitarian aid in the Southern Sudan. In such settings, relief cannot be insulated from politics. In 1996, the role of international NGOs continued to be essential, if largely limited to the provision of humanitarian relief. U.S. diplomatic efforts at mediation had not succeeded, largely because the government of the Sudan continued to prefer to isolate itself from much of the rest of the world.

Sri Lanka

For more than a dozen years, civil war has raged in Sri Lanka between the Liberation Tigers of Tamil Eelam (LTTE), a radical Tamil secessionist group, and the largely Sinhalese armed forces. The struggle has left more than 30,000 dead and more than 1 million people displaced. Most of the fighting has taken place in and around the Tamil base area on the northern Jaffna peninsula, but terrorist strikes in Colombo, the country's capital, and elsewhere have killed hundreds of people, including a Sri

Lankan president and half a dozen other Sinhalese political leaders. In 1991, LTTE assassins crossed the Palk Strait separating Sri Lanka from India to murder Prime Minister Rajiv Gandhi in India's southern state of Tamil Nadu, home to 50 million Tamils.

Sri Lanka's is not a story of conflict averted or even conflict contained. But Neelan Tiruchelvam, a leading civil rights campaigner, argues in his chapter that both human rights abuses and his country's humanitarian crises would have been far more acute without the intervention of local and international NGOs. Imaginative and constructive cooperation between local and international human rights organizations prevented severe deprivation among Tamil civilians on the Jaffna peninsula by enabling the International Committee of the Red Cross (ICRC) to deliver relief supplies to the people of that isolated enclave. The ICRC also facilitated a realistic approach to peacemaking by providing a conduit for communications between the two contending sides.

Sri Lanka was the first country in Asia with a true two-party democracy and elections that brought about peaceful transfers of power. But majoritarian democracy also helped to widen the island's ethnic divide between the Buddhist Sinhalese majority (74 percent of the population) and the Hindu Tamil minority (17 percent). In 1956, President Solomon West Ridgeway Dias Bandaranaike, father of the present president, stirred up both Sinhalese nationalism and Tamil resentment with a vote-seeking ploy of declaring Sinhala the country's only official language.

Since then, communal tensions have erupted sporadically, and Tamil protests over discrimination in employment, university admissions, and the use of the Tamil language, have become progressively more militant. In 1983, after the largest-ever communal bloodbath in Sri Lanka, when as many as 3,000 Tamils were said to have been killed, and nearly 60 percent of the Tamils living in Colombo were turned into refugees, the LTTE set out to eliminate less extreme Tamil factions, cut off Jaffna from the rest of the country, and launched a war of unbridled secession.

Three local human rights NGOs began actively documenting abuses and pursuing political solutions in the late 1970s. Even before the onset of all-out war, they proposed constitutional adjustments and alerted political leaders to the need to rectify ethnic inequities. They found minimal support in the Sinhalese community for their activities.

Two other local NGOs provided legal aid to political prisoners and formed linkages with Amnesty International, Human Rights/Asia (Asia Watch), and the International Commission of Jurists, which publicized their findings. This led to a resolution on Sri Lanka in the UN Human Rights Commission in 1986, calling for peacemaking and inviting in the ICRC.

In 1987, international criticism jolted the Sri Lankan government into signing an accord with India that promised political devolution and full civil rights for Tamils, and gave the go-ahead to an Indian army operation that was intended to put down the Tamil insurgency.

India's military intervention was a high-cost, high-casualty, atrocity-laden failure that hardened Sri Lankan government attitudes toward India and toward the Tamil rebels. Subsequent offers of foreign mediation were rejected. But international agencies performed critical services that local NGOs were barred from providing. The ICRC visited prisoners, traced missing persons, ensured the passage of food and medicine to Jaffna, and transmitted confidential messages between the Tamil Tigers and the government. Sri Lanka also became the first place where the UNHCR extended its mandate to assist not only refugees but also peoples internally displaced.

None of this ICRC or UNHCR activity would have happened without the advocacy and documentation of local NGOs, supplemented for some time by local citizens' committees. But it also would not have happened if the Sri Lankan government had been wholly repressive and had not operated within at least minimal democratic constraints.

Imperfect democracy in which majoritarianism overrode protection for minority rights was a cause of Sri Lanka's civil war; it accentuated minority grievances and threatened their identity. Yet democracy also permitted NGOs to operate. In late 1994, the election of a new national government, with a mandate to talk to the Tamil Tigers, offered the best prospects of a peace settlement for over a decade. Both sides agreed on a truce, while government negotiators met LTTE representatives for talks about talks. Local NGOs seized the moment to launch a peace movement.

But by mid-1996, despite governmental concessions, including a reopening of land routes to the north and a reconstruction effort in Jaffna, the peace initiative had failed. Numerous government troops had been killed by LTTE attacks in violation of the ceasefire, the government had retaliated with heavy assaults to gain control of Jaffna and the northern peninsula, and LTTE operations had moved from the far north to the northeast coast. Negotiations were stillborn. In mid-1996, the civil war continued unabated. NGOs resumed their still frustrated and largely fruitless search for ways in which to intervene constructively.

Guatemala

Apart from a decade of reformist government from 1944 to 1954, which was ended by a U.S.-supported military coup, Guatemala's modern history is characterized by dictatorial rule. There have been two phases of NGO activity, punctuated by severe internal conflict: the 1976 earthquake and its aftermath; and the mid-1980s to mid-1990s, when a gradual democratization allowed the creation of an indigenous NGO network.

Before the earthquake, only a few North American and European NGOs had programs in Guatemala. Dozens more arrived to work on earthquake relief and reconstruction, among them Save the Children groups from seven countries. Breaking with a tradition of independent action, these seven fused their resources and staffs to form a Save the Children Alliance, known locally as Alianza, with the Norwegian representative as coordinator.

In response to a growing activism among Mayan workers and farmers and a growing guerrilla insurgency, a new cycle of official violence and repression began. In late 1980, Alianza was forced to close down its Joyabaj and Southern Quiché programs after a local priest was assassinated and relatives of local staff members were killed by government death squads. Other international NGOs in the Chimaltenango region—Oxfam, Norwegian Church Aid, and World Neighbors—left the country. These were warnings that helped to move President Carter's administration to cut off military aid to Guatemala. But when NGOs and churches produced reports of further atrocities in the early 1980s, there was no international response.

The counter-insurgency campaign of the early 1980s left 75,000 dead and 440 villages destroyed. The election of Guatemala's second civilian president in 1985 created a new climate in which NGOs had limited freedom to pursue labor issues, land reform, and human rights. Two kinds of NGOs sprang up: Popular organizations, aiming at righting political and economic injustice; and Mayan groups, formed to promote Mayan rights and preserve Mayan culture. Mayan groups came together under an umbrella Council of Mayan Organizations. Human rights, labor, and peasant organizations set up a coalition called the Popular Action Syndicate (UASP) to mount demonstrations, lobby the legislature, share information and skills, and link up with international NGOs. Among its members were an urban human rights group, Grupo de Apoyo Mutuo (GAM), which documented disappearances and lobbied for the prosecution of those responsible; a widows' mutual aid organization,

CONAVIGUA; a Mayan peasant organization (CUC), which occupied farms and fought for the dissolution of the army's feared Civilian Self-Defense Patrols (PACs); and another anti-PAC group, CERJ, that took its charges against the PACs to the Inter-American Human Rights Court.

Among the targets of the PACs were NGOs. The military believed that NGOs sympathized with the insurgents. NGO activists were accordingly harassed, threatened, and murdered. Demands for the abolition of PACs were endorsed by the UN Commission on Human Rights, but civilian governments at first hardly dared to curb the patrols. Still, under a third civilian president, elected in 1993, the opportunities for NGOs to operate were expanded and democratic institutions, such as the constitutional court and a human rights ombudsman, were strengthened. The president ruled that NGOs were no longer to be described as "subversive."

In 1996 Guatemala has an estimated 700 local NGOs, mostly small, community-based groups. But severe limits on their ability to operate remain. A culture of distrust stops them from sharing reports with one another and with foreigners about potential violence. An erratic telephone system and electricity supply also prevent the timely transmission of information. Amnesty International and Americas Watch keep in contact with Guatemalan counterparts, but verifying indigenous reports is difficult because of restrictions on travel and a continuing climate of fear.

Until there is both greater mutual confidence among NGOs in Guatemala and a withdrawal of the military and their PACs from rural areas, it would have been premature for NGOs to have contemplated an early warning system, writes Rachel McCleary in her chapter. In other words, early warning is not feasible until it is no longer needed.

In Guatemala, that absence of need may conceivably have arrived in early 1994, with the signing of the Global Accord on Human Rights between the government and the rebels. The accord called for the immediate verification of human rights in the country on the part of the United Nations. Mediated by the United Nations, and called "irreversible" by the chief mediator, the accord opened the way for a final peace agreement that was due to be signed in September 1996.

Macedonia

Ethnic tensions continue to run high in this former Yugoslav republic of 2 million people—so high that Violeta Petroska Beška of the Ethnic

Conflict Resolution Project in Skopje sees a possibility of conflict even more consuming than the struggle in nearby Bosnia. Yet, while fear of ethnic violence between Macedonian Slavs and Macedonian Albanians is a part of everyday life, the terrible example of Bosnia gives people pause. External threats to Macedonia's five-year-old nationhood from Greece, Bulgaria, and Albania exert a similarly sobering effect. Another explanation advanced to explain the preservation of fragile peace is national character: The same passivity and fatalism that has blocked the building of civil society in Macedonia seems to have retarded the escalation of ethnic disputes into violence.

Profound mutual mistrust has led to an almost complete separation of the two main ethnic groups, the Macedonians (67 percent) and the Albanians (23 percent). This separation, in turn, lessens the likelihood of random clashes' igniting a conflagration. Ethnic hostility in eastern Europe is often an expression of other post-communist discontents. It is rooted more in history than in economics; although Albanians are mostly poorer than Macedonians, even well-off Albanians feel discriminated against. Local NGOs, like all other institutions in this new nation, are divided along ethnic/religious lines; very few are currently working to lower tensions or restore trust. Those groups that are engaged in such work tend to be organizationally weak and under-financed. They welcome financial support from international NGOs but are wary of their intentions.

Mistrust is endemic in Macedonian society, as is an aversion to authority, both legacies of the communist years. The "other" is automatically an object of suspicion. Foreigners are assumed to be pursuing hidden agendas or serving as agents of their governments, or both. NGOs may also be also tarred by association with the government, which has to approve their projects, as Eran Fraenkel warns in his chapter. On the other hand, those NGOs which receive official support for relief or humanitarian work are the best placed to promote democratic values. The sheer numbers of international NGOs that have crowded into Macedonia in the past three years constitutes an early warning of impending crisis.

The outside agencies with the most influence are the UN and the Organization for Security and Cooperation in Europe (OSCE), agencies which have engaged in mediating ethnic conflicts and negotiating agreements between opposing communities.

In this suspicious setting, NGOs have had to collaborate in public, transparent ways so as to avoid charges of having hidden agendas. They also have had to be very careful about information sharing with diplomats. Yet USAID-funded NGOs have no choice but to keep the local USAID director and the American embassy informed, as Fraenkel notes.

For NGOs in Macedonia, the advantages of formal information-sharing arrangements would not offset the risks, unless there were an assurance of responsive action—something no government would or could provide. Fraenkel, director of Search for Common Ground in Macedonia, concludes that the most sensible course for NGOs is to explore informal information sharing, not only among themselves and with the local diplomatic community, but also with NGOs in neighboring countries that pose threats to Macedonia.

Petroska Beška proposes a division of labor among NGOs, with local ones tackling ethnic conflict at the grassroots level, while international agencies focus on problems with neighboring countries and deal with the central government. She also urges international agencies to lend support, money, and training to local groups. Locals will judge foreign partners by whether they are truly independent of their governments. Trust has to be built up over time. She suggests that sustained action will be necessary to reestablish communication between the Macedonians and the Albanians and to dispel stereotypes and misapprehensions. Collaboration between indigenous and international NGOs would facilitate such a process.

Nigeria

Ethnic and religious divisions are sharper in Nigeria today than at any time since Biafra's secessionist war in the late 1960s. Those divisions are compounded by a collapsing economy, high levels of corruption, wholesale official abuses of power, and the snuffing out of democracy by the ruling military junta. Additionally and dangerously, these societal strains are for the first time being reflected in the ranks of the army. Ethnic violence capable of embroiling the entire country of 100 million may very well erupt first in the army and then spread to the rest of the nation.

Although ethnicity exercises a pervasive influence on social relations in Nigeria, there were only occasional, localized ethnic clashes in the two decades after the Biafra war. But a political crisis, incited by the cancellation of the presidential election of 1993, has now turned into an ethnic struggle that pits northern Islamists allied to the military junta against southerners, many of whom are Christians or animists.

Nigeria has several active human rights groups, mostly Lagos-based, among them the Constitutional Rights Project (CRP), which pursues a lonely, non-political course. Some of the local groups do not even have working telephones and are in need of technical assistance and training. The local press is closed, intimidated, or self-censoring.

CRP and other local NGOs gave early warning of the government's anti-democratic intentions in the period leading up to the 1993 vote and then led massive demonstrations after General Ibrahim Babangida annulled the apparent victory of Moshood Abiola, one of two presidential candidates that he himself had handpicked. Protests continued after another military takeover later in the same year, by General Sani Abacha. Since then, as human rights violations have worsened, and as Melissa Crow and Clement Nwankwo's chapter documents, local human rights groups have adopted a strategy of "mobilization of shame," targeting foreign governments, oil companies, the UN, and the press in a campaign to embarrass the Nigerian government into restoring democracy.

In 1995, the CPR filed suit in the Lagos High Court, seeking to compel the junta to hand over power. Human Rights Watch/Africa, Amnesty International, and the International Commission of Jurists echoed this call. In 1995, Transafrica Forum set out to mobilize Americans, particularly African-Americans, about Nigeria, on the model of its crusade against apartheid in South Africa. A roundtable of international NGOs is also focusing on Nigeria, including representatives of the AFL-CIO, the U.S. labor union. But there is no sign yet of common cause between human rights groups and developmental organizations.

Human rights NGOs are urging international diplomatic intervention and a tightening of sanctions on Nigeria's military regime, particularly in the wake of the hangings of Ken Saro-Wiwa and other Ogboni activists in 1995, and the country's continued defiance of the international community and the British Commonwealth of Nations. Internally, the government has continued to jail more dissidents and discharge military officers who appear to oppose the continued leadership of Abacha.

Notes

1. The title of the lengthy Väyrynen and Leatherman paper was "Early Warning and the Prevention of Intranational Conflict." It is not included in this volume. Mary B. Anderson also wrote a paper, "The Experience of NGOs in Conflict Intervention:

Problems and Prospects," that is not included in this volume but that informed the opening pages of this introduction.

2. The notion of field diplomacy was introduced by several persons at the meeting that preceded the book. None of the chapters in this book discusses field diplomacy by name, but its existence is implicit in the chapters by Tom Lent and Alison Des Forges.

3. From notes of the 1995 meeting.

4. Meeting notes.

5. Meeting notes.

CHAPTER ONE

International Preventive Action:
Developing a Strategic Framework

Kalypso Nicolaïdis

CASSANDRA'S FATE was to live with the knowledge that her doomsday predictions would always come true but would never be believed. But even if she had been believed, would Troy not have fallen anyway? Preventing deadly conflicts requires foresight, warning, and action. This book is about the interplay among these and asks who should be the Cassandras of this "new world order" and what initiatives are necessary to overcome Apollo's curse. The aim of this chapter is to situate this set of questions inside the overall debate on preventive diplomacy—international preventive action—and to suggest the broad outlines of an integrated strategic framework for effective prevention.

The end of the Cold War seems to have dispelled in many minds the fear of a global apocalyptic conflict. At the same time, the mushrooming of deadly conflicts within the confines of nation states, the flows of refugees, and the regional destabilization and economic and environmental devastation that ensue have led to growing calls for the international community to intervene more systematically to prevent or manage domestic conflicts. Yet, it seems safe to predict that states will continue to hold competing claims over territory, resources, and hegemonic status, and that traditional diplomacy will continue to concentrate on preventing interstate conflicts.

Both the motivation and the institutional underpinning for intrastate preventive action are still very much lacking. Without a credible threat of conflict propagation or an unbearable humanitarian crisis, public opinion does not, on the whole, support the massive expansion of resources that would be necessary for world order to cope with intrastate conflicts. The development of accepted norms and institutional capacity for intervention in internal conflicts is still at an embryonic state.

In the wake of the crises in Kurdistan, Somalia, and Bosnia, the UN notion of a "threat to international peace and stability" which justifies collective action has been stretched to include situations that do not cross borders but require humanitarian assistance. The underlying theory behind such cautious normative evolution is that state sovereignty can be partially bypassed only as a state stops fulfilling the basic responsibilities and functions that go along with sovereignty. Preventive action is one step removed from such a grounding. It is called for, by definition, when a dispute or a crisis has not reached its peak, and may not have even started to lead to institutional breakdown. The earlier the intervention, the harder it is to establish the link and the greater the burden of proof for legitimate intervention. Thus, one of the most widely shared precepts of human experience, that prevention is better than a cure, is bound to be highly contested when it comes to applying it to the prevention of intrastate conflicts by the international community.

In the UN's 1992 *Agenda for Peace*, UN Secretary-General Boutros Boutros-Ghali defines preventive diplomacy as "actions to prevent disputes from arising between parties, to prevent existing disputes from escalating into conflict and to limit the spread of the latter when they occur."[1] Stated in positive terms, preventive diplomacy seeks to promote the peaceful settlement of disputes between nations or groups within nations. Preventive diplomacy is that part of preventive action undertaken by governments acting in concert or individually that keeps the disputes that arise between or within nations from escalating into armed force and violence. International preventive action is a broader notion that includes tools that are not targeted at particular disputes and actors beyond governments. An international prevention regime would designate actions, norms, or institutions that strengthen all alternatives to violent conflicts.

After Boutros-Ghali called for systematic efforts in preventive diplomacy in the *Agenda for Peace*, he obtained a mandate from the Security Council to give priority to preventive diplomacy and peacekeeping. Four years later, it is not only the sobering tone of the *Supplement* to the *Agenda for Peace* that gives cause for cautious reassessment. Neither the creation of a UN Department of Political Affairs to centralize functions related to these activities, nor the proliferation of non-governmental initiatives to analyze and promote international conflict prevention, has really started to bear fruit.[2] To be sure, stunned by the shame of their helplessness with regard to Yugoslavia, the European Union (EU) and the Organization for Security and Cooperation in Europe (OSCE) have engaged in a multi-tiered approach to prevention in Eastern and Central Europe. But these initiatives are still in their infancy.

Intrastate conflict prevention, nevertheless, is bound to be at the heart of twenty-first-century international diplomacy, if only because the outcome of domestic conflicts will reconfigure the international system itself. The whole construction of the UN system and of international networks of cooperative arrangements since World War II can be seen as a grandiose scheme to prevent the scourge of war at the interstate level. To what extent can this model be transposed to deal with civil wars rooted in ethno-nationalism and the escalation of inter-group conflict within states?

The threat and use of force, on the one hand, and traditional diplomatic intervention on the other, will undoubtedly continue to play a role in preventing internal conflicts, but they have obvious limits. There is a great range of other actors and actions that can serve a preventive aim in complementary or alternative ways. For example, the recent success stories resulting from OSCE intervention point to the promise of a new kind of active mediation by global, regional, or local organizations. The incentive of promised institutional membership gives the EU added leverage in its preventive efforts. Increasingly, organizations that deal with crises related to violent conflict stress the need to address underlying causes in cooperation with local actors, in particular, "moderates," who constitute the most reliable as well as the most vulnerable beacons for the peaceful resolution of conflicts. Prevention can rely on a better use of existing international instruments, from the enforcement of human rights to the targeting of development aid, or on the design of new instruments, such as adaptable approaches to minorities' rights enforcement. Similarly, NGOs operating in emergency situations look for ways in which they might have been able to help avert the crisis, either by having expanded the scope of their proven methods or by having devised new approaches. At the core of the prevention challenge is the question of how best to articulate and coordinate these disparate dimensions.

The extensive experience accumulated in other fields, from public health and the prevention of diseases or epidemics, to the prevention of accidents, fires, or pollution, points to a number of important lessons which can be replicated in the realm of conflict prevention, even if metaphorically. By definition, preventive action needs to be more systematic and must cast a wider net than curative action: False positives are required to avoid false negatives. Second, progress in preventive medicine has often meant unlinking prediction and prevention. Third, when the target of prevention depends in part on free volition, the most effective approaches seek a balance between providing incentives, blueprints, and capacities for choosing the desired alternatives.

The following does not present a theory of prevention effectiveness. Rather, the aim is to suggest an analytical framework for thinking about the relationship between various types of prevention and their relative effectiveness, and to suggest some hypotheses, the most noteworthy of which is that "blind prevention"—that is, prevention independent of prediction—is likely to be the most cost-effective approach for the international community. This calls for three types of focus: 1) prevention of recurring conflict, at the post-conflict reconstruction stage; 2) prevention through systemic application of institutionalized rules and procedures, which apply to all like a "conflict vaccine"; and 3) development of a capacity and standard procedures for rapid reaction—be it through force or counter-propaganda—once a conflict has started to escalate.

A prerequisite for increasing the effectiveness of international preventive action must be to take criticisms of the idea seriously. Prevention advocates need to accept the challenges of their critics. Yet, these criticisms do not have the same relevance at each of the stages of the conflict cycle which prevention targets. This should be kept in mind when examining alternative tools for prevention, as illustrated by a schematic analysis of the landscape of preventive action that distinguishes paradigmatic approaches according to two criteria: whether they focus on changing the incentives or the capacities of the actors for turning to alternatives to deadly conflicts; and whether the approach is taken on an ad hoc or systemic basis. Such a typology allows us to deepen the widely used distinction between addressing short-term versus root causes of conflicts. It points to two directions for broadening the scope of conflict prevention: internalization within and generalization across countries.

With such a conceptual framework in place, we can ask specific questions: What is the comparative advantage of NGOs and how can they best collaborate with governments? What is or should be the role of early warning in international preventive action, and what should be the role of NGOs in providing what types of early warning? Under what conditions should NGOs be involved in formulating and even in helping to implement responses to early warning? More important, to what extent does prevention require early warning at all, and what can be done to strengthen the prediction-free dimension of prevention?

The Critiques of Prevention: Delusion, Perversion, and Diversion

The first step in promoting any grand idea whose implementation involves significant efforts and resources is to acknowledge its critics. Actually, many advocates will themselves complain that conflict prevention is "just" a new fad with little operational relevance and cite that "prevention has come to mean everything and nothing," or means "something different to every person." But there is little acknowledgment of the substantive criticisms of prevention; where they are mentioned, they are often too easily dismissed. A holistic program of conflict prevention involving a plethora of actors and a radical change of norms and operating procedures for governmental and non-governmental actors and agencies requires taking the rhetoric of anti-prevention seriously.[3]

The Delusion Thesis

The first type of argument against investing in conflict prevention is straightforward. We are deluding ourselves if we think we can foresee future chains of events and design actions to prevent them. Accordingly, attempts at prevention will not make a difference. The idea that the humanitarian tragedies of Somalia, Rwanda, or the Balkans could have been averted at little cost or risk is wishful thinking. In other words, "we neither know what nor how to prevent." Even while analysis and experience may enable us to identify factors making violent conflict more likely to happen in certain places, there will always be enough unpredictable factors—starting with the actions of individuals—to make attempts at prediction futile. This becomes all the more true the further we move from structural explanations of conflict and the more we believe that triggering factors are their principal determinants.[4] Moreover, even if we could gather credible information about impending conflicts, we would never be capable of deriving prescriptions from prescience. There is no satisfactory blueprint for intervening effectively in national ethnic conflicts.

Alongside this challenge to validity is the challenge of collective action. Even if we could determine in advance what an effective preventive course of action should be, we would not be capable of mobilizing the resources necessary to implement it. In order to persuade public opinion of an action whose measure of success is that nothing happens, the counterfactual needs to be plausible and terrible. Any kind of prevention—be it in medicine or in equipment safety—runs against the challenge of having to justify costs with respect to accidents that have not yet happened. In the international arena, this fundamental barrier is compounded by several factors: Those asked to bear the costs are not themselves the target of prevention, potential remedies vary too much across cases to be administered in a systematic manner, and the data-set on internal conflicts is neither extensive enough nor homogeneous enough to support persuasive before-and-after statistical demonstration of the cost effectiveness of prevention. Moreover, and paradoxically, too much preventive activism can lead to a collective "cry wolf" syndrome—warnings multiply, but "nothing" happens, and costly measures to increase preparedness turn out (or so it seems) to be unnecessary. Thus, when intervention is needed, the guard is down. In an era of increased introvertedness, prevention is not a good candidate for international activism. Prevention is wishful thinking, a waste of resources, and simply a delusion.

The Perversion Thesis

The second argument goes one step further than the first, stressing that prevention not only is unlikely to work but is actually likely to exacerbate the crisis. Intervening in potentially violent processes that we do not understand may have unintended consequences and perverse effects. It is likely to bring about what it is trying to prevent. Proposing actions to avoid or contain a developing crisis could trigger it. In other words, "acting, even with good intentions, can always backfire." Foreseeing conflict would become a self-fulfilling prophecy. Cassandras are ignored not for reasons of indifference but for fear—a healthy fear!—that even to listen is to invite the catastrophe. In volatile situations, warnings can sound like provocations or invitations to retaliate; incidents cited as warnings in a report can be magnified through manipulation by partisan media or in public pronouncements and be used as propaganda tools by one party. Some parties may interpret preventive action as a means of ostracizing their community and weakening their cause. Early warning may lead the targeted community precipitously to flee before any preventive actions solutions have been attempted.

If preventive action is perceived as serving the cause of only one party, chances are that the tensions will escalate. The risk of perverse effects may be heightened by NGOs' attempts to practice preventive diplomacy, as such attempts may often run afoul of governmental attempts at peacemaking. The lack of accountability of NGOs may lead them to take action in ways that benefit a particular group rather than a society as a whole. In seeking to prevent harm to their local clients, NGOs may, in fact, increase overall tensions.

Another variant of the perversion thesis may be that even if prevention succeeds in averting escalation in the short run, it is detrimental in the long run. This argument reflects the inherent status quo bias of conflict prevention, since prevention may merely delay the need to resolve deep societal divisions. Because not all parties may benefit from the diffusion of conflicts at an early stage, attempts to reach peaceful settlements may plunge societies into states of "suspended conflict." Preventive action may simply mistake unstable equilibria for resolution. The very process of development, the redrawing of lines between groups and classes within societies, and the political transitions from authoritarian or military regimes to civilian rule are fraught with conflicts—conflicts that act as the necessary mechanisms for redesigning the social contract. As underlined in a recent indictment of preventive diplomacy, a focus on prevention ignores the role that conflict plays in driving political change in societies. Grievances must be vocalized and sometimes amplified into conflict. Conflicts must be intensified before they are resolved.[5] In short, not all conflicts need to be avoided. In some cases, the challenge is to let a conflict emerge and unfold, while guarding against its most violent expressions and dealing with its side-effects. To be effective, intervention—either through coercion or mediation—must be introduced when the conflict is "ripe," when it has run its course so that the parties have an incentive to seek a peaceful resolution.[6]

The belief in perverse effects is a powerful deterrent to potential external intervenors. As stressed in the supplement to *Agenda for Peace*, this is the reason why states are often reluctant to accept preventive action in a conflict to which they are party or potential party. The very act of engaging in prevention, especially at a very early stage, locks in external intervening actors by increasing their stake in a conflict's resolution.

More generally, the weight of the perversion argument is due in part to the fact that policy-makers are usually more concerned about Type I errors—expanding resources to do something, with a risk of negative consequences—than about Type II errors—not doing something, with a probability of positive consequences. Type I errors are usually much more visible, and specific individuals, governments, and agencies are accountable for them.

In short, external intervention to forestall an internal conflict is often likely to exacerbate it by defining it, tipping the scales, or delaying necessary adjustments. And the cost of "perverse" intervention is higher than that of the foregone benefits of successful prevention.

The Diversion Thesis

The third set of arguments shifts the focus away from the feasibility or effectiveness of prevention. It argues, instead, that while prevention may be desirable in and of itself, a greater emphasis on international preventive action involves unacceptable costs to the system of international cooperation as a whole because of the tradeoffs that it induces. In other words, the money and energy could be better spent elsewhere. From the point of view of governments concerned with safeguarding traditional national interests, an emphasis on ethnic conflict prevention diverts energy away from their main missions. Preventive activism can ultimately be destabilizing if it involves muddling distinctions between external actions to protect vital and non-vital interests.

Prevention may also divert investment away from competing goals by becoming a "must" of development action. United Nations agencies do a lot well. Why should they need to attach the conflict prevention label to their activities? The *Agenda for Peace* asks that the Economic and Social Council provide reports on economic and social developments that may, unless mitigated, threaten international peace and security. Does this request imply that if such developments do not threaten international peace, but "only" constitute humanitarian disasters, that they should constitute lower priorities? There is already a sense that security and peacekeeping are increasingly attracting more resources and efforts than the socio-economic activities of the UN. The focus on prevention makes this paradoxically more pernicious. On the one hand, it does emphasize the causal link between the socio-economic conditions prevailing within countries and their contribution to world security and, conversely, the likelihood that these countries will eventually require peacekeeping operations. On the other hand, a focus on conflict prevention implies a new kind of biased approach to dealing with undesirable socio-economic conditions. Some, for instance, see the risk that development projects will not be supported for the sake of development but rather for the extent to which they prevent conflict. In doing so, there will be a diversion of resources away from countries possibly more worthy of their benefits. A country that is more likely to make good use of funds, but that has fewer downside risks, will be overlooked in favor of a country that may squander the same resources but that has a higher risk of conflict. In the same vein, NGOs whose main function is emergency response may endanger themselves by becoming involved in prevention, with much less tested, uncertain results.

In short, whether for governments, UN agencies, or NGOs, the opportunity cost of preventive action is simply too high, given the potential diversion of resources away from other worthy missions, countries, and recipient groups.

Taken together, these arguments against strengthened international norms, tools, and institutions for conflict prevention require at least that we do not assume that preventive action is always desirable but that we ask, instead: Under what conditions is it desirable? Second, these arguments imply that making decisions about which tools to use for preventive action involves difficult tradeoffs that must be assessed on a case-by-case basis. Finally, these arguments remind us that for those involved in prevention in the international arena, humility is in order.

Assessing Requirements for Preventive Action: The Conflict Prevention Cycle

The customary approach to defining preventive action operationally is through a categorization of different phases to be addressed in the cycle of conflict. In the field of public health, preventive actions are generally categorized according to the phase of the accident cycle or the disease cycle. Primary prevention involves minimizing the number of accidents or illnesses. In medicine, this is the goal of immunizations and vaccines. Secondary prevention minimizes the gravity of such accidents or illnesses, and of the side and after effects. In medicine, it includes early detection and cure. Tertiary prevention minimizes the recurrence of accidents or illnesses.

Similarly, intrastate conflict prevention can be viewed as occurring during three different phases. First, early preventive action consists of intervening in latent conflicts, where disputes have not yet escalated into violent outbreaks. This is sometimes called "conflict prevention," as contrasted with preventive diplomacy. Intervention at this phase attempts to prevent disputes from turning into conflicts. Late preventive action occurs when hostilities have already broken out, and when international action is aimed at controlling escalation or managing deescalation. It refers both to vertical escalation into increasingly violent conflict and the horizontal spread of conflicts across national boundaries. In the field of conflict resolution, intervention at this stage is usually referred to as conflict management. Finally, continuous preventive action, or what the UN now refers to as post-conflict peacebuilding, seeks to prevent conflicts from recurring where they have already taken place.[7] To some extent, one can argue that all early preventive diplomacy is also continuous, in that some version of the conflict at hand has at some point in the past already escalated into violent conflict. Here, continuous prevention is restricted to situations in which the prevention is incorporated into an actual reconstruction effort—that is, where managing reconstruction and prevention are intimately related.

What are some of the barriers to, as well as the opportunities for, prevention present at each of these stages?

Early prevention occurs, by definition, when tensions have not yet materialized into open conflict or, at least, when a conflict has not shown signs of violence. At this level, prevention can address three sets of factors: structural causes of tension in a society, the existing institutional capacity to deal with such tensions, and the search for solutions to specific disputes around specific issues. At this stage, prevention can either maximize or minimize the risk of resource diversion. There is a weak link between investment of resources by outside parties and conflict avoidance, and the assessment of prevention needs is likely to be broad and diffuse. At the same time, obviously, early investment can save greater costs later.

The core barrier as articulated in the delusion thesis has to do with identifying the need for prevention itself, distinguishing, in particular, between situations where conflicts are likely/unlikely to erupt into violence. In discussing the causes of violent conflict, it is customary to distinguish between the structural background, on the one hand, and escalatory dynamics, on the other. (This is not the place to discuss the types of conflict nor interactions among sources of conflict.)

FIGURE 1-1. The "Prevention Cycle"

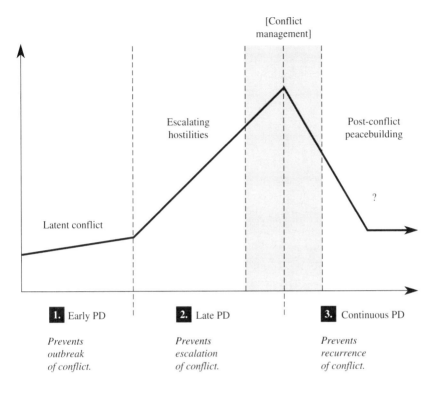

a. PD = preventive diplomacy.

Structural factors generally encompass those which amplify societal conflicts over tangible or symbolic resources such as economic decline, ethnic cleavage, environmental degradation, and governmental repression and corruption. The assault on or lack of democratic institutions is certainly one of the core determinants of a potential for violent conflict. In Africa, for instance, conflicts are associated with the traumatic evolution linked to state formation and nation building, complicated by colonial intervention and post-colonial policies and responses.[8] The manipulation of state institutions to channel power, wealth, and employment opportunities to one group, or rather to the elite members of a single group, creates almost inexorably a level of popular discontent that can be ignited at any time. A wide or growing gap in political participation and economic distribution based on racially, ethnically, or religiously determined forms of identity provides the context for internal conflict. But such patterns do not necessarily lead to violent conflict. Structural factors point to conflict-prone societies (societies at risk), but may or may not lead to the breakdown of political legitimacy, the collapse of the state, and/or civil war. Whether the underlying sense of injustice can be addressed short of a breakout of violence, or, conversely, whether it will be exploited for political gain, depends to a great extent on the makeup of national elites and the relative weight of mass vs. elite factors in the causes of civil wars and ethnic conflicts.[9]

A group's increased demands for recognition by the state as well as by other groups is a general feature of modernity. Even in well-established Western democracies it can produce a fundamental tension between the need for indiscriminate participation in the national creed and the desire for differentiated treatment.[10] Nation building—or at least the prospect of mass participation, if not all-out democratization—contributes to making the politics of identity acute in nations in transition. This is all the more true when a hegemonic group in power refuses that recognition. Group identity and loyalty increasingly translate into political demands—resisted by a group in power—as soon as an intellectual and political space opens up for such demands to be expressed. The space may be created by decolonization, the stepping up or the end of the Cold War, and external power involvement in internal events.

These observations, however, are too general to constitute operational warning. Early warning involves reading specific indicators as signals and patterns of signals, and translating those patterns into some kind of prediction about the likelihood of the emergence or escalation of conflict. It requires an extensive understanding of and sustained interaction with local histories and realities. Early warning also requires a capacity to track emerging disputes and assess, on the basis of underlying factors, their potential for conflict. The primary task involved in systematizing the use of early warning for conflicts will be to establish shared standards for translating such understanding into operational information.[11] The challenge for early warning systems is not so much in identifying societies at risk, in general, but in recognizing patterns of change that will lead to the acceleration of conflicts. Operational warning implies an ability to spot change very rapidly and to publicize trends rather than snapshots.[12]

Responses to warning at an early stage must take into account the risk of the perverse effects of prevention. This means distinguishing between "good" and "bad" conflicts, where the former, even if violent, may be preferable to the status quo. It also means undergoing a systematic assessment of how alternative courses of action are likely to change the incentives of relevant actors. It becomes important to distinguish between alternative roles on the basis of potential perverse effects. The tasks of warning, policy formulation, and implementation often need to be separated. Thus, warnings may emanate from the actual or potential victims of a conflict, while recommendations for action may require a second tier actor with a reputation for impartiality in the conflict at stake. Regional organizations may prove more effective by bringing parties together over less conflictual issues than by attempting to mediate highly conflictual disputes.[13] International fact-finding and monitoring missions often need to operate on a basis different from external mediators in disputes. Journalists have long demonstrated that, in some circumstances, they can be effective warners. They can be trained to be even more effective. But will they be seen as "taking sides"? And is it really compatible with their mission? NGOs face similar tensions.

Late preventive diplomacy does not require the same kind of extensive understanding about an impending conflict to be effective. Instead, it relies on prevention tools that contribute to "readiness" and "rapid reaction" at an early stage of the escalatory cycle, and therefore, to a greater understanding of how conflict escalation works. A primary barrier to prevention in this phase is the heightened risk of perverse effects.

There are numerous models of escalatory dynamics.[14] They usually consist of assessing levels of escalation, by examining overall societal levels of polarization and mobilization, on the one hand, and identifying specific "signs" along the road, on the other. Some analysts distinguish between *signal flares* for the intensification of conflict, such as statements and actions which increase the confrontational nature of a latent conflict; *conflict triggers*, which are specific events like an assassination or the sudden breakup of a governing party, that are precipitators of violence; and *accelerators* of these triggers, like propaganda, which feed on background conditions in order to fuel escalation. Prevention requires learning to recognize these factors better, as well as finding points of leverage where intervention might work.

One key to assessing such dynamics is to evaluate how the incentives and cost-benefit calculations of local leaders change at different levels of this escalatory spiral. In particular, escalation often results when one party feels that it deserves concessions because of past injustices.

The process by which escalation leads to a stalemate is a form of entropy. Options for the victory of one party over the other slowly wither away, and stalemates arise as the attempts by each side permanently to claim value fail. Intervenors need to create conditions of stalemate (for example, failure of contentious tactics, exhaustion of necessary resources, and loss of social support in recognition of the unacceptable cost of further escalation) before entering a dynamic of deescalation.

Finally, continuous prevention at the post-conflict stage is meant to prevent the recurrence of conflict; therefore, the predictor it relies on is simply the recent occurrence of conflict. Post-conflict prevention requires not early warning *per se* but rather an assessment of the effectiveness of conflict resolution patterns. Because the occurrence of past conflicts is the single best predictor of future conflict, ensuring the sustainable character of conflict resolution is at the core of long-term prevention. Here the essential goal is to avert a relapse into violent conflict during the post-conflict peacebuilding stage through the creation of structures for the institutionalization of peace.

The difficulties in operationalizing early warning may mean that it is at this phase that opportunities for prevention are the most promising. International communities know where to act, and populations with fresh memories may be more prone to push for action in those regions. Potential perverse effects are dampened by the temporary focus on reconstruction, and even feeble efforts at reconciliation provide an environment conducive to systematic prevention efforts. The circumscribed nature of this type of intervention also makes it less vulnerable to diversion criticism. Prevention needs to start where the lessons from previous failure are still vivid.

Categories of Preventive Action

When considering whether and how to intervene preventively, outsiders must also assess when intervention is most likely to work, precisely what they are seeking to prevent, what the risk factors are, and whether the differences between prevention and cure are likely to be significant. They need to identify what the relevant parties stand to gain or lose through employing peaceful alternatives and assess whether these calculations, and their incentives, can be altered at any of the different phases of the conflict.

Before outlining a typology of preventive tools, we need to ask what constitutes preventive action. Developing a consensus for what type of actions ought to be included is important for strategic as well as conceptual reasons. On the one hand, if "prevention" is defined too narrowly, the international community may overlook potentially effective tools as well as the need to develop appropriate norms and institutions to maximize their effectiveness; or it might also fail to generalize lessons from one experience because of an inability to understand their inherently similar preventive character. It may also fail to optimize the simultaneous use of different preventive instruments in a given situation. Finally, action by parties other than governments, such as indigenous and international NGOs, may be overlooked.

On the other hand, it may be all too easy to broaden the scope of prevention beyond relevance. To some extent, the creation and maintenance of almost every international institution can be considered as a part of a global preventive strategy. Was the UN not set up "to prevent the scourge of war" for the generations to come? Most international institutions justify their existence not only through short-term benefits but also through their role in preventing long-term conflicts. The EU is a prime example because its raison d'etre is to avoid war in Europe. At some point, prevention is so late that it becomes treatment, in which case, continuing to call it prevention makes failure inherent.

"Hands-off" vs. "Hands-on"

What are the criteria for distinguishing between broad categories of preventive action? The classic debate over prevention in the social field has to do with balancing punitive and proactive strategies. In the field of delinquency, one distinguishes between preventive surveillance and providing assistance. Similarly and schematically, conflict prevention strategies can first be distinguished insofar as they operate either by enhancing the incentives of the relevant parties in favor of peace, or by changing the capacity of societies to deal with disputes through peaceful alternatives. I differentiate two broad categories of "hands-off" and "hands-on" preventive strategies.

"Hands-off" has two connotations in the present context. 1) When outsiders intervene to try to change the incentives of actors, they do not get involved directly *inside* the conflict at hand, nor should they seek to *transform* the conditions that led to the conflict. They may nevertheless be very active or "interventionist." 2) What they seek to influence are the external incentives of the relevant parties. They tell these parties: "hands-off"!

Hands-off approaches operate through both "coercive prevention" and "inducive prevention." In their coercive version, they rely on deterrent or *compellent* threats, as distinguished by Schelling.[15] Deterrence is obviously the classic basis for preventing international conflict, culminating in the Cold War's nuclear balance of terror. Deterrence "discourages or hinders (a given behavior) by fear or dislike of trouble," while a threat is a declaration of an intention to punish or to hurt contingent on a modified behavior. In both cases, outsiders seek to persuade the relevant parties that "the cost and/or risks of a given course of action outweigh its benefits."[16]

Deterrence, in its most coercive incarnation, involves the display and positioning of force to signal a willingness to respond militarily if certain actions are taken. A preventive threat of use of force is designed to persuade a party not to take a given action. Compellence also involves a threat, but in this case, the threat is conveyed through some minimal show of force or through the initiation of international sanctions in order to alter the cost/benefit calculation of the party contemplating an action.

These coercive actions can be preceded by softer persuasion and inducement strategies. Inducement strategies can also be used independently from coercion. In all cases, the ultimate behavior of the outside intervenor is *contingent* on a specific desired behavior of the internal parties. This contingency is supposed to enhance the attractiveness of alternatives to violent conflicts and decrease the desirability of violent conflict.

Alternatively, prevention can be conducted by hands-on approaches. In such instances, outside intervention is unconditional; rather than changing the consequences of different potential courses of action, an intervenor seeks to change the underlying preferences that lead local actors to consider violence in the first place. Prevention moves beyond changing the incentives of the relevant actors to building up the capacity of societies to ward off the disease of violence. Such capacity includes developing or strengthening alternative means for peaceful settlements and addressing so-called root causes of conflict by providing external support and resources.

Hands-on strategies, to a great extent, imply that outsiders become insiders through their preventive efforts. These approaches can be more or less "transformative" in that they can, to varying degrees, change initial conditions. In contrast to hands-off approaches, hands-on approaches stem from a belief that any results obtained by manipulating incentives from the outside through rewards and punishments are not likely to endure in the long term.

Clearly, both hands-off and hands-on approaches resemble other diplomatic options. As conflicts explode into crises and ultimately war, hands-off preventive strategies develop into curative strategies, and preventive actions turn into classical intervention. Compellence ceases to be prevention as the degree of intervention increasingly reflects an escalation of the conflict. In this case, the more successful the preventive action, the less likely it will turn into classical intervention. Similarly, hands-on preventive activities may simply turn into actions to cure broadly defined and observable ills (malnutrition, poverty, and environmental disaster) rather than being geared specifically to prevent those ills from degenerating into conflict. Contrary to the previous category, success in conflict prevention does not necessarily imply a reduced need for curative strategies with regard to the broader goal.

Ad hoc vs. Systemic Prevention

A second distinction is made between ad hoc and systemic approaches. This distinction is akin to that between malaria pills for the adventurous traveler and polio immunization for a whole population. On the one hand, actions can be undertaken on an ad hoc basis in response to a specific event identified in the target country. That they are reactive does not imply that they do not occur early in the prevention cycle. Indeed, ad hoc intervention may be based on very early signs of potential conflict.

Alternatively, the approach to prevention can be systemic, in that certain actions apply proactively and systematically to a category of countries, group of countries, or agents within a country. This does not necessarily mean that the actions are *universal*. The criterion for falling under a systemic approach can simply be that of jurisdiction. Preventive norms and institutional procedures may affect parties by simple virtue of jurisdictional coverage, either because they are members or potential members of an institution.

Actions connected to systemic prevention, since it tends to be proactive, usually cast a broader net than ad hoc strategies. During recent years, however, ad hoc attempts at prevention have proliferated along with the identification of incipient conflicts. To be sure, ad hoc interventions may follow an increasingly systematic pattern and become institutionalized into some structural design. If the motivation and trigger for ad hoc preventive intervention are recognizable, it may not need to be institutionalized to benefit from the force of precedent. Nevertheless, systemic prevention, to the extent that it can become an automatic component of broader agenda and strategy, will tend to encompass an increasing set of countries and situations.

Four Paradigms of International Preventive Action

Any attempt at drawing typologies is necessarily an oversimplification. Identifying alternative paradigms for prevention is useful, however, in order to organize a discussion of appropriate tools for intervention. Crossing the two sets of criteria described above provides four broad paradigms for preventive action, each corresponding to a cluster of preventive policies or tools. Under what conditions and in what circumstances is each of these paradigms most appropriate? I broadly assess their comparative advantages at different phases of the conflict cycle.

Coercive Diplomacy

Hands-off ad hoc strategies usually seek to prevent the escalation of disputes into violent conflicts or the spread of an existing conflict through more or less coercive methods. In these cases, the focus of the external intervention is *enforcement* of a desired solution. In short, this refers to the potential use for preventive purposes of either multinational intervention or of UN Chapter VII instruments as well as gray area measures traditionally referred to as "Chapter VI and a half" measures.

"Coercive diplomacy" refers to a defensive strategy sometimes employed by policy-makers hoping to secure a peaceful resolution of a serious dispute.[17] This strategy primarily involves the threat of force or sanctions. Beyond it, if a conflict has already broken out, coercive diplomacy may involve a limited exemplary use of force or sanctions as a means of restoring peace in a crisis. The use of threats as an instrument of peaceful diplomacy is preventive by definition since threats are meant to prevent the escalation of a given conflict into war. The hope is that

FIGURE 1-2. International Preventive Action: A Framework for Analysis

	Scope	
	a. Ad hoc *Mitigating escalatory dynamics on an ad hoc basis*	**b.** Systemic *Long-term strategies embedded in norms and institutions*
Method **1.** "Hands off" *Threats and promises* ——— *Signaling of contingent actions*	**Coercive diplomacy**	**Institutional inducement**
2. "Hands on" *Capacity building* ——— *Providing the means to address root causes*	**Cooperative management**	**Systemic transformation**

early use of force will avoid a much greater use of force later—in other words, prevent war.[18]

In the cases discussed by George (Vietnam and Cuba), attempts were made to persuade opponents— governments—to stop or undo aggressive actions already embarked upon without resorting to all-out military responses. Military and economic threats and sanctions were used extensively as alternatives to war. The key is to back one's demands on adversaries with a threat of punishment for non-compliance that is credible and potent; force is used to establish the credibility of one's determination to use more force. Finally, external intervenors do not need to rely exclusively on threats but should add conditional inducements of a positive character for face-saving purposes.[19]

While George and others analyze strategies to prevent interstate conflicts, coercive diplomacy can be applied as well to refer to interventions by third parties in intrastate conflicts. In cases of intrastate conflict, deterrence strategies are obviously targeted at different parties depending on the sources of the conflict and the goals of the intervention. Situations where a strong state persecutes and/or seeks to drive out a subset of its population resemble most interstate conflicts. The threat is aimed at persuading a government to stop or undo a given action. It is likely to be issued in response to a call for help by a minority group, as in the case of Iraqi Kurds.

Conversely, a weak state—such as a fledgling democracy—may call for preventive international intervention to help maintain or restore law and order either because it is not able to control ethnic tensions internally or because it is under threat by a "rebel" minority group, with or without support for a neighboring state. In this case, the target of the threat may be the external supporting power or the rebel group, but is generally less identifiable. In cases of state breakdown, where no particular party or group calls for intervention but where preventive coercion is envisaged in order to prevent a civil war and humanitarian tragedies, the target of a potential threat is even less identifiable. Here, coercive prevention seems bound to involve minimal use of force since there is no space for the language of threats.

Whether aimed at inter- or intrastate conflict, coercive diplomacy in general, and credible threats, in particular, are more likely to work under two core conditions: 1) perceptions—if the target of the ultimatum is convinced that the outside party is willing and able to carry out the threat of intervention (the motivations of the outside party must be clear and strong, and there must be domestic and international support for the threat); and 2) alternatives—the targeted party must actually fear the threatened action. The assessed costs of such coercion must fall dispro- portionately on the actors who are responsible for the conflict escalation. There must be precise terms of settlement which can end the crisis. When are these conditions most likely to be met in an intrastate conflict?

One of the keys to the issuer's credibility will be his perceived ability to carry out a threat of intervention in the case of non-compliance. Many writers argue for a strengthening of the international community's capac- ity for rapid intervention in the form of prepared forces in order to prevent the escalation of a conflict (stage two). There is no doubt that the existence of a UN brigade or rapid reaction force would increase the plausibility of effective intervention at an early point in stage two, if only because its mobilization would involve a less cumbersome decision- making process than in the current system of multinational forces. But even intervention by a rapid reaction force would eventually necessitate member states' consensus. Whether a rapid reaction force would be effective in preventing escalation would seem to depend on a host of factors, including the type of technology and character of mass partici- pation in the conflict involved.[20]

Ultimately, the issue is whether the *threat* of intervention by a rapid reaction force could become a relatively credible deterrent over time. In this regard, in addition to developing the capacity to intervene, develop- ing a set of explicit criteria for the legitimate use of threats of force or sanctions for preventive purposes (while at the same time enhancing their automatic character) is critical. Preventive coercion relies dispro- portionately on the power of precedent. As the gospel of forceful per- suasion, the gradual stepping up of the pressure and the "turning of the screw" advocated by George would need to be codified under an inter- national manual for coercive preventive action.[21]

But capacity and a normative infrastructure are not enough. Given that the effectiveness of a threat is based to a great extent on the asymmetry of the motivation between the issuer and the target, it is not the case that leaders of powerful countries or even the UN itself can easily intimidate relevant actors in weaker countries when what is at stake is survival or power and when alternatives to escalating violence do not seem viable with respect to the target. Bargaining power is, in large part, a function of the differences between what is at stake for the different parties to a dispute.[22] A threat can be ineffective, depending on the differences in military strength. If the stakes are too high, the weaker party may refuse to change its behavior, in effect calling the bluff of the stronger one and testing the degree of international support behind preventive intervention.

Whether parties will be led to opt for alternatives to conflict escalation depends in part on whether the external party is able to create in its target a sense of urgency for compliance. Typically, given that power asymmetry *within* the domestic arena is often the catalyst for violent conflict, one way to change parties' incentives is to try to equalize, actually or potentially, the power positions of the internal parties to the conflict.[23] Under this approach, the potential for a gradual loss of superior power may be enough to stop escalation. Also, the kinds of punishment threatened are likely to be more effective if targeted to the specific parties that contribute directly to the escalation of violence.[24] In all cases, what is demanded of the parties must be made clear, carefully thought through, and limited to realistic goals. Given the strategic dimension of the choice of the objective on behalf of which coercive diplomacy is employed, the accomplishment of broader goals can be left to other preventive tools.

Two general propositions follow. First, coercive diplomacy is most likely to work at the late prevention stage simply because threats are more credible as a response to an encroachment already taken. Using methods of coercive diplomacy short of visible escalation to violent conflict in the targeted country—that is, in phases one and three of the conflict cycle—runs the greatest risk of perverse effects. Moreover, coercive prevention is a blunt all-or-nothing instrument. Again, halfway coercive prevention is most likely to accentuate rather than dampen internal deadly conflicts.

States that eventually engineer large-scale persecutions of their populations, leading to genocide, typically have tested international reactions at an earlier stage and are most likely to engage in their enterprises if earlier threats that have been issued have not been followed through.[25] As a general rule, engagement is more advisable than containment when sensitive disputes have not yet degenerated into significant violence, but coercion must be decisive and credible *as soon as* signs of violence can be used as a basis for counter-violence.

Second, even if one grants that the use of force should be a last resort, in some circumstances the threat of force should be moved upstream for preventive purposes. This is especially true for passive or "tripwire" types of coercion. In this case, the use of force is threatened in response to a potential use of force against the intervening party itself. One example of such an approach which stands in between interstate and intrastate prevention is preventive *deployment* as introduced in Macedonia to prevent the spread of the Bosnian conflict as well as, secondarily, to provide assistance in maintaining local security. Preventive deployment could become more systematic in the future, but will still be severely constrained by the UN's limited resources and its consequent incapacity to identify the "right" conflicts.

Another step is to implement more systematically the setting up of intrastate "safe areas" (referred to by the militaries as protected or security zones), either with the agreement of all sides as a means of separating potential belligerents and removing pretexts for attack or in order to protect a specific group against a state. Operation Provide Comfort was an important first experiment of the latter type. It gave a military shield to the Kurdish population of Iraq after its revolt against the Iraqi government in 1991, at the end of the Gulf War.[26] In this case, the international community acted swiftly to prevent large-scale persecution of a minority through the creation, monitoring, and air protection of a security zone within the territory of a sovereign state. The demarcation between the UN relief operation, conducted in cooperation with the Iraqi government, and the five-nation military operation to secure a security zone was clearer in Iraqi Kurdistan than in Bosnia.

There clearly are fundamental limits to coercive approaches to prevention. First, there is the issue of *legitimacy*. While there is a growing consensus regarding the legitimacy of external intervention in cases of state breakdown, the burden of proof is greater in cases of prediction or signs of breakdown. Even if the duty to intervene in order to protect life as well as international peace comes to be widely accepted as an international norm, it is unlikely that the mere threat of loss of life would suffice to justify coercive intervention. When life is threatened by strong states rather than state breakdown, the bypassing of sovereignty seems an even more remote possibility. Second, is the issue of *effectiveness*. Classically, deterrent strategies must be accompanied by an appropriate communication with the target so that the target understands the overall deterrent system. In cases of civil wars, there are compounded uncertainties as to how threats may be received and interpreted. While ultimata always run the risk of provoking preemptive reactions, their having been singled out for preventive coercion may lead parties to act proac-

tively even if they do not expect to win. Given these limits, more institutionalized and hands-on preventive approaches are likely to constitute
priority options prior to or alongside coercive diplomacy.

Institutional Inducement

Contrary to ad hoc approaches, systemic approaches imply that a country
becomes the target of preventive action by virtue of actually or potentially
falling under the jurisdiction of some agent or organization that can act in a
preventive capacity. This jurisdictional dimension in turn lends added leverage to attempts by outsiders to influence developments inside countries.
Such influence can take the form of deterring certain actions but most likely
involves compelling a party *to do* something, which is more compatible
with the proactive character of institutional mandates; the action demanded
then constitutes visible proof of jurisdictional compliance. Building permits
provide a useful analogy. Building permits are granted subject to conditions
for construction, which may vary with local circumstances. They compel
builders to abide by certain standards that are meant to prevent accidents
while at the same time serving as blueprints for effective compliance. The
approval stamps of building inspectors guarantee the legality of a building—that is, its right to belong in a given neighborhood. Similarly, prevention through institutional inducement—if not outright compellence—
implies that the rights and benefits associated with membership in or
association with a given institution should be conditioned upon compliance
with a "blueprint" that embodies preventive mechanisms.

The most basic tool of hands-off systemic prevention is the conditional
recognition of statehood. The weakest form of conditional membership is
recognition of new states by the United Nations and its members. Clearly,
until now, deliberations regarding or denial of recognition has been principally motivated by the reluctance of a majority of member states to
override highly sensitive vetoes (for example, Taiwan and Macedonia)
rather than by attempts to apply pressure that may affect the likelihood of
domestic conflict. The fiasco associated with the circumstances of
Croatia's and Bosnia's recognition and the unheeded recommendations of
the Badinter Commission are cases in point. Nevertheless, it is not clear,
even with hindsight, that a more conditional recognition strategy would
have succeeded in preventing the Bosnian conflict.

Nations must affirm themselves first before caring about belonging to
the community of nations. Moreover, recognition is a two-edged instru-

ment: Its denial can be used as a tool for prevention, but granting it may also facilitate preventive intervention by creating a more firm legal basis for intervention as a civil war is transformed into a war across borders. The creation of a recognition committee at the UN that would apply stringent criteria for recognition explicitly related to minority rights would therefore appear to constitute a limited inducement mechanism. It would be helpful only in cases where conflict occurs alongside state disintegration and where conditional recognition (and de-recognition) is seen as a prerequisite for the short-term sustainability of a new state.

Conditional membership has been used in a much more effective manner by the EU and the Council of Europe as a source of influence over the domestic laws and practices of Eastern and Central Europe. The EU has been using the leverage of membership as an effective tool for preventing conflict in eastern and central Europe by introducing conditions related to political and human rights as requirements for membership and by monitoring their application. It went one step further in 1995, when it persuaded Hungary and Slovakia, as well as Hungary and Romania, to enter into so-called stability pact negotiations regarding their treatment of minorities. Clearly, the EU did not compel these states *per se*, but without the implicit inducement of membership, they would not have been likely to enter into such constraining agreements. EU officials are hopeful that such stability pacts will play a central role in forestalling minority frustrations in these states and spell out the rules of the game for the democratic and peaceful settlement of such disputes. The stability pacts were not presented as an explicit precondition for membership but rather as part of a package that would facilitate the accession process.

Since membership in global institutions is increasingly universal and membership in regional organizations covers most potential members, accession may simply become an obsolete tool. For membership to prove a credible inducement mechanism, international practice must include the possibility of reversal. While rogue states have *de facto* been expelled from the international community of nations, there is no formal mechanism for "recognition" of exit. Expulsion can be purely symbolic, as in the expulsion of Russia from the Council of Europe over the war in Chechnya. In this case, the Council wanted to emphasize the blatant violation of its most fundamental principles by a member, but the threat of expulsion could not be thought of as having any serious deterrent effect whatsoever. The current revision of the Maastricht Treaty in Europe may provide a more effective model as it is likely to introduce the possibility of exclusion in the case of blatant human rights abuse. But expulsion is clearly a very blunt instrument whose deterrent impact will be all the more reduced at an advanced stage of conflict escalation. It is not likely to be used as a tool of early prevention.

Another category of institutional inducement exists for client states of international financial institutions, including the International Monetary Fund, the World Bank, and regional development banks. The instrument of aid conditionality can be geared at inducing the client government to adopt peaceful approaches to ethnic disputes by connecting the disbursement of funds directly to thresholds of political risk assessed on the basis of the capacity of the recipient country to deal with incipient conflicts peacefully. Aid itself might not be designed to help prevent conflict, but the need for funds on the part of leaders or affected communities can constitute an inducement to resolve conflicts peacefully. These strategies must be distinguished from strategies of systemic transformation—where the form of aid itself becomes an instrument of prevention.

A final but important instance of institutional inducement is that of the possible creation of a permanent war crimes tribunal. To some extent, the ad hoc tribunals on Yugoslavia and Rwanda are already starting to deter—to the extent that they can be interpreted by belligerents as the beginning of a pattern (clearly, they had no preventive effects on the actual cases of Yugoslavia or Rwanda). The creation of a permanent tribunal would constitute a powerful means to target the threat of retribution to those actually responsible. At the same time, it can be argued that the kind of perpetrators of crimes against humanity who are likely to be prosecuted are the least amenable to these kinds of threats.

Institutional inducement is most likely to work early, when the sunk costs borne by the parties to a conflict are not so overwhelming as to dwarf the public good provided by the institution, or at a post-conflict stage, when institutional membership is sufficiently valued to constitute an effective inducement for the peaceful resolution of disputes. Above all, its influence is mostly limited to parties who identify their interests with that of a state, either the government of a strong state or of a fledgling state seeking inclusion in the community of nations.

Cooperative Management

With respect to hands-on approaches, unconditional actions can be undertaken by the outside world which are meant to help the parties involved find, create, or use alternative means to settle disputes as well as develop a capacity to address the very root cause of these conflicts in the long run. By definition, these actions rely on the consent of the internal parties. Cooperative management of disputes and conflicts between local and external actors is done on an ad hoc basis. It is always geared to addressing a specific dispute, between specific parties at a specific moment in time. Outside intervenors help provide the means for dispute resolution and reconciliation while persuading the parties to forego violent options. While coercive diplomacy has been referred to as forceful persuasion, this kind of approach may be labeled soft persuasion. It encompasses a great deal of what is traditionally meant by preventive "diplomacy"—or even by diplomacy *tout court!*—that is, the practice of seeking accommodation between conflicting interests.

In its purest form, prevention of this sort does not rely on pressure but on persuasion; it relies on enhancing internal capacity rather than on bringing to bear external incentives. Individual governments routinely capitalize on their special relations with given countries to offer their services to mediate disputes. Actors in the international system, national or international organizations, and government or non-governmental organizations have made it their mission to promote dialogue, confidence, and cooperation among parties in the throes of protracted ethnic conflicts.

Traditionally, international mediation intensifies as domestic disputes turn into conflicts and conflicts turn deadly. At a minimum, the goal of an outside intervenor is to keep channels of communication open between disputants. Even words or actions by one party that may indicate its desire to deescalate, halt, or settle an ongoing conflict before it explodes are all too often ignored or misinterpreted because of their ambiguity. Intervenors can help convey such "gestures of conciliation" to prevent conflict escalation.[27] Traditionally, however, mediation efforts by the outside world have been based on the further assumption that there exist peaceful solutions to disputes that intervenors can help parties identify and refine. (Assessing the preventive effectiveness of external mediation in the post-Cold War era is beyond the scope of this chapter.)[28] The question that scholars need to ask is the extent to which mediation practice and negotiation theory need to be adapted when the ultimate goal is preventing deadly conflict inside states. Under what conditions can outside actors intervene effectively for the cooperative management of conflicts?

In the post-Cold War era, countries are increasingly turning to international organizations and other institutions for assistance in resolving disputes when attempts at direct negotiation fail. The good offices of the UN Secretary-General have, since the creation of the UN, been devoted to helping obtain the peaceful resolution of interstate disputes as mandated by Chapter VI of the UN Charter. The UN is now also becoming involved in internal conflicts. But the UN cannot impose its services and still suffers from a reluctance of member states to empower it more fully. The *Agenda for Peace* notes: "Experience has shown that the greatest obstacle is not a widely supposed lack of information, analytical capacity, or ideas for UN initiatives. Success is often blocked at the outset by the reluctance of one or other of the parties to accept UN help. Collectively, member states encourage the UN Secretariat to play an active role in this field; individually, they are often reluctant that he should do so when they are a party to the conflict." For Boutros-Ghali, "the solution can only be long term. It may lie in creating a climate of opinion or ethos, within the international community in which the norm would be for member states to accept an offer of UN good offices."[29] There is no doubt that the progressive establishment of a new "ethos" favoring prevention will help countries accept the very notion that the international community, in one guise or another, may intervene to settle domestic conflicts.

At a very general level, it seems that the conceptualization and practice of mediation in the international realm have followed, with a lag, the changes apparent in the mediation field in general. They are evolving toward a more "transformative approach," which needs to be enhanced even further.[30] The shift that needs to be consolidated is multifold: toward an increasingly "insider" approach to conflict prevention; toward earlier mediation; and toward bottom-up approaches aimed at societies as a whole.

In the last few years, the OSCE has developed a new approach to prevention which has been characterized as that of an "insider third party."[31] The long-term presence of missions on the ground and the mandate and approach taken by the High Commissioner on National Minorities have represented a subtle paradigm shift in conflict prevention.[32] The OSCE has turned away from the paradigm of the mediator as a "resolver" of conflict toward becoming a facilitator and an adviser over the longer run. In his intervention, the High Commissioner has been increasingly concerned with the process by which the parties are dealing with their conflict, focusing on "satisfying the interests and alleviating the fears of all the parties involved," rather than on determining or interpreting rights.[33]

This approach has led to success stories for the OSCE in places like Macedonia, Romania, Albania, Estonia, Ukraine, and Crimea.[34] But it does have its limitations, especially to the extent that it relies in part on the implicit link between the acceptance of its activities and the hopes of accession by its target countries to institutions like the EU or the Council of Europe. Most important, the OSCE has not been able to help establish institutions inside the countries where it has intervened that can sustain long-term dialogue and transform the conflicts or that could ultimately be taken over by local actors.

In more general terms, Western countries and international institutions "should consider not only what might be called 'hard mediation'—efforts to find specific solutions to specific disputes—but also 'soft mediation'—the broader question of what outsiders can legitimately and usefully do to ease tensions among ethnic groups who share the same states or between states across whose borders ethnic communities spill."[35] At the very least, these efforts should contribute to an atmosphere that facilitates the resolution of conflicts if and when they occur. Soft mediation implies, above all, that intervention occurs at very early stages of disputes and is aimed at establishing a capacity for internal conflict management rather than providing channels from the outside. For instance, soft mediation can help to broaden the acceptance of judicial review or at least third-party involvement in all disputes concerning minorities.

The most ambitious current set of efforts in grounding cooperative management of disputes within a long-term and insider perspective is embedded in the comprehensive peace plan operations conducted by the UN in cooperation with other organizations in countries that have emerged from protracted conflicts in the post-Cold War era. In countries like El Salvador, Mozambique, and Cambodia, where the UN has committed resources to national reconciliation and reconstruction, it has put in place new kinds of peacemaking operations. These are designed to supervise the implementation of comprehensive peace agreements and the transition to democracy. These plans include a range of actions which are meant to help manage disputes domestically. To start with, the UN has set up mechanisms—such as supreme national councils—intended to establish a degree of common interest, as buffers in cases of potential conflicts related to reconstruction. The plans also establish new judicial systems, promote and verify respect for human rights, ensure that the voices of individual citizens are heard, supervise constitutional and administrative reforms, provide training to government personnel, strengthen official structures, register voters, organize and monitor elections, and reintegrate refugees. In such a comprehensive approach to post-conflict prevention, integrating populations and leaderships under common institutional umbrellas is essential not only to prevent a relapse into violent conflict but also to overcome the renewed polarization of society.

At what stage of the cycle and under what conditions is prevention through cooperative management most likely to be effective? The arguments for intervention at stage one are the same as those for early prevention in general: An external mediator with clout can employ resources that may assist resolution even while internal alternatives to conflict have failed; the longer parties to protracted conflicts live with the situations created by these conflicts, the less capable they are of picturing the alternative world of reconciliation. The longer that disputes are allowed to continue, the more entrenched the positions of the parties are likely to be. Early soft mediation will empower the parties themselves by enhancing their capacity to talk.

At the same time, too great a focus on early intervention through cooperative management is vulnerable to all three criticisms of prevention. For one, even if it were possible to identify the most potentially violent conflict around the world, assessing where external intervention could make a difference and where it could not would still be difficult. Generally, the people within societies that will engage in and lead deadly conflicts are the least amenable to techniques of persuasion. But excluding extremists from mediation efforts is not an effective means of preventing a recurrence of conflict, as demonstrated by the case of Afghanistan. Arguments of ripeness also come into play. With conflicts that may become violent, mediation is the last resort that parties will accept. They welcome the peaceful resolution of disputes if they have been shown that they cannot win. Again, early "cooperative management" can have perverse effects in that mediation often forces parties to state positions explicitly and broadcast them, which may actually freeze a situation.

If these latter arguments hold, then the question becomes whether it is better for an international conflict to be engaged at the late prevention stage or not be engaged at all. One response to the issue of when to intervene is that the cooperative management of disputes should focus on alternative tools, depending on the conflict cycle stage at which it is sought and provided. In situations where disputes are serious but violence does not seem imminent, the best route is to support institutions that can address disputes non-violently. In situations where violence is imminent or has started on a small scale, preventive action should be aimed at providing short-term alternatives to violence. In all cases, cooperative management of disputes to prevent deadly conflict stands little chance of being effective without the will of the parties themselves.

Transformative Prevention

The last broad category of preventive tools encompasses hands-on approaches that can be applied systematically when countries come under the jurisdiction of specified institutions. This involves creating preventive institutions or refocusing existing ones. To the extent that transformative prevention requires that the activities of existing international organizations be refocused, these approaches are most vulnerable to the criticism of diversion.

Transformative prevention consists of implementing unconditional actions inside a country, with the aim of changing the country's long-term propensity for violent conflict. Analogies are social policies to prevent crime or physical fitness programs to promote health. Obviously, the boundary between cooperative management and transformative prevention blurs to the extent that ad hoc efforts to create and maintain channels of communication become increasingly systemic and are delinked from attempts to resolve specific disputes at specific moments in time. Nevertheless, transformative prevention encompasses a much broader substantive agenda, including developing international regimes that address the "root causes" leading to the emergence of the conflict in the first place.

Ultimately, transformative prevention consists of spreading respect for the rule of law and the fundamental mechanisms of democracy even though they may be adapted to local contexts. This adaptation enhances the authority of the International Court of Justice and promotes the universality of Article 36 jurisdiction. While the Court arbitrates between states, the ethos of dispute resolution through law may, eventually, spill over into domestic contexts. Most important for our purposes is the systematic build-up of the institutions of law in the context of post-conflict reconciliation. This includes the creation or strengthening of domestic courts, ombudsmen for human rights (as in the case of Guatemala), and the office of a public prosecutor, as well as the most difficult challenge, the training (maybe international) of an army and police force that are servants, not makers, of the law.

At the international level, there is a fundamental need to build on the existing international regimes for human rights and, above all, for minority rights, to enhance their preventive character. As stressed in the last report of the UN High Commissioner for Refugees (UNHCR), today's human rights abuses are tomorrow's violent conflicts and flow of refugees. Actual or anticipated human rights violations are usually the immediate cause of flight. The UNHCR concludes: "Rather than war refugees it would be more appropriate to describe refugees as people whose human rights have been violated or threatened."[36] Given that international norms for basic human rights exist, the need here is to focus on patterns and trends of violations, rather than on ex-post complaint procedures, and create regional mechanisms to monitor and enforce these rights before they lead to conflict.

Focusing on minority rights is the next step in this process. The Council of Europe and the UN and other organizations are currently engaged in a major overhaul of the regime of minority rights in order to develop a body of international law to bestow rights on groups of people who wish to preserve a distinct identity without being subjected to forced assimilation, segregation, or discrimination. Again, the core issue is that of the connection between rights and enforcement. But, from the point of view of conflict prevention, it is also important to reflect on the threshold of minority rights that may increase rather than dampen ethnic tensions by legitimizing exclusion and enhancing fragmentation in societies.

Minority rights must be aimed not at creating safer ghettos but at engineering mutual recognition and mutual engagements among groups in a society. Whether establishing minority rights actually reaches to the deepest causes of conflict, such rights do constitute a key part of the equation.[37]

Another broad category of transformative prevention is that of preventive development. The starting point is not controversial: Disputes are more often than not economic in nature. They arise as a result of competition between different groups over access to scarce resources. This competition is often expressed in ethnic terms as different groups perceive that their own poverty and deprivation is due to discrimination. The UNHCR cites statistical studies showing a correlation between a country's development indices and its propensity to be affected by conflict. Clearly, correlation does not mean causation, and there is little doubt that civil war itself creates poverty. Underdevelopment alone does not create civil wars and refugees. But poverty, inequality, and the competition for scarce resources can play important roles in creating the conditions for armed conflict and the mass displacement of people.

That developmental tensions are often a contributory factor is exemplified by the case of Rwanda, which confronted the huge developmental challenge of having the highest population density in Africa.

Central America also provides clear examples of mass violence rooted in conflicts among social classes created by the unequal distribution of resources. More generally, as Boutros-Ghali and many others have argued, strategies to avert conflict cannot be expected to succeed if they fail to address the "silent crisis of underdevelopment"—chronic and growing poverty, mounting population pressures, unemployment, and widespread environmental destruction. Beyond the traditional array of UN developmental activities, what can be done to focus emergency humanitarian actions and long-term development strategies on conflict prevention?

Simply increasing aid or changing the beneficiaries of aid will not do the trick. As one critic expressed it, "conflict prevention proponents suffer from economic and ecological determinism, by assuming that since shortages of resources may lead to violent conflict, increased aid will prevent it."[38] International financial institutions can use their leverage and economic programs to dampen societal polarization and support processes of transformation that de-emphasize ethnic categorization and encourage integration among groups. These results can be achieved gradually, so that development aid will not divert resources from conflict-poor to conflict-prone countries even if the latter are less likely to use resources effectively. International financial institutions should focus first on indirect and then on direct preventive measures.[39] Indirect measures are those designed to avoid inadvertently creating or intensifying tensions among ethnic groups. Direct measures proactively target potential causes of ethno-national conflict by investing, for instance, in the transport and communication infrastructures of deprived regions where minorities are often marginalized.[40]

Perverse effects can occur. In cases where tensions between groups have gone too far for integrative strategies to be implemented, such measures may actually exacerbate tensions. In these latter cases, transformative strategies need to encourage peaceful separation rather than integration. But who is to decide? International institutions must take their cues

FIGURE 1-3. International Preventive Action: Complementary or Alternative Approaches?

	Scope	
	a. Ad hoc *Mitigating escalatory dynamics on an ad hoc basis*	**b.** Systemic *Long-term strategies embedded in norms and institutions*
Method		
1. "Hands off" *Incentives* ——— *Signaling of contingent actions (threats and promises)*	**Coercive diplomacy** e.g., • Arms embargo • Threat of limited use of sanctions • Threat of limited use of military intervention • Rapid reaction force • Preventive deployment • Safe havens and demilitarized zones *phase 2 (1, 3)*	**Institutional inducement** e.g., • Conditionality for membership in international institutions • Stability pacts in Eastern Europe • Aid and trade conditionality • Arms control and IAEA monitoring • Permanent war crimes tribunal *phase 1 (2, 3)*
2. "Hands on" *Capacity building* ——— *Providing the means to address root causes (blueprints and resources)*	**Cooperative management** e.g., • Official good offices (UN or bilateral), and mediation • "Third-party insider": High Commissioner on National Minorities (OSCE) • Unofficial or grassroots dialogue • Promotion of cross-conflict learning • Country-specific transition programs incl. institution building, elections • Comprehensive peace plan • UNHCR *phase 2, 3 (1)*	**Systemic transformation** e.g., • Rule of Law and World Court • Frameworks of principles for sustainable peace • Adaptation of minority rights regime • Promotion of preventive development • Regional confidence-building measures, risk reduction centers, OSCE conflict prevention center *phase 1, 3 (2)*
Cost:	*False negatives (targeted)*	*False positives (broad net)*

from societal forces and act to help strengthen pre-existing social contracts rather than seek to engineer new ones.

Combining Approaches: A Strategic Road Map

The above survey of preventive action may be seen as corresponding to the underlying worldviews of alternative schools of international relations. These include realists, who favor deterrence strategies; institutionalists, who believe that institutions can affect behavior through changing the incentives and expectations of actors; idealists, who believe in the force of interaction, persuasion, and mutual understanding to foster peaceful management of conflicts; and liberals, for whom changing underlying domestic structures is the key to conflict prevention. Nevertheless, while this categorization is one possible way of differentiating the core characteristics of diverse preventive strategies, it is also clear that the boundaries among these categories are often blurred. Ad hoc strategies become institutionalized progressively, and cooperative management may progressively turn into transformative strategies. These strategies can often constitute different elements of a multifaceted approach. At the same time, however, it is clear that different emphases correspond to different necessities and serve different purposes under alternative circumstances. Given the array of possible preventive tools, each with its own limitations, we need to ask which set of tools should be used in conjunction with others and when they should be considered alternatives.

As discussed extensively above, the classic understanding of prevention in international diplomacy has to do with deterrence. Although deterrence need not be considered as the point of departure for internal conflicts, it can be seen as the most direct and short-term mechanism for prevention, irrespective of our assessment of effectiveness. From there, the scope of preventive action must be broadened in two directions which have to do with addressing causes rather than symptoms of conflicts. On the one hand, outside intervenors can shift from hands-off to hands-on approaches, which I call internalization. On the other hand, they can shift from ad hoc to systemic approaches, a shift that I call institutionalization. In both cases, preventive tools may at times be seen as alternatives and, at others, as complements.

Internalization: From Threats to Promises to Blueprints to
Resources . . . and Back

Preventive strategies are focused simultaneously on manipulating incentives through threats and promises (hands-off), and enhancing capacities through blueprints and resources (hands-on). Under what conditions should capacity building be added to incentive-based strategies and should intervention become more unconditional? To what extent can a deterrent threat continue to be effective if the issuer also becomes an insider with shared responsibility for the target's agreement to desist? When does prevention require engagement rather than containment? In the other direction, when should military force or threats be used to enhance a mediator's credibility and leverage, making her a "peacemaker with muscle"? Conversely, when does persuasive power risk being overshadowed by coercive power? Where institutional inducement is used as a preventive tool, in which cases is it also incumbent on the institution to provide not just the stick and blueprint, but also the resources, to help countries abide by set conditions?

This set of questions must be addressed on a case-by-case basis, whether the case is a target country or an institution taking on the prevention agenda. There are many trade-offs to take into account. Hands-on approaches usually involve less risk, while hands-off approaches usually involve fewer resources. The former are seen as more effective by those who argue that sustained prevention depends on changing the internal constraint on violent action. The latter use a "language" that may be the only one understood by some of the instigators of conflicts around the world. Hands-on strategies aimed at societal factors may need to be combined with threats and promises targeted at key actors from the elites, to the extent that elites play the central role in instigating conflicts and may seek to manipulate transformative strategies in their favor.

A fundamental argument for combining hands-on with hands-off approaches relates to the underlying rationale for preventive intervention in the first place. The international community argues that state sovereignty can legitimately be superseded when a state stops fulfilling its primary law and order function, which in turn legitimizes coercive preventive action. It must then be the case that the targeted state cannot fulfill its functions that have to do with capacity building. Consistency requires that those who support the right (or even the duty) to intervene coercively in case of state breakdown also support internalizing these strategies through hands-on approaches.

One of the most promising developments of the mid-1990s that illustrates how the same institution can act both on incentives and on capacity building has been the setting up of war crimes tribunals. Beyond their role as a deterrent for other potential conflicts, war crimes tribunals today serve as tools of nation building that may, in the long term, prevent the recurrence of the conflict under scrutiny. Since the recurrence of violent conflicts is likely to be based in part on the continued polarization of societies and the desire for retribution, the tribunals may play an important role by attributing guilt to the perpetrators and permitting victims to voice their grievances. Nevertheless, whether "truth commissions" can be as effective when set up from the outside remains to be seen.

Institutionalization: From Ad hoc to Systemic Strategies

The second strategic question has to do with the need to systematize ad hoc approaches through institutionalization while at the same time retaining flexibility in the implementation of systemic approaches. How can strategies be developed that are both comprehensive and selective? In which cases is it sufficient to create a consistent pattern of ad hoc prevention to shape expectations of actors, and when is it appropriate to codify intervention as institutional rules and norms? To what extent is it plausible to rely increasingly on inducements linked to the accession or expulsion of institutions, given the externalities involved in such strategies? Can deterrence strategies be made more systematic and institutionalized? As the involvement of international institutions in ad hoc attempts at cooperative management of disputes rises, to what extent should this involvement be organized under a single set of blueprints and rules? In other words, is it advisable to develop universal methods for such capacity building? To what extent are more transformative long-term approaches to prevention compatible with the less intrusive ad hoc nature of prevention through mediation?

It can be argued that systemic strategies have several broad advantages over ad hoc strategies. First, in the long run, the fact that a preventive strategy is embedded in an institution may be enough to signal threats and promises on an ongoing implicit basis. This, in turn, diminishes risks of perverse effects, counterthreats, and escalation. But the differences here should not be overemphasized. Ad hoc strategies, if repeated with enough consistency, can serve the same purpose. Connected is the fact that a move toward systemic institutionalized strategies signals a move toward less discriminatory preventive intervention since prevention is embedded in an institutional context. Actors may react less defensively if they are not singled out. Finally, such strategies allow us to develop economies of scale for policy-making. But doing so can also be seen as the major drawback of systematization: While the costs associated with ad hoc strategies are false negatives—conflict not attended to on time—the costs associated with systemic strategies are false positives—actions which may not have been necessary and may have diverted energy, good will, and resources.

Assessing the Role of NGOs

What can and should be the role of NGOs in international preventive action? Two broad sets of questions that concern NGOs are: What should their role be in early warning and what should their role be in translating early warning into early action?

There seems to be a conventional wisdom regarding NGOs and international prevention: First, NGOs are the actors least able to take preventive action because they lack the coercive powers of governments to affect the incentives of local actors as well as the resources to provide themselves with the capacity to explore alternatives to conflict and escalation. On the other hand, NGOs have a clear comparative advantage when it comes to early warning since they are "close to the field" and possess an understanding of and the trust of local actors. The evidence collected in this book presents a much more nuanced picture, ultimately turning the above argument on its head. The potential for effective early warning on the part of NGOs is severely limited by factors that cannot be alleviated overnight, including the vulnerability of NGOs and the difficulty of their sounding a warning, and staying and appearing to stay neutral. At the same time, indigenous and international NGOs have not yet achieved their full potential for preventive action. They have a comparative advantage over governments or inter-governmental institutions that must be exploited better.

Achievement and Limit of NGO-based Early Warning

Early warning on the part of NGOs and other actors involves three steps: gathering, interpreting, and communicating information. As many of the chapters in this book show, NGOs are often the first external actors to become aware of a conflict, and they usually are the ones who remain in an area the longest. Since credible early warning requires verification and selection of the relevant information by an agent who is able to identify critical danger signs, familiarity with the field is crucial to the warning function. As stressed in the Guatemalan case, international NGOs definitely play a key role in rumor-driven societies where accuracy of information is often in question. But NGOs confront a number of serious obstacles in providing early warning of an impending crisis.

One of the first difficulties that they face relates to the tension between voice and neutrality. In all cases, one must wonder whether the concept of impartial warning is an oxymoron. While warning can reflect a general level of tension, it most often relates to the action of a particular person or group. Its function is to identify the people involved. Yet, international NGOs, even more than governmental agencies, need ongoing and full governmental approval for their operations. At the same time, as several of the cases illustrate, local NGOs frequently encounter tension as they become increasingly involved in domestic political processes while simultaneously trying to remain impartial. When the local NGOs in Guatemala joined the opposition's National Revolutionary Front, for example, the military called them subversive.

Representatives of international NGOs often are or are perceived to be advocates for the underdog, the oppressed minority (for example, Albanians in Macedonia and southerners in the Sudan). If they do not fuel a conflict directly, at least they are often used as pretexts for parties acting aggressively under preemptive guises. This loss of impartiality leads to a kind of "Trojan horse syndrome," whereby the activities of local NGOs increasingly come to be perceived as preludes to external intervention. This conclusion is all the more true for international NGOs, which are perceived as working for their home governments. On the other hand, maintaining neutrality to ensure continued access may be akin to endorsing human rights abuses.

A related tension is that between voice and safety. Not surprisingly, people working in or for NGOs are often more vulnerable than others, especially if they are from the local community (Rwanda is a case in point). This vulnerability can be in part remedied by strategies of higher visibility, but it can in turn be counterproductive. The use of information technologies shows promise in helping to minimize the vulnerability among certain groups.

Many authorities have remarked on the strong link between effectiveness of early warning and the connection between warners and actors. If prevention does not work, it is not for lack of intelligence. But information that is not relayed does not reach decision-makers. This has to do with the kinds and choices of information that are conveyed and the channels of communication that are available. It also depends on whether the information itself conveys recommendations for action. NGOs are unlikely to provide the same warning as will potential external intervenors. For a warning to be credible, the parties involved must be identified, and the sources of escalation must be analyzed. Moreover, indigenous and international NGOs do not have direct access to decision-makers. It may be preferable, instead, to focus on the horizontal ties at the local level between NGOs and official representatives in the field.

Most important, if warning is not to get lost in the noise, it is necessary to create institutions that are dedicated to early warning and prevention. Such institutions must be responsible both for gathering information and making recommendations for action. As in other realms of life, advice is usually ignored. But because such a new institution would have the authority to issue recommendations for action and because potential actors would have mandated it to do so, such a device might work. The center for prevention proposed by the European parliament provides a possible model; so do embryonic regional centers set up in Africa to monitor conflicts there. Better systems must be designed to collect input from NGOs. But NGO-based warning cannot be at the heart of international preventive strategies.

NGOs risk being taken less seriously if their warnings are not expressed in terms of recommendations for action. Sounding a warning about potential conflict escalation from the field raises important risks of perverse effects. It is clear that issuing warnings without the assurance of action may be dangerous. If issued at all, they must be issued through discreet and unofficial channels rather than through the mass media. Finally, too much early warning activity can detract from the original missions of NGOs. Early warning must be developed with a full awareness of its limitations.

Preventive Action by NGOs: Internal Warning and
Conflict Dampening

Do NGOs have a comparative advantage with respect to early action when a conflict, or even long-term transformative action, can be foreseen? Clearly, they have very little to contribute to hands-off approaches, except to the extent that they have a prominent role in issuing the warnings that may lead to coercive diplomacy. The domain of NGOs is that of hands-on strategies, both of the ad hoc type and of the transformative type. In each case, should NGOs go it alone, or, if not, how can they most effectively work with governments to encourage early action? If NGOs do engage in some degree of preventive action, how should they approach this role, and how should it be related to their initial mandate? If they decide that they should not be in the business of early action, what are some of the strategies for demanding that governments and international organizations respond to warning signs? At all these levels, what are the most effective preventive actions in which NGOs can engage?

NGOs can act by engaging in what may be called "domestic warning," or "internal warning." This is especially the case for NGOs involved in conflict resolution and human rights issues but may apply to other NGOs in the context of their broader activities. NGOs should alert both the outside world and local actors. They can promote awareness about the sources, likelihood, and consequences of conflicts as well as about possible alternatives. International NGOs can also use their knowledge of similar conflicts to help provide a clear picture of unfolding events.

In a more transformative way, NGOs have a fundamental role to play in helping to demonstrate the benefits of peace to local populations. NGOs can be most effective simply by opening channels of communication that would not have occurred spontaneously between communities and opposing sides, and offering these groups fora for dialogue (in Macedonia, Albanians and ethnic Macedonians do not go to the same schools, restaurants, entertainment centers, or sporting events). They can attempt to help restore mutual trust, dispel mutual stereotypes, and educate people about the tools of conflict resolution.

NGOs can contribute to soft mediation by supporting media that foster peaceful dialogue and counter hate propaganda, as illustrated by radio broadcasts organized by Doctors Without Borders in Burundi. Similarly, the International Committee of the Red Cross has employed a variety of alternative dispute resolution strategies that are starting to bear fruit. In short, NGOs can help increase mutual understanding within a society as a whole as a basis for compromise at the political level. In doing so, they can help prevent a struggle between national parties from expanding into a conflict among ethnic communities. This is what happened in Angola and Cambodia and is in the process of happening in Macedonia.

In asking to what extent NGOs should cooperate with governments in prevention, it is important to keep in mind the incentive/capacity equation. NGOs might be considerably more effective if they could increase incentives for conflict management by providing disputing parties with access to useful resources. Offering such "packages" requires, in turn, that they work with other NGOs as well as with governments. But NGOs have another great comparative advantage that may force them to continue to act as autonomously from governments as possible. It is less sensitive for NGOs than for governmental agencies to link developmental aid to ethnic reconciliation. Such a linkage formally established by the latter risks being labeled as unduly interventionist and is vulnerable to the criticism of diversion. NGOs have more freedom to divert resources from "worthy" countries to countries at risk.

Conversely, in some instances, coordination between NGOs and governments has led to successful prevention. Operation Provide Comfort in Iraq was the first large-scale effort to foster cooperation among the military, the UN, and the NGO communities in the post-Cold War era. "Kurdistan became a seminal experience for American [NGOs] in their relation to U.S. forces, as it showed them they could work together productively in a humanitarian emergency, something that even organizations not opposed to U.S. government policies or to close association with the U.S. military doubted."[41] This has significantly increased the mutual respect between the two sides and may provide a model for similar actions in the future.

NGOs can seek to influence socio-political systems from the inside through assets that only they possess. While they have comparatively fewer resources than governmental organizations, they also have greater credibility and freedom of maneuver. Such preventive actions on the part of NGOs may, however, prove to be increasingly incompatible with their being warners calling for potential outside intervention. NGOs may have to choose.

Conclusion: Building a Culture of Prevention

This chapter illustrates the broad potential of international preventive action. It recognizes its limitations by highlighting some of the conditions that hinder as well as favor the prevention of deadly conflicts. Ultimately, it argues for a gradually implemented, long-term institutionalization of prevention to put it at the core of international affairs in the twenty-first century. In this context, NGOs have a circumscribed but crucial role to play.

The real danger today is not that the international community may intervene ineffectively, but that it will not intervene at all. However sophisticated our warning systems, it is only when conflicts are "on the screen," literally as well as figuratively, that they receive attention. Often, that is when it is too late. We should thus strip prediction from prevention to the greatest extent possible. In the same vein as the distinction between "preventive" and "predictive" medicine, blind prevention may be the most cost-effective strategy with regard to domestic conflicts. Rapid reaction capacities need to be enhanced and relied on automatically. Provided that they can be designed to minimize perverse effects, systemic transformative actions should progressively become part of the operational design of international institutions and NGOs. Priority should be granted to preventing the recurrence of conflicts through adequate reconstruction and reconciliation programs.

Even with a focus on blind prevention, there will still be a crucial role for early warning and targeted action on the part of NGOs. But warning needs to be addressed to insiders as well as outsiders. Alongside the obvious risk of self-fulfilling prophecies, self-negating prophecies can also be exploited.[42] Local NGOs can work in conflicted situations with their international counterparts to publicize past examples of successful reconciliation efforts and to paint likely scenarios of peace or violence for a community.

The chapters in this book nevertheless invite caution by showing that NGOs' effectiveness depends in part on the local civic culture, such as ingrained attitudes of deference to public authority and the role of civil society in the political arena. On the whole, NGOs may be better equipped for soft prevention, such as creating channels for expressing grievances, than for official action, such as mediating and helping to implement agreements between opposing sides.

Whether they seek to intervene at an early or late stage, actors of prevention should join forces in order to act on both the incentive and the capacity side of the prevention equation. Governments are best equipped to use carrots and sticks to shift the incentives of the most influential parties to a conflict while international institutions and non-governmental actors can help empower local proponents of peaceful resolution by giving them a voice and additional resources. There needs to be a new consensus in favor of coercive international intervention on behalf of human rights—not only in response to threats to international peace. This consensus should include the threats to use force at a prevention stage. Governmental and non-governmental agencies could bolster their claim for additional resource distribution by analyzing and publicizing the "cost of non-prevention" in the international arena.

In the long run, contributing to the capacity within all societies to develop "infrastructures for peace" is likely to require an increasing degree of institutionalization and long-range planning. Whether in the realm of domestic or international policies, emergency operations have become the central mode of collective action. Prevention is an abstract idea, which rests on rendering visible the shadow of the future. In this light, the main benefit of embedding prevention in longer-term institutional strategies may be that doing so would help foster a culture of prevention where the cries of Cassandras might better be heard, before the logic of an emergency takes over.

Notes

I thank Mia Bloom, Jendayi Frazer, Robert Rotberg, and Ann Hannum for their helpful comments.

1. Boutros Boutros-Ghali, *An Agenda for Peace* (New York, 1995, 2nd ed.), 13.

2. This department has developed an early warning system to monitor political developments worldwide. The first systematic effort of this kind dates to 1975, when the Food and Agriculture Organization (FAO) put in place a Global International Warning System to forecast droughts and other natural catastrophes leading to famines. In 1987, the UNHCR set up an office for research and collection of information. It later established the Refugees and Emergency Alert System (REAS).

3. The typology used here is inspired by Hirschman's typology of the arguments used by conservative thinkers against the left in the last three centuries. See Albert Hirschman, *The Rhetoric of Reaction, Futility, Perversity, Jeopardy* (Cambridge, MA, 1991). There clearly is a conceptual affinity in the critique of state intervention internationally and domestically. In both cases what is derided is the notion that human agencies can have a significant impact on history and engineer progress. Caveats must be introduced, however. Arguments against international preventive action do not necessarily have a conservative flavor. Such arguments can be made to militate against rather than for the status quo; also arguments against prevention can be made in order to protect other, arguably even more ambitious types of intervention. Above all, at an ideological level, anti-interventionism in the international sphere has retained some of its original "anti-imperialist" flavor, which is not appreciated by conservative thinkers.

Because it would risk suggesting a one-to-one parallel between the critics of progressive politics and preventive action, it does not seem appropriate to transpose wholesale the actual categories or labels used by Hirschman. I have therefore adopted categories that fit the purpose of my analysis.

4. For an argument to shift the focus back on triggering factors rather than on underlying structural causes of conflict, see Michael E. Brown (ed.), *The International Dimensions of Internal Conflict* (Boston, 1996), 1–32.

5. Stephen John Stedman, "Alchemy for a New World Order—Overselling 'Preventive Diplomacy,'" *Foreign Affairs*, LXXIV (1995), 20.

6. For a discussion on the notion of "ripeness" and its relevance to conflict resolution, see I. William Zartman, *Timing in Deescalation* (Syracuse, 1990).

7. Although the UN does not formally categorize post-conflict reconstruction as preventive diplomacy, it is currently the area in which preventive approaches are developed systematically.

8. See the chapter by Francis Deng in this volume.

9. For a recent analysis which argues that elite factors usually predominate in the causes of ethnic conflict, see Brown, *International Dimensions*, 1–32.

10. See Charles Taylor, *Multiculturalism and the Politics of Recognition* (Princeton, 1993). Also, in his chapter, Deng stresses how the myth of superiority associated with the dominant group runs against the countermyth of defensive assertiveness of disadvantaged minorities.

11. As argued in the introduction to this book, the relevance of famine and human rights warning mechanisms is limited in that they rely on well-established but idiosyncratic standards.

12. There is a proposal in the European Parliament to create a Center for the Active Prevention of Conflicts. Its main tasks would be to centralize information about "countries at risk," to issue regular reports categorizing these countries according to the degree to which they are at risk, and to monitor change in those areas.

13. See the contested role of the OAU's new early warning system for conflict prevention, management, and resolution.

14. See for instance, Dean G. Pruitt and Jeffrey Z. Rubin, *Social Conflict: Escalation, Stalemate, and Settlement* (New York, 1986); Janie Leatherman and Raimo Väyrynen, "Early Warning and the Prevention of Intranational Conflict," a paper presented at the World Peace Foundation conference on NGOs, Early Warning, and Preventive Diplomacy, Cambridge, 1995.

15. Thomas Schelling, *The Strategy of Conflict* (Cambridge, MA, 1960).

16. Alexander George and Richard Smoke, *Deterrence in American Foreign Policy: Theory and Practice* (New York, 1974), 11.

17. Alexander George, *Forceful Persuasion—Coercive Diplomacy as an Alternative to War* (Washington, D.C., 1991), xi.

18. Preemptive or preventive wars can be seen as extreme versions of preventive coercive diplomacy. They are not a direct concern since they do not constitute alternative strategies to war but rather attempts to avoid defeat in war. (According to one definition, preventive wars are entered into in order to prevent a war from occurring later, when the adversary would have accumulated disproportionate force. In contrast, in preemptive wars, the attacking state fears that it is about to be a target.) While academics have argued that preemption is a very likely path to armed conflict

between states, in actuality, preemptive wars rarely occur. From a prescriptive stand-point, the question that needs to be addressed is how and when can preventive and preemptive wars be avoided? For a recent discussion, see Dan Reiter, "Exploding the Powder Keg Myth," *International Security*, XX (1995), 5–34.

19. George, *Forceful Persuasion*, 8.

20. The case of Rwanda seems to lend credence to the fact that even the appearance of minimal intervention at an early stage, before a conflict explodes out of control, can have a disproportionate effect. Many eyewitnesses testified that the violence stopped in Rwanda when French airplanes were thought to be bringing inter-position forces rather than flying out foreign residents.

21. George, *Forceful Persuasion*, 8.

22. See Jeffrey Z. Rubin and John Zartman, *Power and Negotiation*, forthcoming.

23. For a discussion, see Bertram Spector, "Creativity Heuristics for Impasse Resolution: Reframing Intractable Negotiations," *The Annals of the American Academy*, DXLII (1995), 81–99.

24. For instance, freezing financial assets seems to be more effective than impos-ing undifferentiated sanctions.

25. See Mia Bloom, "The Road to Hell is Paved with Good Intentions," (unpub. manuscript, Harvard Program on Non-Violent Sanctions and Cultural Survival, Center for International Affairs, 1996).

26. For a detailed history of the military operation, see Larry Forster, "Operation Provide Comfort: A Shield for Humanitarian Intervention in Iraqi Kurdistan," (Harvard University, CFIA Research Paper, April 1996).

27. See C. R. Mitchell, "A Willingness to Talk" (working paper, Fairfax, VA, 1993).

28. For a recent overview, see, for instance, Jacob Bercovitch (ed.), *Resolving International Conflicts: The Theory and Practice of Mediation* (Boulder, CO, 1996).

29. Boutros-Ghali, *Agenda for Peace*, 13.

30. For a general description of the evolution of the mediation field, see Robert Bush and Joseph Folger, *The Promise of Mediation* (San Francisco, 1995).

31. See Diana Chigas with Elizabeth McClintock and Christophe Kamp, "Pre-ventive Diplomacy and the Organization for Security and Cooperation in Europe: Creating Incentives for Dialogue and Cooperation," in Abram Chayes and Antonia Chandler Chayes (eds.), *Preventing Conflict in the Post-Communist World* (Wash-ington, D.C., 1996), 25–99.

32. Member states have an obligation to accept fact-finding missions for inves-tigative purposes. The High Commissioner on National Minorities has the authority to initiate conflict prevention activities without seeking prior political approval. After visiting countries to collect information and promote dialogue, he may request a mandate for early action through a more formal program for conflict resolution.

33. See Chigas, "Preventive Diplomacy," 66.

34. In addition, OSCE has set up a Conflict Prevention Center, which is sup-posed to assist the Council in reducing the risk of conflict, in part by supporting mil-itary aspects of conflict prevention, including military exchanges.

35. See Jenonne Walker, "International Mediation of Ethnic Conflicts," *Survival*, XXXV (1993), 102–117.

36. UNHCR, *The State of the World's Refugees, In Search of Solutions* (Oxford, 1995), 58.

37. For a discussion, see, for instance, Jean Manas, "The Council of Europe's Democracy Ideal and the Challenge of Ethno-National Strife," in Chayes, *Preventing Conflict*, 99–146.

38. Stedman, "Alchemy," 19.

39. For a discussion of this distinction, see Wolfgang Reinicke, "Can International Financial Institutions Prevent Internal Violence? The Sources of Ethno-Conflicts in Transitional Societies," in Chayes, *Preventing Conflict*, 312–313.

40. See Ted Gurr, "Give Us the Means to the Future: The Mobilization of Grievance, Minorities at Risk" (Washington, D.C., 1993), 68–69, 71–72. See also Faisal Farooq-Khan, "The De Facto Regimes and Foreign Interests, Toward a Contextualized Approach for Managing the Afghan Crisis" (unpublished manuscript, 1996).

41. Andrew Natsios, "The International Humanitarian System," *Parameters* (Spring 1995), 69.

42. An example of a self-negating prophecy would occur when a broadcasted prediction of a traffic jam induces everyone to stay home in order to prevent the traffic jam, or when the prediction of a landslide drives supporters away from the polls. See Thomas Schelling, *Micromotives and Macrobehavior* (New York, 1978), 118.

GUATEMALA

CHAPTER TWO

The Search for Peace and Justice in Guatemala: NGOs, Early Warning, and Preventive Diplomacy

Tom Lent

THE WORK of NGOs in Guatemala during the past two decades has addressed a myriad of concerns that range from relief, reconstruction, and development to the protection of indigenous Guatemalans from the state, and broader human rights issues. Through their relationships with actors at all levels, NGOs have evolved into organizations capable of providing early warning of conflict and exercising preventive diplomacy. One such experience in Guatemala was that of Save the Children.

The Earthquake

On 4 February 1976, Guatemala suffered an earthquake of disastrous proportions (6.5 on the Richter scale) that left over 25,000 people dead, 75,000 injured, and 1 million homeless. The human response was impressive. Amid the rubble, destruction, and tragedy, neighbors began to help neighbors, and community committees joined together to start rebuilding damaged structures. Most of the wealthier sections of Guatemala City were left unscathed, but several of the poorer and working class neighborhoods, where construction was older and/or less sturdy were heavily damaged. *Departamentos* (provinces) around the Motagua River were even more devastated, leaving many rural towns and villages with hardly a structure standing. Regardless of—or because

73

of—the physical and emotional damage resulting from this devastating event, a contagious spirit of solidarity, resilience, and individual and collective strength evolved within the population as a whole.

International organizations quickly arrived on the scene. A few North American and European NGOs (CRS, CARE, and Oxfam/UK) already had offices and programs in the country, but literally dozens of others arrived in Guatemala and joined the reconstruction efforts.

An alliance ("Alianza") of seven Save the Children organizations—those from Norway, Sweden, Denmark, Austria, Canada, Great Britain, and the United States—joined forces to support the reconstruction and development efforts in Quiché, a highland department of Guatemala. Initially, upper-level staff positions were held mainly by persons from overseas; over time, however, Guatemalans assumed all of these positions.

Regardless of our nationality or position within the team, none of us could have known that, while participating in reconstruction, we would become part of the next chapter in Guatemalan history, which would make the destruction caused by the earthquake appear mild in comparison.

From Disaster Relief to Development

On seeing the widespread devastation and rubble in the aftermath of the earthquake, the agencies that had come to Guatemala to provide relief promptly concluded that the first priority of the country and the people should be reconstruction. After holding community meetings in Quiché, however, we learned otherwise. In Guatemala's moderate climate of "eternal spring," shelter was important, but not the highest priority of local people.

In these meetings, local residents described their daily struggle for survival. Their concerns included increasingly poor farming conditions (depleted soil and small plots of land); subsistence wages and inhuman living conditions on coastal plantations where they were forced to work to supplement their incomes; illiteracy (especially among the women); child malnutrition (80 percent of children were malnourished); and infant mortality. Although the earthquake took 25,000 lives, 40,000 children in Guatemala died each year of malnutrition and related causes. Which was the greater "disaster," and which issue should receive greatest priority? Community members also spoke of the lack of schools and potable water—many people had to walk one to three kilometers a day to fetch water from contaminated sources—and described the degradation and racism that dominated their relationships with many of the powerful ladinos (a sociological term describing people of primarily Spanish or mixed descent, or those who have left behind their Mayan customs) in positions of authority and control.

In order to respond most effectively to the needs of the communities, we decided to take a holistic view of the communities' problems as the people themselves saw them. Our belief was that solutions and options should be the result of community discussion and analysis, not remedies that outside agencies created and imposed upon them. Our role would be to help strengthen the problem-solving process within each community.

We would therefore have to focus our efforts more on a "community process" of short-, medium-, and long-term problem solving than on the construction of "community projects." In practice, doing so meant that the building up and/or strengthening of community committees and groups was integral to whatever we did. For example, community agricultural promoters were taught agricultural techniques to increase and diversify crop production. They were then encouraged to form groups in their communities in order to replicate these improved methods. These same groups, in turn, could buy agricultural goods at reduced rates and obtain higher market prices. In another example, after receiving training in primary health care and pre- and post-natal attention, midwives and health promoters formed an association in order to receive medicines, training, and support. Similarly, local home builders involved in reconstruction efforts formed committees in order to obtain needed supplies and to learn seismically appropriate building techniques. Literacy groups were also started to share materials, discuss common problems, and create community learning centers and libraries.

At no time did we view the community as a homogeneous entity with a common vision, interests, and goals. To the contrary, what was most obvious were the divisions that existed within and among communities. Racial, class, language, religious, political, and gender conflicts were chronic. What we did contend, however, was that these conflicts could be overcome by helping individuals and communities to develop a common awareness of the differences among them and respect for those differences. Through dialogue and analysis, a new, common vision and a set of priorities could be generated. We hired local ladino and Mayan staff for responsible positions, ran training courses for them together, and supported joint projects.

Another part of this strategy involved working with the groups who traditionally had not been represented or heard in the adult male-dominated community committee meetings. Training and discussion sessions for women's groups, children's groups, and groups of the poorest community members helped provide them with confidence; therefore, when they discussed their respective issues and priorities in community forums, they were able to do so with greater clarity and conviction than in the past. For instance, the men on the community committee in one village decided that the community's first priority was to build a road so that fertilizers could be brought in more easily and crops could be transported out to markets. The women, however, envisioned a different priority: Through their preparation and focus group, they advocated a water project because they and the children had to walk daily up and down steep mountain paths to a stream to bring water back up to their houses. In the end, the women and children prevailed.

After the earthquake, community committees constructed more than 100 schools, dozens of potable water projects, health clinics, bridges, and roads. Organized groups taught numerous literacy classes, sponsored income-generating projects and vaccination campaigns, and fostered family vegetable gardens—all testimony to the mystique and vision of the rural Mayan population. These projects also reflected their commitment to their communities and their belief in their own capacities and futures.

Our work over several years generated stories of both success and failure with community organization. Both our professed intentions as well as our programmatic actions were centered on building bridges among groups, encouraging forums for analysis and action, and creating greater confidence in local capacities, resources, and technology.

Our approach was far-reaching, and went beyond the philosophy that, "If you give a man a fish, you feed him for a day; if you teach him how to fish, you feed him for a lifetime." What happens if an NGO "teaches how to fish," and the people they are working with live in a desert? Furthermore, the issues affecting the communities were not particular to individual "fisher*men*." Problems were shared; solutions could be shared as well. The challenge for an NGO is to commit itself to listening and learning, and never to assume that it has answers. Development is fundamentally a question of values. We must discover what people value and why.

Much of what Alianza tried to do was motivated by the ethics of development and relief: Avoid creating dependencies, encourage people to do as much as they can for themselves, respect local values and traditions, build on what people have and know, and listen to and learn from the people in the community. This had a practical side to it as well. We had neither the resources nor staff to rebuild the *municipios*. Furthermore, people needed to learn earthquake-resistant construction techniques for themselves. Home building in rural Guatemala consists mostly of self-construction from adobe. A neighboring carpenter or mason may give a hand, but most construction is of the self-help variety. As years go by and children marry and bring spouses back to live as an extended family, new rooms are added. When the inevitable tremor or quake occurs, the results are often fatal.

Early Warning Signals?

To speak of "early warning signals" in the case of violence in Guatemala is to miss the point: More than signals, we saw pre-existing patterns with historical roots. Conflict was omnipresent and cyclical, more than "early," and what could be interpreted as "warnings" were also opportunities to emerge from a paradigm of injustice.

While the reign of violence from 1981 to 1984, which affected hundreds of thousands of people, certainly had been accompanied by "early warning signals," most events that led up to and induced the wave of massive repression were seen at the time by most of us in development and disaster relief as positive signs of popular organization and mass mobilization, and as non-violent expressions in favor of a more just society, or the efforts of groups affirming their rights to better social and economic conditions. The agendas for the great majority of these groups had more to do with the need for clean drinking water, more school rooms, fair wages, evening literacy classes, and the development of community projects than the revolutionary transformation of society. Change, however, even on a small scale, was seen as a threat to the existing order and resulted in violent responses by the government, landed elites, and security forces at local and national levels. In Guatemala, as has been the case in many countries, not all the early warning signals of impending violence were negative or violent in nature; rather, they were most frequently articulated by daily actions that sought peacefully and collectively to construct fair and equitable means of survival and to ensure the well-being of the greatest possible number of people.

In the 1980s and early 1990s, divisions within Guatemala in general, and in Quiché specifically, were extensive. Beneath the remarkable beauty and drama of the country—the imposing volcanoes along the piedmont that separate the coastal plantations and the highlands; the colorful market days brightened by traditional Mayan clothes and weavings; the richness of the country's twenty-two cultural-linguistic groups; the impressive ruins of Tikal; and many other noteworthy geographical and cultural features—lay feelings of deep discord and friction.

Class, race, gender, religion, geography, and political affiliation all contributed—with varying intensity from community to community across the highlands—to the overall sense of divisiveness within these areas. In most of the Quiché work areas, the *cabecera municipal*, or county seat, was an "urban" area of about 2,000 to 3,000 inhabitants, many of whom were ladinos. Even where ladinos were not a numerical majority, they still controlled much of the commerce in town and were the elected officials, policemen, and teachers. They also contracted workers—mostly Mayan—to pick cotton, harvest coffee beans, and cut sugar cane. Almost all of the rural areas were populated by *indigenas*, people of Mayan descent who, to varying degrees, continued to live according to Mayan traditions. In the Quiché highlands, ladinos represented approximately 5–10 percent of the population; indigenas represented 90–95 percent.

Of the many divisions that existed, those related to religion were among the most profound. Guatemala has the largest Protestant population (over 30 percent) in Latin America. The friction between Catholics and Protestants was evident, and serious schisms existed within each of these denominations as well. Some focused on the peace to be attained in the afterlife, while others were concerned with justice in this one. The Catholic Action community groups became a principal movement for change; the charismatic and fundamentalist Protestant groups came to play a greater and politically conservative role from the 1970s onward. *Costumbristas* continued to practice their Mayan religion, and many mixed that together with Catholicism.

Economic divisions between rich and poor generally had ethnic implications. Two percent of the population (nearly all ladino) owned 62 percent of the land. Most of the Mayan population in the Quiché part of the highlands was so poor that they were obliged to migrate to the plantations for two to six months out of the year in order to supplement their family incomes. These economic divisions determined who had access to education, health facilities, and credit. As a result, Guatemala had among the highest illiteracy, school absenteeism, and malnutrition rates in Latin America and the lowest in per capita expenditures on health and clean drinking water. Only 7 percent of the population obtained 70 percent of the credit.

Political parties and affiliations were taken seriously in the 1970s and early 1980s; (little by little, however, old and new parties alike, as well as the political system in general, have been discredited, resulting in electoral abstention rates surpassing 70 percent in the 1990s). Political parties included the Movimiento Liberación Nacional (MLN); the Partido Institucional Democratico (PID); the Partido Revolucionario (PR); and the Christian Democrats (DC). These parties, however, were "represented" in elections by different military groups competing for political power. Voting, especially in 1974, 1978, and 1982, was marked by fraudulent procedures, and the political system and political parties lost credibility. As time went on, a growing number of people saw the electoral process less and less as a realistic road to democratic change. At the time, the MLN, a right wing party, was led by persons responsible for many of the death squads. Run by an authoritarian strong man, or *caudillo*, the party stood on the platform of anti-communism, when communism was defined as just about anything that represented change, redistribution, justice, equity, or ethnic expression. Even some of the more conservative elements within the *indigena* community formed part of the MLN. PID and PR had become the official parties and represented an odd mixture of old reformers, industrialists, army officers, and the urban middle class. The DC, center left within the Guatemalan context in the 1970s and early 1980s, represented for the progressive Mayan population a political-electoral option for democratic, non-violent change. (The fact that, by the 1990s, all of these "major forces" had nearly insignificant roles is another story.)

Another divisive factor in the 1980s stemmed from the relationship between the civilian populations and the army and security forces. In short, almost all of the officers were ladinos, while most of the foot soldiers were Mayan, many of whom had been forcibly recruited at early ages from their villages. After undergoing a period of indoctrination and spending time in the army, many soldiers found it difficult to return home. In addition, the *comisionados militares* (military commissioners), mostly ladinos, were volunteer agents of the army at the village and hamlet level, and were responsible for maintaining law and order and reporting "subversives" and opposition activity (however narrowly defined) to the army. In fact, many civilian ladinos used this system as well as the security apparatus of the state and the army to further their own control at a local level. Much of the violence in the highlands was a product of official army and state policy and often framed in Cold War terms, but, at local levels, many ladinos used this power structure to settle scores that had less to do with ideology and Cold War justifications, and more to do with the protection of traditional political and economic interests of the elite.

The Crisis Develops

What developed in Guatemala in the 1980s was a kind of "chronicle of an announced death," as depicted by Gabriel Garcia Marquez in *Crónica de Una Muerte Anunciada (Chronicle of a Death Foretold)* (Bogotá, 1981), in which slowly, a whole village comes to realize that a murder is to take place, with the last person to find out being the victim himself. Garcia Marquez describes how the wheels of motion of the crime, the momentum of the decision itself, the paralysis of key spectators, and the pervading surreal atmosphere of the situation, made it nearly impossible to prevent the "logic" of the tragedy from evolving.

In the case of Guatemala, entire populations were subjected to forces similar to those in the novel: They became, in effect, the victims of a tragedy which unfolded slowly and, sometimes, imperceptibly around them. Like the victim in *Crónica*, who was innocent and did not realize that he had been accused, and therefore did not pick up the signals or take precautions, many highland Maya went to their deaths at the hands of the army, not realizing—or realizing too late—of what they had been accused.

After the earthquake in 1976 and 1977, relief and development agencies began to receive news of an increased army presence and occasional clashes with the guerrillas in the Ixcán area of Quiché, to the north of our work area. News then arrived that the cooperative members of the colonization programs were being subjected to intimidation and assassination by the army. Many of the villages affected were within 100 kilometers of our work area, but the dire conditions of rural roads made travel extremely difficult; as such, they were as far away in hours as a flight to Asia. Little news appeared in the mass media about what was occurring.

Throughout this time, however, with the authorization and blessing of at least some sections of the government, we continued to support the formation of local Reconstruction Committees. Concerns about political tensions in areas further north in Ixcán had to be viewed in the context of the progress being made in the highlands by local communities successfully carrying out potable water projects, and building schools and health posts in isolated rural areas. They were "heady" times, when health promoters, agricultural extensionists, women's groups, and other community groups were all receiving training and were mobilizing on community issues. It was a time of optimism, hope, and confidence. The feeling was that, changes for the rural poor probably could not or would not come about in politics at the national level through government policies, land reform, structural changes, or income redistribution in the short term, but could possibly be partially addressed at the community and municipal levels.

As time went on, however, events occurring at the community, regional, and national levels took on increasing significance and started to feed into each other. Tensions heightened as three forces began to take on an unprecedented momentum, virulence, and logic of their own: the army, popular movements, and the armed opposition (the guerillas). It was apparent, even then, that something dramatic and historic was evolving, as the events themselves demonstrated.

In one of the first community meetings in Quiché after the 1976 earthquake, in one municipio, a municipal-wide assembly was called to form a Reconstruction Committee. The mayor, a local businessman and member of the right wing MLN party, and someone accustomed to dominating matters, attempted to appoint the officers and members of the committee. Despite his efforts, however, our staff "successfully" insisted that committee members be elected by the community itself. This "victory," while significant for strengthening unity at the community level, began a history of antagonism between our organization and some of the elite (ladinos) of the municipality.

In May 1978, 150 unarmed Kekchi Indians in Panzos, Alta Verapaz, were surrounded in the town square by soldiers and killed. The Indians had been protesting against the invasion of their lands by outsiders and were told by the army to meet that day in the town square to discuss the issue. Numerous investigations into the events that day indicated that the massacre had been premeditated. Like the repression against the cooperative movement in the Ixcán area, this event occurred outside the reconstruction areas and did not seem to indicate a widespread government policy of terror.

In other parts of southern Quiché, in May 1978, more progressive members of the Catholic Action community-based religious groups created the Committee of Peasant Unity (CUC), and began to address issues involving land, wages, human rights, and the army's forced recruitment of youth. Whereas other organizations that had some local support—the DC, guerrilla organizations, and church hierarchies—were headed by ladinos, the CUC was Mayan.

Later in 1978, Ixtahuacan miners began a long march from Huehuetenango into Guatemala City (over 150 miles) to protest working conditions and salaries. Although their demands were met before they reached the city, support all along the Pan American highway was so great that they continued their nine-day journey, and, by the time that they entered the city, 150,000 people were walking. There was an enhanced feeling of community solidarity and a sense that a great awakening was taking place. Growing numbers of people, especially among the Mayan population, were beginning to expand their traditional focus on local community issues and to create linkages across communities, municipalities, and provinces.

In the 1978 national elections, a municipio in which we worked in Quiché elected a DC mayor whose mother was Mayan K'iche', upsetting the local power elite. For decades the mayorship had been controlled by the official party and the extreme right-wing party. In the national elections, the official party retained control of the presidency. At the time, our staff was optimistic that the election of the new mayor would mean more support for rural development projects. Most resources of the municipality traditionally had been reserved for infrastructural projects for the town county seat.

Rumors spread that the army had a list of people who were considered to be subversive, and that numbers of teachers, DC leaders, progressive Catholic priests, and community leaders in the southern Quiché area had had their lives threatened or had "disappeared." Within a short period of time, many of these rumors were confirmed. We also heard of the deaths of rural teachers who had been active in community development as well as the deaths of cooperative leaders, DC leaders, priests in the Ixil Triangle, and others. The unspoken message from the government was that those who were advocating change and working with "the people" would be selected as targets.

In the late 1970s, a number of our staff members and others in the communities received visits at night by armed, non-uniformed men. The head of the Social Promotion Program, a Mayan and DC leader, was visited at night by "unknown people" who wanted to "talk with him." Our colleague remained inside without answering the door. Believing that the visitors had most likely been secret police and/or death squad members connected to the government (at least locally), we visited the vice president of the country—who was then acting president—and expressed concern over the matter. Because Quiché was well known for guerrilla activity (especially in the Ixcán area farther north), the vice president assured us that the visitors had been guerrillas. Although we did not believe him, we feared telling him that the "visitors" were probably members of the secret police. The vice president's response was consistent with previous and subsequent official responses: All incidents were blamed on the guerrillas.

By the late 1970s, the MLN, the far right political party, had begun an open campaign against the DC. Select DC and CUC leaders were assassinated in many rural villages and towns in the highlands. Known as the party of organized violence, the MLN was not about to relinquish its hold on local municipal and departmental power.

President Carter threatened to cut off military aid to Guatemala in 1978 because of its human rights violations. The Guatemalan government preempted this action, however, and refused U.S. aid, having secured alternative sources of support from Israel, Taiwan, and South Africa. The military structure no longer needed or depended directly on the United States for training, equipment, or technology. In the 1960s and 1970s, the Green Berets had trained special counterinsurgency forces—the Kaibiles—in Guatemala, who, by the 1980s, had achieved such a level of "professional competence" that they had begun training special forces from other countries.

In 1979, the Sandinistas took over power in Nicaragua, far ahead of their own political projections. A sense that progressive change was possible began to permeate other countries in Central America, including El Salvador and Guatemala. Many Guatemalans in both rural and urban areas were emboldened by the political changes that had occurred and openly supported the Sandinistas. They started to become more openly critical of their own government as well. The subsequent fall of the Somozas, the most powerful family in Central America, shattered the previously held belief that the power structure of the region was immutable. What had at one time been considered unthinkable—that the elite could be challenged and overthrown—now seemed to be within the realm of the possible. This change in attitude did not translate into a Sandinista-style movement in Guatemala, however, nor did it mean that the rural population opted for armed struggle. Far more extensive movements for change in Guatemala would eventually evolve according to their own logic and form. Most people saw the period as an opportunity to increase work among community committees, cooperatives, religious groups, and other organizations.

In the same year, Colom Argueta and Fuentes Mohr, two prominent and progressive civilian leaders of political parties, were assassinated in Guatemala City in separate incidents. Argueta had been a well-liked and respected former mayor of Guatemala City and was supported by the popular movement and labor groups. He was killed days after registering a political party. Mohr had been a respected social-democratic economist who had served as minister of finance in previous governments. Both had been considered strong presidential candidates for the 1982 elections, and either of them could have won an open, honest election. The assassinations signaled that civilian presidential candidates and parties of progressive persuasions would not be allowed seriously to participate in the 1982 elections.

On 31 January 1980, over thirty CUC members and university students peacefully occupied the Spanish Embassy in Guatemala City to focus attention on the abuses perpetrated by the army and other authorities in Quiché, the forced recruitment of young boys into the army, and ongoing land problems. The army and police surrounded the embassy; an explosion followed, and all but two people died. One survivor, the Spanish ambassador, left the country. The other survivor, a Mayan and a CUC member, was dragged out of his hospital bed by the secret police the next day, tortured, and left for dead on the national university campus. The message was clear that political expression, even though nonviolent, would not be allowed when it contained information or criticism about military activities in the highlands and Ixcán area.

In February 1980, in an unprecedented move, the CUC called for a strike throughout the south coast, which succeeded in raising the minimum wage from $1.50 a day to $3 a day. The majority of the farmers in the rural highlands migrated (and continue to do so) to the coffee, sugar cane, and cotton plantations seasonally. The large number of people involved in the strike and the organizational power of CUC amounted to a political-military wake-up call to the power elite, who had historically enjoyed cheap, subservient labor.

In August 1980, the Rev. Faustino Villanueva, a Catholic priest in Joyabaj, was assassinated. While the "sisters" in the parish were noted for their progressive ideas, Father Villaneuva had been more moderate and less political. Two men came into town on motorcycles in broad daylight and entered his study. Shouts were heard, gunshots rang out, and the men fled. Witnesses tied the men to the army. It was clear that neither the official nor the unofficial power structure would look the other way while progressive church members attempted to organize people around ethical or social justice issues.

In the same month, our team in Joyabaj met to decide the future of our program. We needed to determine whether we should stay on in the hope of protecting communities, or whether our presence and activities, in fact, jeopardized the safety of community members. After a rather lengthy and painful discussion, the Joyabaj program decided to close down. It was considered too dangerous for staff to continue working with and organizing local communities. "Social promotion," "community organization," and "awareness raising" were branded as subversive activities by many authorities at municipal, departmental, and national levels.

In view of events in Quiché and the decision to close the Joyabaj program, team members from a nearby program met to discuss what steps they should take. The team decided to continue with its program. It felt that it had nothing to hide or fear, and that closing the program would imply to those in power that we were, in fact, guilty of something. Upon returning to Quiché after the meeting, a staff member learned that his brother had been tortured and killed that day by the secret anti-Communist army (ESA), one of the country's death squads. Another staff member learned that his village had been invaded by the army that morning and that his wife had been shot to death in bed, with her nine-month-old son in her arms. Had he not met with us that day, he would have been home. Many other people in his village had died that morning, as well.

The program decided to close down its activities.

Rumors within "politically aware" groups in the city and highlands indicated that parts of Quiché and Huehuetenango were considered "liberated territory," under control of guerrillas. Very little news appeared in the newspapers or on television. The residents of Guatemala City, in general, knew almost nothing of what was happening in the highlands. Some might argue that, because of racial or ideological reasons, these people chose to ignore what they had heard. Nonetheless, the paucity of information at that time was astounding to those of us who knew what was happening.

These events in Quiché rapidly turned threatening as polarization among the many factions increased. By then, the army, death squads, secret police, and military commissioners were aggressive and menacing. To add to the inflammatory situation, people who had had local feuds and disagreements took advantage of the general atmosphere of terror and instability to settle old accounts. "Eliminating" an enemy, perceived or real, could be accomplished, with impunity, by spending a few hundred quetzales: No questions would be asked, and retribution was not a threat.

By 1981–1982, because of the continued threat of violence, OXFAM, Norwegian Church Aid, World Neighbors, and other aid organizations in the Chimaltenango area had closed their programs, and many of their staff had left the country. Alianza had development programs in other parts of the country that had not experienced similar levels of violence. So we stayed.

Those who left were criticized for leaving during a time of such critical need; those who stayed were asked how they could do so, when remaining in the country supposedly lent legitimacy to an illegitimate government. Those who chose to stay were also criticized for believing that their assistance might make a difference to Guatemala; the country, argued the critics, needed deep social change which could not be delivered by the palliatives offered by the programs. In fact, the decision to go or stay was never quite so simple as these arguments would suggest. Many of the NGOs that did leave consulted first with community members, who told them that they could be of greatest help to the communities by informing the rest of the world about events unfolding within the country. In fact, many of these NGOs found ways to support the communities financially and morally even though the NGOs no longer had a physical presence in the country. NGOs that stayed in the country found numerous ways of working without having their work coopted or compromised by the government or army. The great challenges facing them created courageous responses.

Responses to the Early and Late Warning Signals

By 1980, Consejo de Instituciones de Desarrollo (COINDE), a national coordinating council of Guatemalan NGOs, and Asociación de Instituciones de Desarrollo (ASINDES), an NGO umbrella organization composed of national and international NGOs, had begun to meet with greater frequency in an effort to create a united front against the mounting violence.

ASINDES started off as an umbrella group of NGOs whose members, in more "peaceful" times following the earthquake, had decided to meet periodically to share insights, materials, and ideas about their work. As political events increasingly began to affect us personally and to interfere with the work of our programs, we sought to formalize the coordination among NGOs.

During the early 1980s, we held numerous meetings with the president and his cabinet to protest disturbing events in the rural and urban areas. We were invited to the presidential palace on several occasions to express our views, but nothing ever came of the meetings. On several occasions, members of the army even offered to come and explain their policies to the assembly. In short, ASINDES came to be recognized as a representative body of NGOs; however, its capacity to lobby or truly to articulate a voice of protest was limited. We managed to address specific issues with certain cabinet ministers, but we were unable to alter the government's strategic policies of "scorched earth" or "guns and beans," or its practices of intimidation and violence.

Periodically, some NGOs tried to bring international attention to the incidents of violence that they had been witnessing, but their efforts failed to bring about any action. Reports by Amnesty International, Americas Watch, and Cultural Survival exposed violations of human rights throughout Guatemala, and North American and European journalists transmitted stories about atrocities there; however, little outside pressure was exerted on the government.

By late 1981, the Guatemalan government began a scorched earth policy in an attempt to "take the sea away from the fish." What had previously been selective governmental repression against progressive rural teachers, DC leaders, Catholic Action groups, CUC leaders, and cooperative leaders and committee members escalated into a government-sanctioned policy of massive displacement, torture, and massacre. During this period entire villages were targeted for elimination. Government policy at this time was premised on the fact that any political uprising in the Guatemalan rural area like that in Nicaragua or El Salvador would have to be prevented at any cost.

Tensions were mounting, creating a potentially explosive mixture: the growing anti-army—and, by extension—anti-government movement in the highlands; the indignation resulting from the fraudulent elections, crime, and corruption; a sense among rural populations of historical injustice and exploitation perpetrated against them; the "continuismo" that was represented by the uninspiring and uncharismatic president-elect Guevara, a general closely tied to the Lucas government; the success at social mobilization of CUC and reconstruction committees in certain parts of the country; and the feeling that, after the fall of Somoza in Nicaragua, change was possible. This conjunction of forces was altered and distracted, however, by the sudden coup on 23 March 1982 that put General Efrain Rios Montt into power.

The scorched earth policy was intensified. Rios Montt's "guns and beans" policy, which purported to combine social policy with military policy, merely increased military control. While publicly emphasizing national "developmental" issues, Rios Montt focused on establishing special courts and trials for political prisoners. Rios Montt and his associates felt that they were in danger of losing power, and were prepared to take drastic measures to maintain control.

Between 1981 and 1983, an estimated 75,000 people—nearly all of them civilians—were killed; 440 villages were destroyed; 150,000 people fled into Mexico—and at least as many went farther north; 200,000 children were left orphaned by at least one parent; and 1 million people were displaced within the country.

These numbers present only one part of the story. The ongoing crisis and the continued threats to personal safety throughout this period required that many people inside and outside our development program make difficult choices. Some people went to Mexico, others migrated to the capital or the south coast, and still others joined the guerrillas. Many of our former staff members were killed. The fate of people who chose to participate in the armed conflict is still unknown, but many of those who stayed in their villages hoping to wait out the violence were subjected to persecution and death. Among those targeted most actively were the agricultural promoters and people involved with the Social Promotion Program. They represented change.

The 1990s

During the continuing violence in Guatemala there were countless acts of heroism, sacrifice, and honor. That thousands of Guatemalans survived in refugee camps in Mexico, slum areas in Mexico City and Guatemala City, and the jungle and highlands of Quiché is a testimony to human ingenuity and perseverance. In the mid-1990s, however, many of these people have begun to return home, and they still face a great deal of uncertainty.

Each year between the mid-1980s and 1995 was designated "The Year of the Return." After numerous false alarms and dashed hopes, however, the committee of refugees (Commisiones Permanentes/CP) in 1992 signed an agreement with the Guatemalan government that provided a framework and norms for repatriation. The lack of political will on the part of the governments from 1985 to 1995 to address issues of repatriation, and their lack of financial support, aggravated tensions on multiple levels. In short, more than a decade after the eruption of violence in Guatemala, many "early warning signals" remain in place. There is potential conflict. Any future conflict may not resemble the conflicts of the 1980s, but may nonetheless be serious and widespread.

Warning Signals

It was not until late 1995 that Civil Defense Patrols and the Military Commissioners were officially abolished. In spite of what has happened at the official level, however, in 1996, the structure of power and repression is still intact in much of the rural countryside. Furthermore, the army still maintains an official presence throughout many of the "conflict areas." Despite the outward appearance of progress related to the peace process, negotiations, and agreements, peace has not yet arrived in the 6,023 towns and 20,000 hamlets in Guatemala.

The land reform issue is generally neglected in official political discussions. Much of the land that was left behind by those who fled to Mexico or to other parts of the country is now being occupied by other people—in many instances, equally poor peasants—who were relocated there by the army during the mid-1980s.

The army continues to accuse the returnees (retornados) of being either guerrillas or guerrilla sympathizers, and has warned neighboring communities against cooperating and socializing with the returnee population.

The returnees developed strong ties of solidarity and cooperation during their ten years in exile and, as a result, have the capacity to mobilize around issues. They have gained confidence in their own role in civil society and in the roles that they play in the reconstruction of their villages and local economies. Although they are unarmed, and have been civilian victims of a far-reaching, intolerant military policy, most returnees will not likely consider taking refuge in Mexico as a future option should repression reach the scale it did in the early 1980s.

One of the most significant factors in any future political equation is the emergence of Mayan ethnicity in the form of cultural and political expression. Before the 1990s, most indigenas organized politically around their community and *municipio*. They faced considerable discrimination in many aspects of their lives. Within Mayan communities, for example, great pressure existed for people to learn Spanish. School children who did not speak Spanish often faced ridicule by other children and by their teachers as well; many parents, as a result, pressured their children to learn Spanish to save them from such embarrassment.

By the 1990s, however, despite the fact that discrimination against the Mayan people continued, they had begun to take greater pride in their culture, traditions, values, and language. The word "Mayan" was rarely used a decade ago; now Mayan groups have become prominent at the community, municipal, departmental, and national levels and have joined forces around issues related to religion, culture, land, politics, education, and health. Furthermore, community efforts and programs increasingly seek to "rescue" and preserve cultural traditions and language. The focus of these and other initiatives will continue to be primarily community- and municipal-based, but Mayan issues will gain political importance on a macro and national level in the future. Indigena communities were seldom isolated enclaves, but one can now speak of a Mayan movement—or at least, Mayan movements—that gain strength and articulation daily.

In Guatemala, political, economic, and cultural aspirations of a democratic, populist, or ethnic nature have historically been met with resistance and repression of varying degrees. The alliance among different sectors of the power structure in the country—Comité Coordinador de Asociaciónes Agrícolas, Comerciales, Industriales y Financieras (CACIF), the umbrella organization of the economic elite; the army; and certain forces within the government—has helped keep the situation under control. In 1995, however, land invasions took place, and the security forces did not respond with the same degree of repression that they had a decade or so previously. The same consensus among the power elite does not exist as before.

A new political party, Frente Democratica para una Nueva Guatemala (FDNG), emerged and participated in the 1995 elections. The party represented the popular movements, labor groups, NGOs, and similar organizations. Its votes—8 percent—surpassed most expectations in the polling booths, and it won seats in Congress.

Human rights organizations and international organizations, the activities of which were inhibited in the country during the 1970s and early 1980s when the great waves of violence took place, are now permitted to operate, although the extent to which they ultimately will be allowed to work openly and fully is yet to be determined. The diplomatic community is much more active than before, and the UN has a significant presence there, with the UN Mission to Guatemala (MINUGUA) monitoring the peace process and agreements.

Questions for the future are:

— To what degree will the presence and work of national human rights organizations and members of the popular movements be tolerated?

— To what extent will members of the FDNG be free to operate at municipal and national levels, as they gain increasing support among the population?

— To what extent will civilian populations in the area of return be subjected to harassment and military activity?

— To what extent will peace agreements be upheld? Reactions of the conservative sectors within the army and CACIF to the peace agreements and subsequent policies and legislation need to be monitored.

— How will the security forces respond to land invasions by landless peasants, and to the increased militancy of some groups within the popular movement?

— What will be the response of official and unofficial security forces as networks and umbrella organizations in the highlands continue to gain strength and address land, wage, and human rights issues?

— To what degree will members of the media be permitted freedom from harassment and threats as they investigate controversial issues such as degradation of the environment; deforestation by economically powerful interest groups in the Peten and Sierra de las Minas; the return process; corruption; clandestine cemeteries and mass graves; and the peace process?

— To what extent can the safety and security of key NGO staff and leadership, coordinating/umbrella groups be guaranteed?

— How can organizations work with groups that have a history of conflict or non-cooperation? How can they help facilitate group activities based on what unites rather than what divides groups? How can organizations create new terms of reference, commonalities, shared visions, and different perceptions of the "other"? How can they redefine situations so that they can become win-win and not win-lose or lose-lose prospects?

—How can organizations train staff and set up mechanisms within and among organizations so that warning signals are detected and communicated? Part of this orientation involves understanding that signals are frequently ambiguous. A sign that conditions are improving for one group may be a signal that the interests of other groups are being threatened, which may ultimately lead to a conflict. Signals of violence are not limited to incidents of armed conflict, disappearances, or torture; malnutrition, racism, and mental abuse must be viewed as signals of violence as well.

—Once conflict occurs, to what extent is an organization able and willing to act and advocate? Those who work at a local or community level at times find it difficult to denounce violations at a national or international level or to act as advocates at these levels, and vice versa. NGOs which operated in Guatemala could not very easily or openly pass on information to human rights groups outside the country.

—How can organizations inform the outside world during the various stages of a conflict? How can they determine who, in fact, is listening? During the most violent hours in the early 1980s in Guatemala, no one seemed to be listening. The international press provided very little coverage of the "silent war" that was being waged against the Guatemalan population.

—How can organizations develop linkages with each other to use their combined resources most effectively as "leverage" in accomplishing their goals? The demands of their work situations require them to do more with less. They must therefore learn to work more effectively, and this involves eliminating the territoriality that characterizes the approach of many organizations. They also need to seek a reasonable and appropriate division of labor within their programs.

— How do organizations bring out the best in themselves and others, so that their programmatic responses represent the optimal and relevant use of resources and make objective and subjective changes? While recognizing and responding to vulnerabilities, root causes, and effects, they need to recognize, respect, and build on the capacities and potentialities of the people involved. International and national NGOs should focus less on themselves and more on supporting processes that help others become self-sufficient.

CHAPTER THREE

Guatemalan Indigenous NGOs and Their Capacity for Early Warning

Rachel M. McCleary

IN 1985, Guatemala enacted a new constitution and held popular elections, making Marco Vinicio Cerezo the second civilian president in the history of the country.[1] Since then, peaceful and legal transitions have been made to three other civilian presidents. In January 1991, Jorge Serrano Elías was popularly elected, and Ramiro de León Carpio was elected by Congress in June 1993, after a failed coup attempt by Serrano. In 1996, Alvaro Arzù became president. This transition to civilian rule took place while an armed conflict continued—one that began in the early 1960s and culminated in the massacres of the late 1970s and early 1980s.

In 1994 and 1995, the Unidad Revolucionaria Nacional Guatemalteca (URNG) and the Guatemalan government were engaged in peace negotiations. Six substantive agreements were reached: Agreement on Democratization (July 1991); Global Accord on Human Rights (March 1994); Accord for the Resettlement of Populations Displaced by the Armed Conflict (June 1994); Accord on the Establishment of a Commission for the Historical Clarification of Human Rights Violations and Violent Acts That Have Caused Suffering to the Guatemalan People (June 1994); Accord on the Identity and Rights of the Indigenous Peoples (March 1995); and Agreement on Socio-Economic Issues and Agrarian Reform (May 1996).[2] Currently, the two parties are discussing the strengthening of civil society and the role of the military in a democratic society.

Within this context of a transition from authoritarian rule to democratic governance, NGOs within Guatemalan society began to form and express their views on labor issues, land reform, impunity, human rights abuses, the security of the internally displaced, and refugees returning from Mexico.[3] Christian Tomuschat, the United Nations Independent Expert to Guatemala, has described Guatemala as a country "rich in organizations that aspire to promote and protect human rights."[4]

This chapter examines the capability of indigenous Guatemalan NGOs to provide an early warning for potential conflict. It considers whether an early warning system is possible among indigenous NGOs and how such a system, in turn, might assist international organizations in better understanding the situation in Guatemala.

The Guatemalan Context

The transition from authoritarian rule to procedural democracy in Guatemala has been contingent upon the military's victories over the guerrillas. In the early 1980s, the Guatemalan military engaged in a counterinsurgency campaign in which 440 indigenous villages were destroyed; an estimated 75,000 people were killed, an estimated 200,000 children were orphaned, and 40,000 women were widowed.[5] The military's counterinsurgency campaign, as these statistics show, involved not only the eradication of the guerrillas from Guatemalan territory but also the destruction of indigenous communities. In addition to violent repression as part of its counterinsurgency campaign, the military established Civilian Self-Defense Patrols (PACs) as a means of obtaining information from indigenous communities on guerrilla activity and exposing guerrillas living in these communities. Males between the ages of 15 and 60 were—and still are—required to serve periodic twenty-four-hour military stints and to report to local military officials.[6] The Guatemalan army also established civilian representatives—known as military commissioners—in the communities, and the army's intelligence unit relies on an estimated 3,000 civilian informants.[7]

During the early 1980s, the military established planned communities of refugees ("Development Poles"), in which the residents were under continual military surveillance to ensure that they did not participate in the insurgency. Like the PACs, these planned communities were a means of controlling the indigenous populations in the areas where the armed conflict was taking place. In 1994 and 1995, despite objections from Rigoberta Menchú and other indigenous leaders, the Guatemalan government continued to set up new communities for returning refugees.

At the same time that the military was seeking victory in battle, serious disagreements between the military and private business elites began to develop.[8] The economic growth of the country was dependent upon the government's reaching credit agreements with the International Monetary Fund (IMF) and maintaining bilateral relations with countries with which Guatemala traded.

The private business sector, represented by the umbrella Comité Coordinador de Asociaciónes Agrícolas, Comerciales, Industriales y Financieras (CACIF), was in favor of the military regime's reaching credit agreements with the IMF. But the private business sector did not want to bear the economic burden of the fiscal and monetary crises confronting the country—crises that were brought about by the ineptness and policy failures of a succession of military heads of state.

Realizing the extent of its negative image, both domestically and internationally, the military in 1982 initiated a project entitled, "Thesis of National Stability."[9] With military victory over the guerrillas as the prerequisite for the transition to civilian rule, the military drew up a multi-year plan: "Victory '82," "Consolidation '83," "Institutional Restoration '84," "National Stability '85," "Consolidation '86," and "Strength '87."[10] The military's plan continued successfully until 1985, when popular elections were held. During the process of political liberalization, civilian groups had been permitted to organize and began to criticize human rights violations committed by the military. The first such organization was the Grupo de Apoyo Mutuo (GAM), founded in 1984 by families who had "disappeared" relatives. In 1988, an umbrella organization, Unidad de Acción Sindical y Popular (UASP), was formed and eventually came loosely to represent a wide variety of organizations.

The most strident case of such criticism was the civilian response to the massacre of Santiago Atitlán on 2 December 1990, in which the military was publicly accused of killing fourteen members of that community. The community of Santiago Atitlán also accused military personnel of the local garrison of kidnapping townspeople. The community demanded the removal of the garrison and, in an unprecedented move, President Cerezo and the military complied with the townspeople's request.[11]

This case received national attention. *La Crónica*, the country's news magazine, ran an article on the tragedy two weeks after its occurrence, stating, "This time the army has been fingered."[12] The importance of the story running in *La Crónica* was that the magazine was owned by private business sector elites. The Ombudsman for Human Rights, an office that had been created by the 1985 constitution, also criticized the massacre, noting that the office had received complaints of abuses by the military.

The critical role that the community of Santiago Atitlán played in obtaining the removal of the military garrison was not directly linked to any NGO. However, the abolition of the PACs and the removal of the military from indigenous communities (described later) are primary objectives of several NGOs.

The Peace Process and Opportunities for a National Dialogue

With the participation of Cerezo in Esquipulas II, and the signing of a Central American peace plan on 7 August 1987, opportunities were created within Guatemalan society for the formation of a National Commission of Reconciliation, which was convened by the Cerezo administration. As a result, a series of meetings took place in 1990, between sectors of Guatemalan society and the URNG.[13] Representatives of NGOs under the umbrella organization UASP participated in the meeting between the labor and popular sectors and the URNG.[14] The participation of the Comité de Unidad Campesina (CUC) was problematic, as the security of its representative could not be assured.[15] Nonetheless, in the end, its representative did participate and admitted that doing so was a "step forward" in building trust.[16]

With the election of Serrano in 1991, direct negotiations began between the Guatemalan government and the URNG. The peace negotiations included representatives of the Guatemalan government and military on the one side and representatives of the four factions of the URNG on the other, with no place allocated to representatives of civil society. Nevertheless, politically involved members of civil society, including representatives of popular groups, Mayan groups, religious organizations, and unions who had attended the 1990 meeting in Metepec, Mexico, with the URNG, formed the Coordinator of Civil Sectors (CSC) to continue civilian dialogue on issues relating to peace. At around the same time, the Civil Coordinator for Peace (COCIPAZ) was formed by representatives of the cooperatives, professional schools, small businesses, and the Universidad de San Carlos who had attended the meeting with the URNG in Atlixco, Mexico.[17]

When Ramiro de León Carpio became president in June 1993, the peace negotiations were restructured and moderated by Jean Arnault, a representative of the UN Secretary-General. The restructuring also included the creation of an Assembly of Civil Society (ASC), which did not have representation at the negotiating table but could forward proposals to both parties to the negotiations.[18]

A broad range of groups representing different sectors of society participated in the ASC. They included representatives of the groups that had met with the URNG in 1990, as well as Mayan groups, journalists, NGOs, research centers, women's organizations, and vocational bodies.

Although the participation of civil society in the peace negotiations was indirect, it was significant in terms of the effectiveness of the accords reached. Seven of the accords were substantive in nature and touched on fundamental structural issues in Guatemalan society. If the structural changes called for in the signed accords are fully implemented, civil society will have to agree to the content of those agreements. Otherwise, support for those changes will not reach beyond the two negotiating parties. The private business sector represented by the CACIF did not participate in any of these fora. The lack of political will on the part of CACIF to participate jointly with other sectors of civil society to draw up position papers and suggest procedures for implementation could prove problematic for the actual implementation of the agreements.[19]

The Indigenous NGOs within Guatemalan Society

The term "NGO" includes a wide variety of national as well as international organizations. The NGOs in Guatemalan society can be classified, according to their membership, into two different categories: popular and Mayan.[20] Popular groups in Guatemala formed within a context of military repression and violence. The objective of such groups was to fight the granting of any impunity to the military, denounce human rights abuses, and promote the interests of society as a whole. Among the active and publicly prominent organizations are:

Popular Organizations

In 1984, the year before Cerezo was elected president, GAM was formed to pressure the government and the military for information regarding the whereabouts of those who had disappeared. GAM denounced the existence of clandestine military prisons and cemeteries, and sought exhumations through legal channels. However, realizing the narrow focus of its mission, GAM began to seek information on all disappeared persons and condemned violations of human rights, calling for the legal prosecution of those responsible. Although GAM began as a ladino, or non-indigenous organization, as a result of expanding its mission, in 1996, two-thirds of its membership were indigenous women.[21]

In 1988, after a series of organized demonstrations in Guatemala City, GAM joined a labor movement, La Unidad de Acción Sindical (UAS); the Asociación de Estudiantes Universitarios (AEU); and CUC to form the Unidad de Acción Sindical y Popular (UASP).

The creation of UASP was significant. It brought together a rural, indigenous organization, CUC, with an urban human rights movement, GAM. The result was the creation of a support network that addressed a variety of issues. It also provided a precedent for the eventual incorporation of other Mayan groups, making UASP the most organized popular pressure organization in Guatemala City.

After the massacres in the early 1980s, the Maya-K'iche' Indians who made up CUC, like the majority of the indigenous populations in the highlands, migrated to Guatemala City. Some disappeared, others became refugees in Mexico and the United States, and still others became internally displaced persons.[22] During their diaspora, the members of CUC managed to continue communicating with each other, and in 1986, they reunited as an organization, demanding land and decent wages, and advocating the abolition of the PACs and the right of local communities to reject the presence of the military in their districts.[23]

During 1987 and 1988, as it was rebuilding its bases in indigenous communities, CUC actively campaigned against the PACs, whose presence in local communities was an obstacle to CUC's recruitment efforts. CUC was affiliated with the URNG faction called the Army of the Guerrillas of the Poor (EGP), and, because of this affiliation, its objectives were broader than simply ethnic ones.[24] CUC's interests in seeking the disbanding of PACs and occupying farms were thus viewed by Guatemalans as a part of a larger URNG strategy. Along the southern coast of Guatemala, where there are sugar, pineapple, and banana plantations, CUC began occupying farms to protest the lack of payment of minimum wages. CUC continues in 1996 to occupy farms both on the southern coast and in the Alta Verapaz region.

The Consejo de Comunidades Etnicas "Runujel Junam" (CERJ) was formed in 1988, in the department of Quiché, by men who did not want to join the PACs in their communities and who sought the dissolution of PACs. The mission of CERJ quickly expanded to include the protection of human and indigenous rights. CERJ filed a case in the Inter-American Human Rights Court, arguing that the PACs were unconstitutional and violated fundamental human rights. The organization also set up an informal network of delegates to record human rights violations. As a consequence of its work, numerous CERJ members were killed, and its founder, Amílcar Méndez, continually received death threats.[25]

In 1988, indigenous women of the departments of Quiché, Sololá, and Chimaltenango who had lost their husbands organized the Coordinadora Nacional de Viudas de Guatemala (CONAVIGUA). The organization assists women in small enterprises that allow them to earn an income and teaches them basic skills in reading and writing. With regard to orphans—in Guatemala, a child who has lost one parent is considered an orphan—CONAVIGUA demands their right to an education, free meals in school, and teachers. Although CONAVIGUA's 11,000 members are primarily indigenous, the mission of the organization is to represent all of Guatemala's widows and orphans.

Mayan Groups

The organizations that are identified as Mayan consider their primary objective to be the perpetuation of an ethnic identity.[26] As a result, they promote awareness of the Mayan culture, promote Mayan ceremonies through workshops and meetings, and publish materials about Mayan culture. The exception is the Council of Mayan Organizations (COMG), which is made up of fifteen groups and supports Mayan parliamentary and local government candidates and was directly involved in peace negotiations.

The work of the COMG is two pronged. Its members work in the Mayan communities in the countryside, promoting the perpetuation of Mayan cultures and languages. They also engage in scholarly work of documenting and preserving Mayan culture.[27] The Mayan Coordination of the New Awakening (Majawil Q'il) was founded to coordinate the activities of different groups with regard to redefining the five-hundredth anniversary of the discovery of America. After the celebration, Majawil Q'il, through its participating organizations, focused on the promotion of Mayan ceremonies.

Through these and other organizations, the Mayan groups foster legislation regarding such issues as bilingual education and the creation of networks among rural Mayan communities.

The Mayan groups as well as the popular ones, through their participation in UASP, together are able to organize large masses of peoples in ways that as singular organizations they cannot. As members of UASP, their most common tactic is to organize public demonstrations in Guatemala City on a variety of issues of concern to its member organizations. UASP also takes out paid advertisements in the newspapers and distributes leaflets and other written materials stating its position on different questions. In terms of skills and resources, participation in UASP gives leaders of NGOs a support system whereby, for example, a union leader might assist the leader of CONAVIGUA in organizing a meeting. Furthermore, a group like CONAVIGUA, which has not developed strong ties with women's groups in Guatemala City, can participate in national politics through its membership in UASP.

Thus, politically, what is important to individual organizations is that UASP gives them access to Guatemala City, the capital, where national politics take place.[28] Without the infrastructure, support, and know-how of the urban members of UASP, groups such as CERJ and CONAVIGUA, which are primarily made up of indigenous peoples, would not be able to lobby Congress effectively, find out which officials they need to see, or organize large demonstrations in the main square. Finally, UASP provides its member organizations with information about and access to their international counterparts. In a highly centralized country such as Guatemala, belonging to a umbrella organization such as UASP is critical to pressuring the government publicly and to gaining international attention so as to protect the lives of its members.[29]

International Development NGOs

Other NGOs promote development and attempt to alleviate poverty.[30] These organizations were originally established in Guatemala City in response to the devastation brought by the 1976 earthquake, but have expanded their work since then to provide funds for projects throughout the country. These projects are intended to help children and the poor. An estimated 80 percent of the NGOs in Guatemala primarily meet the needs of others—that is, they are not grassroots organizations, such as communities, cooperatives, and neighborhood associations, which meet their own needs.[31]

NGOs whose primary goal is to meet the needs of others can be broken down according to their membership. Some of these organizations are "staffed by individuals elected from and by the grassroots organizations that are themselves members" of the organization, while other NGOs have staff who are, for the most part, urban professionals "who are often socially and ethnically distinct from the grassroots."[32] Staff members of international development NGOs, such as the Christian Children's Fund, OXFAM, and Save the Children, fall into the latter category, and are either urban professionals or foreigners.

Because they are not located in rural areas, where military control is at its highest, international development organizations could not witness outbreaks of armed conflict on a daily basis. As a consequence, as a crisis builds, before violence erupts, their staff should rely on the people from within the local community to read and interpret the "signs" of early warning for them. Staff members must have faith in the judgment of their informers and must establish relationships based on mutual trust.

Non-local staff have access to mediums of communication in Guatemala City and have contacts in other countries. An efficient early warning system is dependent upon a strong bond between the staff of an international NGO and the people it serves. The staff of the international organization can then take the message to other countries, where pressure can be placed on policy-makers.

Early Warning Capability and the Potential for an Early Warning System

Are indigenous NGOs uniquely positioned to sense when intrastate and interstate conflicts are apt to escalate into violence? First, it is important to determine the level of repression in Guatemalan society that would hinder (1) access to information regarding potential conflict; and (2) the ability to communicate that information to others, particularly to those who could assist in ameliorating the situation.

The Guatemalan countryside is divided into twenty-two military command zones—one for each department—and three military bases, all in Guatemala City. The Guatemalan air force has airfields in Guatemala City, Petén, Puerto San José, and Retalhuleu and the navy has bases in Puerto San José and San Tomás de Castillo. The army's military zones have a commander who is responsible for controlling the department in which he is stationed. The military command is able quickly to mobilize troops to block roads or move into villages. As a result, the strength of the military presence throughout the country ensures a high level of monitoring of all civilian groups.

Only by participating in PACs can local communities efficiently learn about potential conflict. For the most part, participation in the PACs is forced, yet their primary function is to monitor the countryside and report any unusual activities to the local military garrison. Ideally, in a non-militarized society, the PACs would serve as the nerve-endings of an early warning system for the civilian population. However, in reality, they serve as an early warning system for the military command of each department.

The leaders of PACs frequently enjoy impunity and, with the protection of the local military, often engage in human rights violations. Members of NGOs have been harassed, threatened, and murdered by PAC members because they are viewed by the military and some members of the private business sector as sympathizers of the URNG or of being directly affiliated with a faction of the URNG. The military has referred to the NGOs as "subversives."[33] Because of these suspicions, the ability of these organizations to gain access to information and to convey early warning is necessarily limited. In a crisis situation, leaders of NGOs are most likely to be targeted for murder.

Since local communities have not had much success in obtaining the removal of the army's garrisons, they seek the demilitarization of their communities through the dissolution of the PACs. The presence of the military, coupled with the lack of any significant judicial system in the rural areas, creates a repressive environment in which NGOs have no freedom of movement or expression without fear of raising the suspicions of the military. Tomuschat said that there was a "tendency in the army to consider as members of the URNG all those who refuse to participate in the PACs."[34] During his tenure as an independent UN expert in Guatemala, Tomuschat consistently called for the dissolution of the PACs, as did the United Nations Commission on Human Rights.

Thus, in Guatemala, it is not possible for indigenous NGOs to sound the bells of early warning. Until the military presence in the countryside is diminished and the judicial system in Guatemala functions effectively, the capacity of indigenous organizations in the rural areas to learn of potential conflict and to tell others before it escalates into violence will continue to be severely limited.

Faxes, telephones, and other forms of electronic communication are not reliable enough for early warning. Within the Guatemalan countryside, electricity is available in only certain communities and on a limited basis per day. The telephone system is inefficient, and even within Guatemala City does not function well. The United Nations Mission to Guatemala (MINUGUA) requested telephone and fax lines for six of its twelve substations. International organizations might help indigenous organizations by purchasing telephones and fax machines so that early alert centers could be set up at strategic places in the countryside.

International organizations can further assist indigenous NGOs by using their contacts with the local and international press to publicize events in the country. Most international NGOs in Guatemala are staffed by urban professionals or foreigners who have access to mediums of modern communication. In a rumor-driven society like Guatemala, where the accuracy of information is often in question, staff of international organizations can play a key role in collecting, verifying, and publicizing it.

The answer to the second question, as to whether an early warning "system" would make sense and how such a system would be arranged, is obvious. An early warning system requires structural lines of communication within an organization as well as among organizations. The organization itself must have clear lines of communication, and the organization must have access to technology and other means of conveying information.

Particularly with regard to Guatemala, when one speaks of a "system" of early warning, other factors, such as the level of trust among representatives of the organizations, must be taken into account. *The source of information will in large part determine whether or not one believes it to be reliable.* The level of trust depends on two levels of familiarity: personal and institutional. Within Guatemala, establishing personal acquaintances with different leaders of NGOs is critical to developing supportive working relationships. Guatemalan NGOs rely heavily on their leaders for credibility and access to resources. These organizations tend to have loose structures and, as a consequence, their existence depends on a "personality."

Staff of international NGOs must trust leaders of indigenous NGOs to provide them with reliable information that can be viewed as an early warning signal, so that effective action can be taken. This trust must, however, be cultivated within the context of a fluid, unstable situation, characterized by constant death threats, a high level of impunity within the country, the lack of a properly functioning judicial system, and a police force that is unskilled and poorly equipped. All point to a lack of an institutional response to human rights abuses and potential violent conflict. In addition, the ongoing armed conflict contributes to the violence and impunity in the country. Achieving a positive result under such circumstances is often difficult.

Another essential aspect of an early warning system is that participating members of indigenous NGOs will need to share similar approaches to specific issues. In a society like Guatemala where there is minimal trust outside one's sector, how to approach an issue is critical to medium- as well as long-term cooperation with regard to information that could prove a matter of life or death. A consensus needs to be reached on how organizations are going to deal with human rights abuses. For, if such a consensus does not exist, the military can successfully isolate and intimidate NGOs.[35]

The groups that belong to the UASP share an interest in human rights violations (disappearances, forced recruitment into the PACs, and repression and murder on the part of the military and national police); labor issues (land distribution and decent wages); democracy issues (impunity in the legal system and the pervasive lack of law and order); and the role and rights of indigenous peoples. As the military withdraws from rural areas and the PACs are dissolved, the rurally based NGOs will continue to grow and begin to assert themselves within their geographical regions. Only within this context will NGOs in Guatemala City be able to develop an early warning system.

Conclusions

Although the peace negotiations were taking place in 1994 and 1995, the armed conflict also continued, but in a limited and more strategic way. This is primarily a result of three factors. First, the destruction of

guerrilla bases and indigenous communities during the early 1980s culminated, for all intents and purposes, in the victory of the military over
the URNG. Second, the destruction of the guerrilla bases and indigenous
communities meant that the URNG endured high casualties, with many
of its members fleeing to Mexico, along with the civilian refugees. In
1995, the URNG fighting force numbered between 500 and 1,000; the
army included about 44,000 soldiers. Third, the suspension of U.S. military assistance, beginning with the Carter administration and completely
suspended by the Clinton administration, coupled with increased international attention to human rights violations, created a negative international image. The Guatemalan private business sector found it difficult to
engage in international commerce.

Some institutions in Guatemala have become increasingly democratic
(the Constitutional Court, Supreme Electoral Tribunal, and the Ombudsman for Human Rights), while others (the Supreme Court of Justice,
Congress, and the Public Prosecutor's Office) are beginning to undergo
structural changes that will strengthen their capacity to perform their
functions democratically. Some institutions, such as the military and the
national police, have yet to be sufficiently reformed and restructured.

Nonetheless, under President de León Carpio, a tolerance for civil
opposition on the part of the executive branch has been critical to the
success of NGOs. By tolerating the expression of opposition views, the
executive branch has set a standard within Guatemalan society; referring
to NGOs as "subversive" is no longer acceptable. Respect for freedom of
expression, particularly during the recent administration of Ramiro de
León, has enabled NGOs to express their views. This includes the
freedom to hold public workshops, publish their views in newspapers,
and demonstrate openly in the streets without fear of military and police
brutality.

As democratic institutions are strengthened in this developing democracy, the role of the military is being redefined. In addition, NGOs will
increasingly exercise their rights and will most likely develop an early
warning system. Until then, networks between international NGOs and
indigenous ones should be strengthened. International NGOs can provide
access to media and policy officials in other countries; indigenous organizations can help provide information about local attitudes and activities.

Within the Guatemalan context, democracy is a goal, not a reality. It
is a goal valued by Guatemalans and members of the international community. As its institutions currently function, Guatemala is a fragile state

moving from authoritarianism to some form of participatory government; it merely has the appearance—a trompe l'oeil politique—of democracy. Because of its history—the manner in which the transition was made from military dictatorship to civilian rule—Guatemala will not be a democracy as it is practiced in other countries. Yet, as Guatemala makes the transition, the international community must continue to play a supporting role in Guatemalan efforts.

Notes

1. Julio César Méndez Montenegro was popularly and fairly elected in 1966. He remained president until 1970.

2. For a comprehensive treatment of procedural and substantive agreements, see Fundación para La Paz, la Democracia y el Desarrollo, *Documentos Basicos del Proceso de Paz* (Guatemala, 1994); Fundación para La Paz, la Democracia y el Desarrollo, *Acuerdos Entre el Gobierno de Guatemala y la URNG* (Guatemala, 1994); Fundación para La Paz, la Democracia y el Desarrollo, *Documentos de la Asamblea de la Sociedad Civil-ASC* (Guatemala, 1994). The calendar for the peace negotiations was renegotiated on 17 February 1995, with a comprehensive peace agreement to be signed in August 1995. Alvaro Arzù became president in January 1996. In May 1996, the Accord on Socio-Economic Issues and Agrarian Reform was signed. The expectation of both parties to the negotiation and the UN moderator was that a comprehensive peace accord would be signed by September 1996.

3. See Centro de Estudios de Guatemala, *La Democracia de las Armas: Gobiernos Civiles y Poder Militar* (Mexico, 1994), II, 75–84. Santiago Bastos y Manuela Camus, *Quebrando el Silencio: Organizaciones del Pueblo Maya y sus Demandas (1986–1992)* (Guatemala, 1993, 2nd ed.); Victor Gálvez, René Pointevin, Carlos González, *Estado, Participación Popular y Democratización* (Guatemala, 1994), 11–56.

4. United Nations, Economic and Social Committee, Commission on Human Rights, *Informe del experto independiente, Sr. Christian Tomuschat, sobre la situación del los derechos humanos en Guatemala, preparado de conformidad con el párrafo 11 de la resolución 1991/51 de la Comisión.* E/CN.4/1992/5 (21 January 1992), 9–11.

5. Government sources cited in *La Hora* (24 September 1988), 3. Also see Jennifer Schirmer, "The Guatemalan Military Project: An Interview with Gen. Héctor Gramajo," *Harvard International Review* (Spring 1991), 10–13.

6. The PACs, according to Guatemalan Decree-law 19-86, function under the command and coordination of the Minister of Defense. The PACs are considered "organizations that are primarily civilian in nature and a ready, mobile and territorial reserve."

7. For statistics provided by the defense minister of Guatemala, see United Nations, Economic and Social Committee, Commission on Human Rights, *Informe de la experta independiente, Sra. Mónica Pinto, sobre la situación de los derechos*

humanos en Guatemala, preparado de conformidad con la resolución 1993/88 de la Comisión. E/CN.4/1994/10 (20 January 1994), 15. On 30 June 1995, President Ramiro de León Carpio announced the dissolution of the military commissioners beginning 1 July, through September 1995. The military was in agreement with this move, recognizing that the military commissioners were no longer relevant. Presidency of the Republic, Guatemala, Comunicado de Prensa, no. 909-95. "Discurso del Señor Ramiro de León Carpio en conmemoración del 124 Aniversario del Ejército de Guatemala."

8. Jennifer Schirmer, "Violence and Democracy: The Case of Guatemala," unpublished manuscript, 5–7.

9. For a description of this plan, see Héctor Alejandro Gramajo Morales, *Tesis de la Estabilidad Nacional* (Guatemala, 1989). Also see Gramajo, "Transición Política en Guatemala: Una Perspectiva desde el Interior de las Fuerzas Armadas de Guatemala," in Jorge I. Domínguez and Marc Lindenberg (eds.), *Transiciones Democráticas en Centro América* (San José, Costa Rica, 1994), 253–300. In 1977, the Carter administration suspended military assistance to Guatemala. During the Reagan administration, although international attention to human rights violations in Guatemala continued, President Reagan renewed both economic and military assistance to Guatemala in his successful attempt to obtain assistance from the Guatemalan military for the Contras in Nicaragua.

10. For a brief description of the goals for each year, see Alfonso Yurrita, "The Transition from Military to Civilian Rule in Guatemala," in Louis Goodman, Johanna Mendelson, and Juan Rial (eds.), *The Military and Democracy: The Future of Civil-Military Relations in Latin America* (Lexington, MA, 1990), 75–89.

11. A copy of Cerezo's letter to the community is reprinted in Victor Gálvez, René Pointevin, and Carlos González, *Estado, Participación Popular y Democratización* (Guatemala, 1994), 96. Two soldiers were convicted of the crime, receiving sixteen and four years in prison, respectively.

12. "Cuestionamiento y Reflexiones, Secuelas de la Tragedia de Santiago," *La Crónica*, 156 (14 December 1990), 14.

13. Meeting of political parties with the URNG, 11 June 1990, resulting in the Agreement of El Escorial; meeting of CACIF with the URNG, 31 October, through 1 September 1990, resulting in the Communique of Ottawa; meeting of the religious sector with the URNG, 26 September 1990, resulting in the Declaration of Quito; meeting of the labor and popular sectors with the URNG, 23 October 1990, resulting in the Declaration of Metepec, Mexico; meeting of the academic, cooperative, business, and professional sectors with the URNG, 27 October 1990, resulting in the Declaration of Atlixco, Mexico.

14. For UASP, the participants were Flavio Pérez Zapeta (Sindicato de Trabajadores de la Educación de Guatemala-STEG); Rosalina Tuyuc (Coordinadora Nacional de Viudas de Guatemala-CONAVIGUA); Otto Enrique Vásquez Peralta (Asociación de Estudiantes Universitarios-AEU); Cruz Zapeta (Comité de Unidad Campesina-CUC); Mario Polanco (Grupo de Apoyo Mutuo-GAM); Julio Rodolfo Delgado L. (Coordinadora de Estudiantes de Educación Media-CEEM); Amílcar Méndez (Consejo de Comunidades Etnicas-CERJ); Armando Sanchez (FENASTEG); Walter Conrado Gaitán Morales (Sindicato de Industria Electrica-

STINDE); Byron Morales (Unidad Sindical de Trabajadores de Guatemala-UNSI-TRAGUA); and Lorenzo Pérez Mendoza (Consejo Nacional de Desplazados de Guatemala-CONDEG).

15. Santiago Bastos and Manuela Camus, *Quebrando el Silencio: Organizaciones del Pueblo Maya y sus Demandas* (Guatemala, 1993, 2nd ed.), 67.

16. Ibid., 67–68.

17. See endnote thirteen.

18. For a brief history of civilian participation in the peace negotiations and the creation of the Assembly of Civil Society, see Fundación para La Paz, *Documentos*, 1-4.

19. Representatives of CACIF stated that they would not participate in the Assembly of Civil Society for the following reasons: First, the decision-making structure of the Assembly was not consensual but rather authoritarian, with the moderator, Rodolfo Quezada Toruño, holding substantial organizational decision-making power. Second, many of the groups participating in the Assembly were not legal or legitimate or representative of civil society. Third, the URNG has representatives in the Assembly of Civil Society, and CACIF finds this unacceptable, as the URNG is not a legitimate representative of civil society.

20. This classification was developed by Bastos and Camus, *Quebrando*, 57–122. It is the standard used by other researchers on NGOs in Guatemala. See Centro Canadiense de Estudio y de Cooperacion Internacional, *Democracia y Derechos Humanos en Guatemala: Un Analisis* (Guatemala, 1994), 95–98; Richard N. Adams, "A Report on the Political Status of the Guatemalan Maya," in Donna Lee Van Cott (ed.), *Indigenous Peoples and Democracy in Latin America* (New York, 1994), 155–186.

21. Richard N. Adams, "A Report on the Political Status of the Guatemalan Maya," in Van Cott, *Indigenous Peoples* (New York, 1994), 163.

22. On 31 January 1980, members of CUC occupied the Spanish embassy in Guatemala City, asking the military to vacate an area of the city. The embassy was burned down by the Guatemalan military, killing the members of CUC, one of whom was Rigoberta Menchú's father.

23. The PACs are estimated at 537,000 members. See United Nations Economic and Social Committee, Commission on Human Rights, *Informe de la Experta independiente, Sra. Mónica Pinto, sobre la situación de los derechos humanos en Guatemala, preparado de conformidad con la resolución 1993/88 de la Comisión.* E/CN.4/1994/10 (20 January 1994), 15.

24. Yvon Le Bot, *Guatemala: Violencia, Revolución y Democracia* (Guatemala, 1992), 10. It is commonly believed in Guatemalan society that CUC is affiliated with the EGP and the FAR.

25. In 1991, in a show of solidarity, President Jorge Serrano Elías received Amílcar Méndez at the presidential palace after Méndez had received numerous death threats.

26. In Guatemala, there are twenty-two linguistically distinct ethnic groups. The 1980 census estimated the indigenous population at 44 percent of the total. A census was taken in 1994, but the results were not public in 1996.

27. Bastos and Camus, *Quebrando*, 107–111.

28. Instituto para el Desarrollo Económico y Social de Centro América (IDESAC) has identified over 700 local and international NGOs working in

Guatemala. Eighty-five percent of these organizations have their headquarters in the Guatemala City metropolitan area.

29. Rosalina Tuyuc (head of CONAVIGUA), Amílcar Méndez (head of CERJ), and Byron Morales (head of UNSITRAGUA) have received international recognition for their efforts.

30. See Gálvez, Pointevin, and González, *Estado,* 11–56; Centro Canadiense, *Democracia,* 87–91.

31. Centro Canadiense, *Democracia,* 91.

32. See Anthony Bebbington, Graham Thiele, et al., *Non-governmental Organizations and the State in Latin America: Rethinking Roles in Sustainable Agricultural Development* (London, 1993), 7.

33. This conclusion has been well documented by different human rights groups. In his reports, Christian Tomuschat describes the various cases of NGO representatives and the PACs. See United Nations *Informe del experto*, paragraphs 90, 103, 116, 120; United Nations, Economic and Social Committee, Commission on Human Rights, *Informe del experto independiente, Sr. Christian Tomuschat, sobre la situación de los derechos humanos en Guatemala, preparado de conformidad con el párrafo 13 de la resolución 1992/78 de la Comisión.* E/CN.4/1993/10 (18 December 1992), paragraphs 67, 68, 73. United Nations, Report of the Director of the United Nations Mission for the Verification of Human Rights and of Compliance with the Commitment of the Comprehensive Agreement on Human Rights in Guatemala. A/49/856 (1 March 1995).

34. United Nations, *Informe del experto* (21 January 1992), 67. United Nations, *Informe del experto* (18 December 1992), 76.

35. In July 1994, Mario Enríquez, the defense minister, accused Rosalina Tuyuc, head of CONAVIGUA, of being a member of the URNG. The psychological intimidation on the part of the military took place in the national newspapers and on local television news programs. The military spokesperson also accused Tuyuc's two brothers of being members of the URNG and of having participated in the burning of a farm.

MACEDONIA

CHAPTER FOUR

International NGOs in Preventive Diplomacy and Early Warning: Macedonia

Eran Fraenkel

IN A WORLD beset by local wars, there is no doubt about the need for and validity of preventive diplomacy, or conflict prevention and management, as practiced by NGOs, both domestic and international.[1]

Examples abound of conflicts that may have been prevented, limited, contained, or resolved more speedily or equitably had the knowledge and experience of NGOs been sought and heeded. The hypothesis being addressed here, however, does not concern the validity of NGOs as a phenomenon or their raison d'etre, but rather the possible systematization of an NGO network to provide early warning signals in situations where tensions promise to erupt into violence. From the perspective of a country that has already endured a civil war, the answers to these questions are relatively clear cut. The perspective from Macedonia, however, a country that has thus far avoided the escalation of ethnic tensions into sustained violent conflict, casts some doubt on the very notion that NGOs should serve an early warning function.[2] It is, in other words, easier to debate retrospectively actions that might or should have been taken than it is to prognosticate about the utility of actions in circumstances that have not yet arisen.

In an effort to address the thesis of whether NGOs *should* serve as providers of early warnings and not only whether they *could* do this, this paper focuses on six topics with the greatest overall bearing on NGOs in Macedonia: Which organizations are actually NGOs? Are NGOs

uniquely positioned in Macedonian society? Do NGOs form a system?
Are monitoring and reporting compatible with being an NGO? To whom
should/would NGOs report in an early warning system? And, what is the
role of NGO-to-NGO relations across international borders?

Background

The name "Macedonia" refers to the newly independent country formally known as the Republic of Macedonia. Similarly, "Macedonians"
refers to all citizens of this new country, irrespective of ethnicity/nation-
ality—for example, Macedonian, Albanian, Turk, and Rom—whereas
"ethnic Macedonians" refers to those people who identify themselves as
Makedonci (Macedonian).[3]

Macedonia's history is a long and tangled one and has been claimed
by Macedonia's neighbors—Greece, Serbia, Bulgaria, and, to a lesser
extent Albania—as part of their national legacies. The country's political
history, however, is simpler to follow: From the mid-fourteenth to the
early twentieth centuries, Macedonia was part of the Ottoman Empire;
part of old Serbia (including the Kingdom of the Serbs, Croats, and
Slovenes, and pre-war Yugoslavia) from the Balkan Wars until World
War II; and then part of the Socialist Federated Republic of Yugoslavia
from 1945 until 1991. Following the secession of Slovenia and Croatia
from Yugoslavia, Macedonia also held a referendum in November of
1991, when its population voted for independence.

The reaction of Macedonia's neighbors to its secession from
Yugoslavia has been mixed, if predictable. Bulgaria, which has historically rejected the notion of Macedonians having an identity distinct from
Bulgarians, was quick to recognize Macedonia's independence as a state,
with the proviso, however, that the country was populated by people
whose "nationality" was Bulgarian. Greece, which also categorically
denied the existence of a "Macedonian" Slav ethos, has maintained its
position by negating the right of any country to use the name Macedonia, thereby rejecting the validity of the Republic of Macedonia as a
country and the people who refer to themselves as Macedonians.[4]

The rump Yugoslavia, until the fall of 1995, had regarded the border
between itself and Macedonia as an administrative rather than an international one, and, accordingly, neither explicitly rejected nor accepted
Macedonia's independent status. Preliminary negotiations for mutual

recognition were announced in Macedonia in late 1995, just days before the attempt on the life of President Kiro Gligorov. The subsequent signing of the Dayton accords ending the shooting war in Bosnia led to the suspension of UN sanctions against Yugoslavia and, in early 1996, to the announcement that Serbian-Macedonian relations were soon to be normalized. This normalization, however, is still contingent on Greece and Yugoslavia's coming to their own mutual understanding over the future of Macedonia, since these two countries have entered into a joint agreement regarding the "Macedonian question," including the legitimacy of the country's name—an issue that, unto itself, has no bearing on Macedonian-Serbian relations.[5] Only Albania has recognized Macedonia's independence without qualification, although disputes between the two countries revolving around the demands for rights made by Macedonia's large Albanian population have caused Macedonian officials to question the sincerity of Albania's commitment to Macedonia's political sovereignty and territorial integrity.

Of the former Yugoslav republics (excluding Kosova and Vojvodina as part of Serbia), Macedonia is the most demographically heterogeneous.[6] Irrespective of the actual population percentages arrived at in the most recent census (1994), and the relative access to political power that these numbers imply, Macedonia consists of a majority of ethnic Macedonians, followed by Albanians, Turks, Rom (Gypsies), Serbs, and Vlachs. The country also has a number of smaller communities such as the Jews who survived World War II, but these are statistically and politically insignificant.[7]

The politicization of virtually all aspects of life in Macedonia in terms of ethnicity, loyalty to the new state, real or perceived irredentist aspirations, and national security—to touch upon but a few factors—has caused a number of political crises, though not to the point of persistent violent conflict either among its constituent populations or with its neighbors. In view of its internal and external situation, Macedonia as an independent country faces two major sets of issues that will determine its ability to survive: how to reconcile its national interests with the demands and positions of Serbia, Greece, Bulgaria, and Albania; and how to reconcile the interests and demands of the country's own diverse populations, which are only now beginning to find their political voices.

Underlying Macedonia's internal and international political difficulties are the country's economic problems. They derive from the two-year (1993–1995) trade embargo imposed by Greece from the south (closing access to the port at Thessaloniki, through which Macedonia formerly imported raw materials and exported finished goods), and, until 1996, the United Nations' sanctions against Serbia, traditionally Macedonia's primary direct trade partner as well as its overland corridor to Western Europe. Without diminishing the magnitude of Macedonia's domestic issues, these extrinsic factors have heightened Macedonia's political and social instability in manifold ways, such as by damaging the country's ability to provide sufficient employment or to guarantee social welfare. Coming in the midst of Macedonia's transition from its Yugoslav-style planned economy to a nascent market economy, these obstacles have only served to aggravate both ethnic and class tensions.[8]

It is within this context of uncertainty and flux that Macedonia has been inundated with American and European NGOs offering to help navigate a course toward "democracy," "modernization," and "pluralism."

NGOs in Macedonia: Reality vs. Perceptions

Western countries have heard a warning bell ringing in the southern Balkans and have committed certain resources to help address some of the region's most pressing needs. The very presence of NGOs in Macedonia is an indication of concern regarding Balkan stability, irrespective of differences in opinion as to how instability should be defined or which measures may most effectively render southeastern Europe more stable.[9]

In post-Cold War Eastern Europe, NGOs have become a premier growth industry, as is amply demonstrated in Macedonia, which has hosted dozens of international organizations calling themselves non-governmental. These range from multimillion-dollar contractors sponsored by the United States Agency for International Development (USAID) or the European Community Humanitarian Organization (ECHO)—with specific and usually short-term humanitarian and development projects—to the Soros Open Society Institute and UNICEF. Then there are smaller-budget conflict resolution organizations such as Search for Common Ground or the Swedish Transnational Foundation for Peace and Future Research (TFF).[10]

Whether it is a lexical or epistemological lapse, the application of the term NGO to this diversity of organizations is misleading. Discrepancies in the size, operational presence, and budgets among NGOs influence resource allocations as well how an organization is perceived by the

Macedonian government and people.[11] With Soros, AID, or ECHO as models, Macedonians routinely associate NGOs with the distribution of funds. Even at its economic and political apogee, Yugoslavia (including Macedonia) viewed the West, and the United States in particular, as a "milch cow: all teats and no horns." Independent Macedonia has retained this view, evident in the common attitude that the country deserves financial support, with no political or social accountability; that is, without obligations to transform its institutions. Accordingly, there is more interest in working with an organization modernizing the communications infrastructure, for example, than with one advancing a process such as the development of civil society.

What does civil society in the so-called information age mean for Macedonia, which has recently entered what may be described as the post-modern Ottoman period? The dynamics of social and power relationships have not changed in Macedonia since the country's pre-industrial period, neither by dint of the conditions imposed by socialism nor through the current changes in the transition to post-communism. In these traditionally constructed relationships there is a premium placed on information: Whom and what one knows has been and remains the best guarantor of succeeding in any undertaking, from the most mundane to the most politically sensitive. Without *vrska* (connections), for example, it may take months or years to have a telephone installed. With it, the only question is whether one's personal ties or information are strategic enough to attain the desired goal.[12]

By these standards, information about oneself or one's activities is held to be leverage that the possessor of that information may use to one's benefit or detriment, depending on circumstances and personal predisposition. It is taken for granted in Macedonia that information should be restricted to people with whom one has mutual confidence. By definition that tends to exclude agencies or agents of government (unless, of course, one has ties of kinship or other mutual obligations to someone in a position of authority). For international organizations working in Macedonia, the question that arises from these considerations is whether suspicions toward local government and authority are projected onto foreign NGOs; and if so, to what effect? A corollary question is whether organizations whose presence in Macedonia depends ultimately on foreign government support can truly function—or claim to function—without representing their respective governments' interests. In other words, which organizations are really NGOs, and what does that actually mean?

For any NGO to work successfully in Macedonia, one of its first tasks is to build trust and to assure the honest use of any information gathered in the process of establishing and implementing its programs. Trust building is constrained for international NGOs because the societal and political experiences of people in Macedonia do not readily accommodate the concept of a "non-governmental" organization working in the public sphere. Not surprisingly, therefore, Macedonians frequently equate foreigners not only with their countries of origin but with the government and politics of that country.

The population in Macedonia is particularly skeptical about the dissociation of NGOs from U.S. government interests. Indeed, throughout the U.S. and European NGO universe, there may be cause for this skepticism, insofar as the majority of these organizations operating in Macedonia are funded by their governments. For American NGOs, this government/non-government dialectic is further complicated by the bitter disappointment that Macedonians have felt toward the United States for the protracted delay in establishing full diplomatic relations between Washington and Skopje. The delay was viewed as the single greatest encouragement to Greece.[13] Macedonians hold a similar, if somewhat less harsh opinion of European governments.

There is, in the view of Macedonians, a clear hypocrisy between the official American and European diplomatic positions and the notion that these same countries are sending NGOs to address Macedonia's salient economic, social, or political issues. NGOs therefore not only confront the generalized suspicion or mistrust of government and authority, with its native roots, but also must overcome the additional wariness created by the politics of their home countries.

NGOs must take into account how such considerations may impede their functional roles. Whereas, on the one hand, Macedonians seek, or feel they merit, help in the form of money and technical expertise, on the other hand they distrust the motives of funders who provide such monies because they assume that the funders must have a hidden agenda.[14] Regardless of the number of activities an NGO has accomplished successfully, for each program or project it proposes, a calculation is made on the part of Macedonians as to the potential fallout—generally measured in that abstract currency of political risk—attached to a program, or attached to being associated with a foreign organization at all. NGOs with large enough budgets offer sufficient benefits to reward Macedonians for entering into possibly risky relationships. Likewise, organizations working in agriculture, finance, transportation, or other infrastructural or technical fields, do not pose the same level of perceived risk as do those focusing on social or political processes: Because the former penetrate Macedonian society to a limited extent, an extent determined, if not managed by the Macedonian government itself, their connections to foreign governmental interests are also of less concern. With some resignation Macedonian citizens acknowledge that, with the exception of Soros, only governments or supra-national agencies are able to fund such large-scale projects.

The most obvious expression of this preference for high-level projects is that the majority of international NGOs deal exclusively with various branches of the Macedonian government. It is critical here to understand the general Macedonian concept of governance and its particularly complicating effect on NGOs. Whereas in the West anything not explicitly prohibited by law is implicitly permitted, in Macedonia the law assumes that anything not expressly permitted is implicitly prohibited. Thus, whereas NGOs are permitted to exist under the ambiguous terms set forth in Macedonia's laws regarding "civic associations," which subsume both domestic and foreign organizations, an NGO may pursue its specific activities only after engaging in a complicated approval procedure that culminates in the submission of an "agreement" between itself and Macedonian government. Once the prerequisite steps have been completed—a process that may take from months to years—each agreement is either accepted or rejected by the Macedonian parliament. By law, an approved NGO is then restricted to those activities itemized in its agreement. Since, however, virtually no international NGO has passed through this parliamentary approval process, most are functioning in legal limbo.

The government of Macedonia is not overtly repressive, and accordingly, international organizations working in the country are not subject to harassment or blatant forms of censure. Rather, subtler hints (for example, getting or not getting a telephone) serve as constant reminders to all NGOs—those active in the social and political arenas most particularly—that they are ultimately beholden to the goodwill of the host government. Just as financing programs depends on the NGO's home government, the realization of these programs depends on the receptivity of the host government. Thus, for example, contractors for USAID or ECHO working in healthcare, agriculture, transportation, or banking are effectively functioning on a government-to-government level, albeit that the contractors are themselves non-governmental. Such projects are negotiated between the

Macedonian government and the NGO, based predominately on an assessment of Macedonia's needs made by the Macedonians and the contractor's sponsor. If the U.S. government, for example, does not deem a certain project important for U.S. interests, it will not be funded by AID.[15] Likewise, if the Macedonian government does not favor a project, it will take the necessary steps to ensure that the project fails to thrive.

Thus, in considering the reality versus the perception of international NGOs, the fundamental paradox is that those organizations most enjoying the blessing of both their home and host governments are least subject to operational vagaries but are the very organizations thought by the general Macedonian population to support the status quo rather than to further Macedonia's transformation toward a new civil society. Such privileged NGOs may be successful in realizing their projects, but this success, and moreso its implicit connotation of ties to the establishment, often distance NGOs from the very populations they are ostensibly meant to serve.

Networking and Information Sharing among NGOs

Given these realities, what defines the ability of an NGO to work productively in the niche it occupies within Macedonian society—that is, to position itself uniquely so that it can perform strategically? In the most literal sense, every NGO is uniquely and strategically placed in Macedonia insofar as it specializes in some activity, whether road construction or the formation of parent-teacher associations. Furthermore, every NGO's view of Macedonia differs somewhat if only because, to continue the previous example, organizations working with mechanical engineers are presented a different interpretation of Macedonia and its problems than are those working with schoolteachers. Organizations with widely divergent mandates such as the National Democratic Institute, Catholic Relief Services, Search for Common Ground, the International Research and Exchanges Board (IREX), the Institute for Sustainable Communities, and TFF, three of which are USAID-funded, have made efforts to go beyond narrowly focused or project-oriented activities and to establish themselves as initiators or supporters of more intensive and far-reaching processes aiming at the transformation of social, political, and cultural dynamics. As a corpus, therefore, NGOs may provide a panoramic view of Macedonian society and the strengths, weaknesses, or points of fissure pertaining to any given segment of that society.

An individual NGO's capacity to position itself uniquely and to act strategically rests on its ability to penetrate society, based on those considerations of access, trust, and freedom from government discussed above. The success of such efforts depends, among other things, on organizational and personal commitment: the long-term presence of an NGO on the ground (with the obvious implications this has for funding); its knowledge of local languages and cultural values; its acceptance of local partners as equals in any program; and so forth. Organizations with some or all of these enumerated qualifications may represent only a fraction of the total international NGO community in Macedonia, but their presence is significant, for the country and for each other. Collectively, these NGOs have established relationships with people across Macedonia's social, ethnic, and political spectrum, from Supreme Court judges to small shopkeepers, from print and broadcast journalists to peasant farmers, and from students and educators to factory workers.

Clearly, no one person or organization is able to become expert in every dimension of Macedonian society, and thus, all benefit from the perspectives and experiences of others working in the field. The strength of such NGOs consists of their having gained the trust of diverse groups of people who are not only willing to be frankly and openly informative but also able to critique the perceptions and ideas put forth by the NGOs. It is at this level of inter-organizational or interpersonal relationships— whether the connection is between an international and a domestic organization or between an international NGO and private citizens—that the accuracy and value of an international NGO's information are assessed and reassessed.

A second level of assessment therefore takes place as NGOs with related activities or interests consult with each other, either formally or casually. Like-minded NGOs constitute an organic network, of which information sharing and feedback on ideas are an integral part. Their purpose is not to disseminate information outside the group, but rather to compare notes on current projects, to discuss possible joint activities or to avoid reduplicating one another's, and to assess the general political and social climate within which each is working.[16]

A separate, formal, mandated network also exists among government-funded NGOs that are expected to meet and report to each other and to their funders on a regular basis; certain organizations do this weekly, others monthly. USAID-funded NGOs (and presumably those supported by ECHO as well) are also required to submit written reports about their projects, which the local USAID officer uses to evaluate the programs and to recommend others for the future. A central difference, however, is that, unlike the informal NGO contact group, USAID or ECHO may use such information to provide their governments with status reports about Macedonia that are then applied to or affected by concerns of foreign policy.

The Macedonian authorities also have established a formal network that revolves around organizations distributing relief aid. All NGOs formally labeled as humanitarian are expected to attend monthly meetings held by the Macedonian Red Cross, at which time they discuss and review their activities. NGOs involved in development or less-directly related activities are also invited but are not strictly required to attend. Although the Red Cross represents itself as a domestic NGO, it is closely affiliated with the Macedonian government, and is, in fact, one of the organizations that must approve the applications of all foreign NGOs during their registration process.

Macedonia may thus be said to have four coexistent networks of organizations that intersect only occasionally, and then only coincidentally: The largest of these is a mandated, government-oriented group of international NGOs, whose projects focus primarily on infrastructure, and whose personnel generally penetrate Macedonian society only minimally. Smaller is the spontaneous network of international NGOs, whose association rests on shared interests, experiences, and attitudes; whose projects focus more on political and social processes than on infrastructure; and whose personnel generally tend to have the skills needed to penetrate society. Third, is the formal Macedonian-mandated association of relief organizations. Fourth are the organic networks among NGOs and their local counterparts or colleagues, irrespective of whether the domestic counterpart belongs to an NGO. In addition to the enumerated networks, personal contacts develop among individual members of NGOs with diplomatic personnel of various embassies, UN organizations, the Organization for Security and Cooperation in Europe (OSCE), and private citizens within the international community, all of which invariably contribute to the broader dissemination of information, albeit on an informal level.[17]

Should NGO Networks Be Systematized?

Whether by necessity, design, or chance, information is constantly circulating within the orbits just described, and to some extent among them. Two options exist for the further systematization of information sharing: either to formalize the process of communication within the existing orbits or to formalize communications across orbits. Each option represents a different perspective, not only regarding the process of creating networks, but also regarding the purposes such a network would serve.

Even assuming the desirability of NGOs' providing early warning signals and initiating early action, three sets of issues arise regarding the formation of formal networks among such organizations:

— What is the correlation between intention and action? Is it possible for NGOs to engage in early warning without becoming, or being viewed as, advocates for a particular side or point of view?

— To whom should information be directed if NGOs do participate in an early warning system?

— Is there a need for NGOs or an NGO network, like their diplomatic counterparts, to establish cross-border connections in order to evaluate their domestically gathered information, since Macedonia faces not only potential internal conflicts but also possible hostile developments in Serbia, Greece, Albania, and Bulgaria?

Intention vs. Action: Warning or Advocacy?

Systematic information gathering in Macedonia takes place on the level of governments and government-sponsored aid organizations, the United Nations (UNPROFOR/UNPREDEP foremost), and the OSCE.[18] Their diplomatic underpinnings, however, predetermine that anything regarded as politically inadvisable, regardless of the source that informs it, will not result in action beyond that already practiced by UN mediators and negotiators. NGOs, in contrast, have little capacity to convert their knowledge into action—that is, no real or potential enforcement powers—regardless of their ability to penetrate society and to become truly well informed. Thus, whereas for the UN, OSCE, or a national government, the issue is one of tactics, for NGOs it is one of purpose since NGOs, with rare exception, are not explicitly engaged in preventive diplomacy.

The quandary in the information-into-action formulation is that in Macedonia, regardless of the circumstances and potential for conflict, it is nearly impossible for an organization to remain or to be perceived as remaining "neutral" except through inaction. The very act of sounding a warning may be interpreted as partisan, prejudicial, or biased by one or more parties to a conflict. It must also be borne in mind that warning, like advocacy, is a matter of judgment. What a given party—either within the dispute itself or among the outside observers—may interpret as something falling within the range of acceptable behavior may be viewed by other parties as something provocative, or possibly worse.

One such example was the alarm expressed by UNPREDEP and OSCE human rights observers to the Macedonian government regarding the deployment of armed police forces in Tetovo by the Ministry of the Interior to prevent the opening of the so-called illegal Albanian-language university in 1995. The government immediately denounced this action as an illustration of these organizations' pro-Albanian stance. Simultaneously, Albanians blamed the same two international organizations for standing by and not condemning forcefully enough what Albanians considered an unjustified attack on civilians by armed police. Albeit that the UNPREDEP and the OSCE are not non- but rather supra- or meta-governmental organizations, this example illustrates some of pitfalls inherent in early warning activities.

Any assumption that NGOs have something to contribute to an early warning system must therefore also presume the presence of an effective system to respond to and act upon the information provided by NGOs. Otherwise, for NGOs to enter into formal information-sharing networks, especially with governmental or diplomatic bodies, does not offset the risk of running afoul of the Macedonian government or losing the trust of the Macedonian population. With their limited range of independent action, NGOs may not be open to the same level of sharp criticism as the UN or the OSCE, but they are susceptible to it, nonetheless. American NGOs, for example, have contended with claims against them ranging from "meddling in the country's internal affairs" (often reframed as advocacy for minority rights generally, or Albanian rights specifically), to being front organizations for the CIA. Although few Macedonians take these accusations very seriously, such charges—spying in particular—are, by their nature, nearly impossible to *dis*prove and potentially can reduce an NGO's credibility and effectiveness substantially. This would be the case even more if NGOs were formally affiliated with governmental or diplomatic bodies. The attendant question thus arises: With which organizations should NGOs cooperate in any systematized early warning or information-sharing network?

To Whom Would NGOs Report?

The seemingly logical recipients of NGO information would be international bodies most able to take action based on such reports—that is, the United Nations and OSCE, with their perceived independence from the agenda of any single country as well as their resources to implement recommended early warning actions. Neither, however, is authorized to engage in measures to quell a situation that threatens to erupt into violence. The experience of the United Nations in the Bosnian war has made Macedonians question the UN's willingness and ability to be a decisive element in conflict prevention. And, although it is not often openly discussed, the popular perception is that UNPREDEP—with its clear mandate to "observe, monitor, and report" and not to intervene—would be the first group to evacuate, should hostile conditions arise.[19]

In view of the already politicized role of the major players in the international arena, should NGOs decide to coalesce into a formal early warning network, it would still be incumbent upon them to identify—or, possibly more effectively, to create—an organization that possesses both the credibility and authority to serve as a center for the collection and distribution of information.

Cross-border Communication among NGOs

For Macedonia, possibly more than for its neighbors, events across its borders may influence internal political, economic, and social developments. For the majority of NGOs in Macedonia, however, a narrow focus on internal issues precludes their involvement in monitoring the international climate as it affects their work. It does not, however, diminish their interest in being kept informed. For that reason, the presence of NGOs in three of the four countries surrounding Macedonia—some are active in Albania, Bulgaria, as well as Serbia—is a potentially useful and stabilizing element.

Unlike diplomatic operations, NGOs maintain little cross-border communication with each other. Only the NGOs in Macedonia with offices in other countries (for example, the Soros Foundation, Catholic Relief Services, the Institute for Sustainable Communities, the National Democratic Institute, Opportunity International, or the Central and East European Law Initiative) are able to keep track of important events through contacts with their local representatives. Others such as IREX are intended to function as regional centers for the southern Balkans, and their officers attempt to stay current by making periodic site visits. NGOs without these resources benefit by having the chance to consult with organizations that have first-hand sources of information.

A number of attempts have been made to bridge this communications gap, not necessarily with the purpose of strengthening a specific network or of promoting a particular agenda. Rather, international conferences focusing on the need for NGO networking, or examining problems with international implications, have sought to encourage regular channels of communications among NGOs throughout the Balkans.[20] Whereas participants in these conferences generally agree that improved inter-NGO communication is valuable, it still remains to be seen whether these efforts will yield sustainable results.

Conclusions and Recommendations

Similar to many other institutions in Macedonia's nascent post-communist society, NGOs—both domestic or foreign—are a new and, as yet, untested political and social force. Accordingly, rather than existing as a value-free representation of Western notions of "civil society," international NGOs are perceived and related to on the basis of the Macedonians' previous experiences with government, poles of authority, problem-solving mechanisms, social stratification, and so forth. For the West, whether out of justified self-interest or genuine concern for "world order," political stability per se is held to be a desirable goal, and the absence of such stability is interpreted as a sign of impending danger.

Macedonia has clearly been identified as being in such potential danger, for nothing else explains the presence of so many international NGOs in a country of just over 2 million inhabitants. The issue is not whether NGOs are best qualified or situated to provide early warning signals: The early warning bell has been rung! Rather, this question should better be rephrased to ask whether the signals are being interpreted properly and how future responses may best be formulated.

To arrive at cogent and well-reasoned answers, concerned members of the international community must look to the competence, expertise, and experience of NGOs, since these organizations, regardless of their shortcomings, have a collective hand on the pulse of the country. Yet, too frequently, if NGOs are consulted at all, they are among the last organizations to be approached on issues of importance. This paradox speaks more to the nature of relations between governments and NGOs than to the relationship between NGOs and the country in which they work, at least in the case of Macedonia.[21] Much like the Macedonians who calculate the risk involved in their association with foreign NGOs and their programs, NGOs themselves are in an analogous position when assessing how to interact with governmental and other diplomatic bodies. Furthermore, NGOs have not yet assessed the dynamics within the NGO community itself in order to determine whether NGOs do, in fact, represent a definite counterpoint to the diplomatic sphere. They also would benefit from determining how the two spheres might intersect.

Can NGOs assume an active role in evaluating conditions (early warning, broadly defined) in Macedonia and in formulating responses (early action)? Yes, but only if this role is based on a clearer understanding both of the relationships among NGOs and between NGOs and other organizations with which they might cooperate in an information-sharing or policy-advising capacity.

Recommendations

Inter-NGO Relations and Communications

— *Organization of a voluntary in-country NGO forum*

Such a forum would enable all NGOs, irrespective of their mandates, to assess and clarify their common and unique needs.[22] International NGOs with shared interests in Macedonia's social and political spheres hold regular monthly gatherings to facilitate not only inter-NGO communication but also collaborative programs. In conjunction with the forum, a monthly or quarterly newsletter or bulletin could serve as a venue on both an internal and community-wide basis for publicizing NGO activities, plans, and views on pertinent issues.

— *Organization of an NGO board authorized to represent its members*

NGOs have thus far presented themselves only individually, if and when they have been invited to attend conferences or other professional gatherings. This board, which could be a function of the NGO forum, would represent their collective concerns and views in such settings. NGOs functioning under USAID regulations may not be permitted by those regulations to delegate authority to a body not under the direct jurisdiction of USAID. Nonetheless, even an informal association with such a board would at least permit the voice of the NGO community as a whole to be heard.

— *Organization of an information-coordinating body to permit NGOs to stay aware of pertinent events in neighboring countries*

The Soros foundations, with their local offices, are perhaps the most logical locus for such activities, which could include meetings on a regular or per-need basis, and the publication of a bulletin.

NGO Relations with Foreign Governments and Diplomatic Bodies

— *Cautious exploration of cooperation*

To assume that NGOs derive no benefit from contacts with the diplomatic community is to ignore the value of information uniquely available to NGOs from these sources. The existence of informal information sharing among NGOs and governments clearly demonstrates that individuals on both sides acknowledge the advantages gained by maintaining open channels of communication. The risks of formal association with governmental or diplomatic bodies cannot be minimized, and yet NGOs must not be precluded by this risk from fully exploring the potential benefits of such relationships. For the time being, therefore, the most sensible compromise for NGOs is cautiously to explore regular information sharing on an informal basis, without entering into programmatic cooperation.[23]

— *Formation of an international NGO lobby group*

The Brussels-based Verona Forum exists already as a lobby organization for Balkan domestic NGOs at the European Parliament. A similar organization, which may or may not coincide with the in-country NGO forum, could represent the views and concerns of international NGOs to diplomatic bodies that are responsible for formulating policies affecting Macedonia.

NGO Relations with Host Government

— *Maintaining an open and above-board relationship*

All of the foregoing recommendations are of minimal benefit if an NGO is prevented by the Macedonian government from pursuing its programs. The perception of a hidden agenda could derail the plans of the most well-intentioned organization. It is therefore imperative for NGOs to be forthcoming about their objectives and the methods that they use to achieve them. Publication of an NGO newsletter or other public awareness measures will ensure that NGOs operate with the same degree of transparency that they themselves are expecting of the country in which they work.

Notes

1. There are numerous opinions about which term should be applied to NGOs' work in the field of preventive diplomacy: conflict resolution, conflict prevention, or conflict management. Each has connotations or implications about the nature of conflict and the ways of dealing with it constructively. Nafi Saraçini, of the Catholic Relief Services in Macedonia, offered the term "conflict navigation," which, although originally suggested in jest, we have begun to use more in earnest.

2. This statement and the analysis that follows have been made, keeping in mind the clashes between Albanian civilians and the Macedonian police in the predominantly Albanian town of Tetovo/Tetovo (Albanian, Tetovë/Tetova) in western Macedonia in 1995, in which one civilian was killed and twenty people, including ten policemen and one journalist, were injured. As this paper will argue, the warning bell for Macedonia has already been rung; the question, however, is whether the incident in 1995 and its repercussions will significantly increase the decibels of the warning. See the editorial by Iso Rusi, "Averting Another Balkan Wildfire," *New York Times* (4 March 1995).

3. I am deliberately refraining from applying the vestigial Yugoslav taxonomy used in Macedonia, whereby a community is classified as a "nation" (*narod*), "nationality" (*narodnost*), or ethnic group (*etnička grupa*), each of which has constitutionally defined rights and limitations. Within Macedonia now, only the Macedonian Slavs are considered a *narod*, the Albanians, Turks, Bulgarians, and Serbs are each a *narodnost*; and the Rom (Gypsy), Vlachs, and Jews are each an *etnička grupa* or *zaednica* (community). One central point of contention between the Macedonian Slavs and Albanians is the latter's demand to have their community considered a *narod*, that is, a constituent or formative nation of Macedonia. This, among other things, would raise Albanian to the status of the country's second official language, and would also further justify the establishment of the Albanian-language university in Tetovo.

4. Greece's objection to the use of "Macedonia" in the name of any country outside its own borders is one of several volatile issues that Greece and Macedonia have been negotiating. (The name "Former Yugoslav Republic of Macedonia" resulted from an interim arrangement allowing Macedonia to be admitted into the United Nations. Its usage was to be limited to that body.) This disagreement over the name appeared to be an unbridgeable difference between the two countries, and indeed was the dispute that provided Greece an excuse for imposing its long trade embargo.

5. Until the proposal for mutual recognition in early 1996, the Macedonian-Serbian border had been treated as an international one when economic issues such as the UN sanctions were in question. The Serbian (Yugoslav) army tested both Macedonia's and the United Nations forces' commitment to Macedonia's territorial integrity by sending troops close to or just over the border. On several occasions only the presence of UN troops prevented low-level confrontations from escalating into more serious military clashes.

6. In the Albanian orthography, which uses the Latin alphabet, *Kosovo* is spelled *Kosovë/Kosova*, whereas in the Slavic languages using the Cyrillic alphabet, such as Serbian and Macedonian, *Косово* is transliterated as *Kosovo*.

7. The July August 1994 census provides the following demographic data: Macedonians, 66%; Albanians, 23%; Turks, 4%; Rom, under 3%; Serbs, under 2%.

8. See Violeta Petroska Beška's article, in this volume, for the root causes of inter-ethnic tensions in Macedonia.

9. Debates are ongoing within the international community, for example, as to whether economic reform is a necessary precondition for social and political stability or whether yet-unsolved economic problems are only a convenient excuse for delaying social and political reforms. Now that the Greek and Yugoslav obstacles to Macedonian economic development have been removed, the questions regarding the tempo and credibility of political reform are coming into sharper relief.

10. The number of ECHO-funded NGOs has diminished significantly in the past year, due mostly to the perceived reduced need for humanitarian relief, which is ECHO's primary mandate. (Much of this aid had been targeted at Bosnian refugees in Macedonia, whose repatriation to Bosnia began long before the signing of the Dayton agreement.) ECHO has made it clear that conflict resolution and development are outside its scope, and ECHO therefore arguably may be excluded from discussions of preventive diplomacy until the organization's policies change.

11. Connie Bruck, "The World According to George Soros," *New Yorker* (23 January 1995) contains an analysis of the role played by George Soros and his foundations throughout Eastern Europe, including a lengthy discussion of the Soros Foundation's activities in Macedonia.

12. *Vrska* must sometimes be supplemented by *mito*, or *bakšiš* (bribe/payoff), but these are only sometimes effective substitutes for *vrska*—for example, when crossing the border with smuggled or contraband merchandise, for which customs officials must be paid off in order to avoid import duties.

13. Whereas a U.S. Liaison Office has been in operation in Skopje since shortly after Macedonia's independence, the United States refused to establish full diplomatic relations until the disputes between Skopje and Athens were settled by the accord signed in New York in 1995. Not surprisingly, Macedonians viewed the U.S. position as a surrender to pressure exerted by the Greek-American political and economic community, especially under the Clinton administration.

14. Public perception of the Soros Foundation (Open Society Institute) has been negatively affected by an anti-Soros campaign waged in 1995 by the pro-government media, in which Soros personally and his foundation were accused of political meddling and harboring ulterior motives. A number of the foundation's functions have been transferred to its regional center in Prague, and rumors circulate routinely that

the Open Society Institute is about to close its doors, either voluntarily or by official request.

15. The United States Congress's decision to diminish the USAID program may result in a dramatic reduction in the number of NGOs present on the ground, followed by a hardening of attitudes toward the remaining organizations.

16. Search for Common Ground in Macedonia has organized a regular but informal monthly discussion among U.S. and European NGOs whose focus is broader than humanitarian relief or development. These meetings have already produced collaborative projects and, because of Search's specific focus on the deescalation of conflict and inter-ethnic tensions, have stimulated other NGO directors to consider the impact of their programs on intercommunal relations.

17. Networking and information sharing among domestic NGOs does not occur in any regular or sustained fashion. Ways of improving inter-organizational communication were one focus of a conference of international and domestic NGOs from throughout former Yugoslavia, together with international funders, organized by the Erasmus Guild and the Center for Strategic and International Studies in Zagreb, 10-11 March 1995.

18. UNPROFOR was renamed UNPREDEP following the separation of the command of the UN Croatian forces from those in Macedonia. I am using UNPREDEP to refer to those forces both previous and subsequent to this separation.

19. Observation and monitoring have included periodic efforts at mediation between Albanian and Macedonian political leaders, mostly in the area unclearly defined as "human rights." Nonetheless, public pronouncements by the Macedonian government generally refer to UNPREDEP positively as a preventive force (see, for example, *Nova Makedonija* 16 March 1995).

20. The Erasmus Guild/CSIS Zagreb conference in 1995 was one. Another was the Helsinki Citizens Assembly's pan-Balkan conference in Skopje (9–10 March 1995), which produced a report recommending a common platform for the discussion and possible resolution of issues relating to minorities in southeastern Europe.

21. In the months since the writing of this chapter, the United States diplomatic staff in Macedonia, as well as individuals from the OSCE and UNPREDEP, have regularly sought NGO opinions. It is unclear, however, whether these opinions are heeded. The visit to Skopje in late 1995 by a working group from the Council on Foreign Relations—and its red-carpet reception by the U.S. and Macedonian governments—also illustrated that not all NGOs are created equal.

22. NGOs in Albania have established such a forum that might serve as a model for international organizations in Macedonia.

23. In 1994, the Balkans Peace Project of Cambridge, Massachusetts, convened a seminar in Austria called "Exploring the Potential for Collaboration by the OSCE and NGOs on Preventive Diplomacy." In the seminar's summary statement, the participants concluded, "There is no need to further formalize the relationship between the OSCE and NGOs at this time." Numerous recommendations, however, were made for strengthening the informal relationship between NGOs and the OSCE that could also be applied to other governmental and diplomatic organizations.

CHAPTER FIVE

NGOs, Early Warning, and Preventive Action: Macedonia

Violeta Petroska Beška

BEFORE THE DECLARATION of its independence in 1991, Macedonia was one of the republics of Yugoslavia. It lies at the heart of the Balkans, a region whose very changeable and complicated history has contributed significantly to the current unrest in the area.

Background

Despite the Republic of Macedonia's peaceful transition to an independent state in 1991, it is a country in the midst of a crisis brought about by its failure to win unanimous international recognition of its independence and exacerbated by economic and political instability and increasing tensions among its ethnic groups.

Disputes over International Recognition of Independence

Neighboring states have either not accepted the independent status of Macedonia or have accepted it only on conditional terms. Bulgaria has recognized Macedonia only as a territorial unit; it refuses to recognize the Macedonian nationality, claiming that the Slavic population, in fact, consists of Bulgarians. Albania has recognized Macedonia as an independent country, even though, in reality, Albania acts in ways which may

133

be perceived as a threat to Macedonia's territorial integrity. It constantly interferes on behalf of ethnic Albanians in Macedonia. Serbia (in the name of the present Yugoslavia) has not recognized the independence of Macedonia—it acknowledges its border with Macedonia only as an administrative, rather than an international border.

Greece has only recently promised to accept the existence of the Republic of Macedonia. The earlier objections from Greece were over the use of the name "Macedonia" for the country, and "Macedonians" for its Slavic population, which Greece claimed should be applied only to certain parts of Greece and the Greeks living there. Because of these objections from Greece, the country was recognized by the United Nations in 1993, under the provisional name "The Former Yugoslav Republic of Macedonia." Since then, Macedonia has received bilateral recognition from the international community under the same provisional name and, in 1996, grudging recognition by Greece.

Economic, Social, and Political Difficulties

The Macedonian economy has always been dependent on trade (primarily with other Yugoslav republics) based mainly on exporting agricultural products, importing equipment for its industrial base, and exporting manufactured goods. The war in Bosnia and Croatia, and the UN sanctions against Serbia have cut the country's traditional markets and trade routes, aggravating the difficult economic situation that was inherited from the past. Agricultural production cannot find a new trade market, and industry and construction have suffered considerably. In addition, the embargo imposed by Greece against Macedonia (due to the "name issue") made the import of goods extremely difficult, exacerbating the country's economic problems.

For the last five years, per capita income in Macedonia has fallen more than 50 percent, placing the country economically among the poorer countries of the Third World. Over one-third of the potential working population is unemployed, with an additional 25 percent of the employed being on forced holiday. About 25 percent of those who go to work do not receive wages. Industrial production has fallen 30 percent, and the social welfare case load has been constantly growing while government resources have been depleted.

Macedonia is making efforts to replace the previous unique form of Yugoslav socialism with a new capitalistic system. Doing so, however, has created additional economic, social, and political problems. In order to obtain international loans through the International Monetary Fund, the country must operate according to an imposed stabilization plan, which has resulted in an increase in the unemployment rate. Besides worsening the strain on the overburdened social welfare system, this situation is squeezing the economy and intensifying the social tensions that put the government under additional political pressure. At the same time, the transition has influenced changes toward the democratization of the country. The most obvious changes in that direction have come through the introduction of political pluralism as well as legislative reform. However, it cannot be said that the average citizen has understood the full meaning of the concept of "democracy"—he/she must first understand his/her role in a democratic society and act accordingly, if the process of democratization is to be speeded up.

Ethnic Tensions

The existing economic, social, and political problems intensify those related to the ethnic heterogeneity of the population. The majority of the population of 2 million consists of ethnic Macedonians (66.5 percent according to the most recent census in 1994), followed by Albanians (22.9 percent), Turks (4 percent), Roms/Gypsies, Serbs, and Vlachs. Most of the ethnic Albanians are concentrated in certain parts of western Macedonia—in some regions they are the majority of the population.

Since the declaration of its independence, Macedonia has constantly faced the problem of ethnic tension, which has emerged as a consequence of both the present economic decline and the current political climate in the country, and in the Balkans as a whole. In their efforts to gain support from the people, most political parties have given priority to ethnic interests, contributing to the growing nationalism of all ethnic groups in the country. With respect to the ethnic backgrounds of their members and followers, the most influential political parties can be divided into two opposing groups. One involves the parties which represent the interests of the Macedonian majority, and the other represents the interests of the Albanian minority.

Continuing historical, social, and religious differences between ethnic Macedonians (mostly Orthodox) and ethnic Albanians (mostly Muslims), together with the growing national ethnic tensions, have already created a pre-conflict situation in the country. Ethnic Macedonians are the dominant group demographically as well as socially, politically, and economically. As the second largest ethnic group in the country, ethnic Albanians argue that they are treated as second-class citizens and are discriminated against with respect to education, employment, and political representation. They demand equal status with ethnic Macedonians.

In order to overcome the present situation, representatives of the Albanian political parties, formally or informally supported by the government in Albania and the political leaders from Kosovo, call for the recognition of Albanian as an official language, and for Albanian-language education at all levels. They also seek free use of Albanian national symbols as well as recognition in the Constitution of the Republic of Macedonia of Albanians as a constitutive nation. In addition, they have demanded proportional representation in the government, as well as in the police force, the army, and other public institutions—all of which have so far been "reserved" for ethnic Macedonians.

At the same time, representatives of Macedonian political parties object to the Albanians' demands because they find the demands dangerous for the integrity of the country. They also question the Albanians' loyalty since almost all members of the Albanian ethnic group, under pressure from their political leaders, boycotted the national referendum calling for sovereignty and independence of the country, and voted for a culturally autonomous territory in their own referendum. Furthermore, the Albanian representatives in the Parliament refused to vote for the new constitution.

In addition, nationalistic passions within both ethnic groups have been stirred up by the continuous political battle for dominance among the Macedonian political parties as well as among the recently divided Albanian political parties. In order to strengthen their political power and overtake the supreme position among the members of their ethnic groups, these extremely nationalistic political parties have exaggerated their "need to get more," on the one hand, or their "need not to give anything more" on the other. These tensions are serious threats to the stability of the country, as well as to the stability of the whole region.

Ethnic Conflict as a Source of Crisis

The Republic of Macedonia is currently in a pre-conflict stage, or in a stage of nonescalated conflict with a high probability of an outbreak of violence. The escalation of the present ethnic tensions can very easily provoke inter-ethnic conflicts with consequences even worse than those in Bosnia. An open, violent confrontation between the ethnic groups in Macedonia might lead to the disintegration of the country, and also start a war that would involve other neighboring countries.

The existing intolerance between the Macedonian and Albanian ethnic groups is a result of mutual mistrust. That mistrust has its roots in the past but has been strongly encouraged by the restrictions on certain rights previously enjoyed by the Albanian ethnic group (as well as by the other minority groups in Macedonia) during the last fifteen years. Within the context of insufficiently integrated relations, these restrictions added fuel to the fire: Macedonian nationalists and chauvinists showed their appreciation of the "proper" attitude of the government, whereas the Albanian nationalists and separatists claimed that living together with Macedonians on the basis of equal rights was not possible. With the additional significant influence of the mass media, which serve the current political regime and support the actions undertaken by the government, ethnic distance and intensification of the ethnic intolerance progressively widened. Although some of these restrictions have since been removed, little progress toward better relations has been made. On the contrary, the existing mutual mistrust has become so strong that it has already caused ethnic Albanians and ethnic Macedonians to fear each other. The average ethnic Albanian feels threatened by the Macedonian ethnic group as much as the average ethnic Macedonian feels threatened by the Albanian ethnic group.

Perhaps the most serious consequence of this high level of mistrust has been the almost complete separation of both ethnic groups. Most of the ethnic Albanians have enclosed themselves within their ethnic group, taking into consideration only the interests of their own group. The same has happened to the ethnic Macedonians: Most have retreated into their ethnic group to unite in defending themselves against the Albanians. As a result, communication between the two ethnic groups has broken down in many areas of everyday life.

One example of this lack of communication can be seen among Albanian and Macedonian students at elementary and high school levels. They attend separate classes where each group is taught in its mother tongue. Even in the ethnically mixed schools, where Albanian and Macedonian students study under the same roof, separation of the two groups, and lack of communication between them, are obvious during the breaks, as well as in extracurricular activities. All student disputes are regarded as having an ethnic dimension.

This segregation also extends to most public gatherings. Ethnically mixed audiences are rarely, if ever, seen at art openings and never at music festivals, for example. Sporting events also reflect ethnic intolerance: Football (soccer) matches between teams of different ethnic backgrounds are always potential sources of violence among fans.

Ethnic separation is even more evident in the mixed parts of western Macedonia. Very few Macedonians enter restaurants owned by Albanians, and very few Albanians enter restaurants owned by Macedonians. They rarely shop at the same stores. The situation with regard to discotheques and youth clubs is very similar: Young people go out to different places and never dare date someone from the other ethnic group.

The mass media have played a significant role in fueling the crisis originating from ethnic conflict. The present situation in the mass media is a consequence of accumulated ethnic intolerance and, at the same time, is a cause of further expansion of the ethnic distance between the groups. The most influential newspapers, television channels, and radio programs are characterized by a high degree of separation and lack of communication between the ethnic groups. With the present variety of private TV and radio channels and programs, and newspapers in their mother tongue, ethnic Albanians usually choose to watch and read what is offered in Albanian. Similarly, ethnic Macedonians never watch or read anything that is not in Macedonian, not only because of language constraints but also because of personal preference. This would not create a problem if most of the mass media were not biased in favor of one or the other ethnic group. As it is, however, the media are biased. Events are portrayed with a clear bias toward one side or the other, with each side defending the actors that are members of its own ethnic group and attacking and blaming the members of the opposing ethnic group. As a result, instead of reducing the tensions, almost all members of the mass media have been adding to the atmosphere of hostility.

What began as a conflict between the national political parties has been turned into a conflict between the two major ethnic groups. The battle for political power could very easily be replaced by a battle for territorial redistribution. What has developed is a potentially volatile situation of intolerance between ethnic Macedonians and ethnic Albanians, characterized by a very high level of tension. The fear of conflict escalation is becoming a part of everyday life.

Indigenous NGOs: Roles and Activities

The disintegration of former Yugoslavia, with all the accompanying occurrences, has rapidly increased the number of NGOs in the region. Most of the indigenous and international NGOs currently operating in Macedonia have appeared within the last five years. This recent proliferation may be attributed to the change in the political atmosphere, favoring pluralism, as well as to emerging economic, social, political, and ethnic problems. The rapid increase in the number of NGOs should be regarded as an early warning signal of an impending crisis.

Indigenous NGOs currently operating in the country include humanitarian, ecological, youth, women's, and human rights organizations. Many of these mostly humanitarian organizations are divided along ethnic lines, such as humanitarian organizations for Muslims or for Roms, the League of Vlachs, the Union of Roms, or the League of Albanian Women in Macedonia, as opposed to the Organization of Women of Macedonia, and so forth. Only a few, such as the Helsinki Citizen Assembly, have active members from different ethnic backgrounds or work for the benefit of all ethnic groups.

Besides the purely humanitarian NGOs, not many NGOs are really active. Many of those established to promote the idea of democracy and to contribute to resolving some of the acute political and ethnic problems have either grown passive or have ceased most of their activities.

In order to function properly as an actively engaged NGO, an organization should include members who are interested in and thoroughly aware of emerging problems and who are willing to listen to the needs of all parties. In other words, they must have strong and independent personalities—they should be creative, inventive, and brave enough to disclose opinions that are different and even opposite from the ones expressed by the majority of their ethnic group. However, in Macedonia, most people fear and feel threatened by public authorities from opposing backgrounds. Very few among them dare to oppose the majority.

Within the former Yugoslavia, Macedonia was organized according to a very strict hierarchy; all power was distributed among a very limited number of people at the top of that hierarchy. NGOs that existed under those circumstances were, in actuality, working for the government and/or with its approval. It is thus understandable that whole generations of people brought up in that society do not yet realize how powerful citizens' associations can be. As a result, the prevailing belief has been that indigenous

NGOs are powerless to contribute to changing the crisis situation. This belief not only has the effect of lowering the status of NGOs in society, but also leads to a feeling of helplessness within the NGOs themselves.

The limited influence of the indigenous NGOs also results from the narrow scope of their activities. Most of them have not yet developed an appropriate strategy for action since either they are relatively new organizations, or they have not enjoyed adequate leadership. Another limiting factor is the lack of local professionals to attract and train strong leaders as well as the lack of necessary resources to help the organizations function effectively.

Despite these serious constraints on indigenous NGOs, they may be able to exert a significant influence on the current political situation. To what extent have they and could they get involved in early warning? What actions have they undertaken, and what actions could they undertake to prevent the escalation of conflict and outbreak of violence?

Indigenous NGOs in Macedonia which take into consideration the needs of both sides in the conflict might not be able to become involved in warning in a direct way. Those who do usually risk being misunderstood— they are seen as taking one side against the other. However, by organizing meetings where people from opposing sides can listen to each other's perspectives, and by arranging contacts which would not otherwise be made spontaneously, in numerous instances they have opened up a process of promoting awareness about the possible consequences of conflict. Although some individuals have engaged in sending warning messages, NGOs have very rarely, if ever, used the mass media for that purpose.

Very few of the indigenous NGOs have carried out preventive actions aimed at lowering the tensions and restoring mutual trust. One of them is the Ethnic Conflict Resolution Project, whose basic goal has been to increase understanding of the sources of present and potential conflicts as well as to provide training in conflict-resolution techniques. In fact, it has aimed at helping people understand and manage ethnic conflicts from the grassroots up, mainly through training seminars for ethnic Macedonian and ethnic Albanian participants.

The efficiency of indigenous NGOs in resolving, containing, or preventing ethnic conflicts could be increased by broadening the range of their activities as well as by recruiting members of opposing ethnic groups to work with them to achieve common goals. NGOs need to coordinate their efforts by setting up a network to help share information, exchange ideas, and assist each other more generally.

International NGOs: Roles and Activities

For the last five years, the number of international NGOs operating in the Republic of Macedonia has been growing constantly. Some are concerned mainly with the distribution of humanitarian aid and/or support of developmental projects. There are also NGOs, such as Search for Common Ground, that are primarily engaged in activities which support the development of democratic processes in the society and try to create mechanisms of dialogue. Somewhere in between are the NGOs like Catholic Relief Services, which are involved in both types of activities, offering humanitarian and developmental aid, and undertaking actions to promote human rights programs. Efforts to advance the development of democratic processes have been easier for those NGOs which offer humanitarian and relief aid as well. Most NGOs that seek government support for a specific cause must become involved in activities which have been given priority by governmental agencies.

Another distinction among the international NGOs can be made on the basis of the amount of money that they are able to spend on their activities. This distinction is very important in achieving success, since it influences the way in which the government and people in Macedonia perceive an NGO. Since the better-funded NGOs (like the Open Society Institute/Soros Foundation) make it appear that the main purpose of all NGOs is to provide financial support for local needs, less well-endowed NGOs are forced to overcome various obstacles in order to proceed with their activities. In addition, the success of the activities undertaken by the international NGOs is very much dependent on the goodwill of the government. If their activities are approved and supported by governmental agencies, they are much better able to carry out their work.

International NGOs in the country, especially those whose activities are related to ethnic conflict, are often criticized for taking one side against the other. Although this does not necessarily occur (since "not being with me" does not always imply "being against me"), the average citizen is under the impression that international organizations focus on the needs of one particular ethnic group, while neglecting the needs of the others. Ethnic Macedonians, in particular, often have this impression, since representatives of the international NGOs are seen as protectors and even advocates for ethnic Albanians. This belief has created a great deal of suspicion within the Macedonian population toward the roles and intentions of many NGOs.

As a consequence, people increasingly have come to believe that NGOs are not there to help resolve the conflicts but to create them. In order to avoid the possible detrimental consequences of this misconception, NGOs need to be more careful in their attempts to maintain neutrality. It is very important to appear more as mediators than as arbitrators, and not as advocates for one particular side in the conflict.

At the same time, most of the international NGOs in Macedonia are not perceived as true NGOs, but rather as organizations working for their home governments. They are perceived as gathering information for their own governments and taking actions according to their governments' instructions. It is commonly felt that many, if not most, international NGOs are self-serving and are involved in Macedonia only on behalf of their respective government's needs and interests.

It is difficult for the international NGOs to find proper ways to sound a warning about the possibility of the escalation of conflict and the outbreak of violence. The difficulty comes from the necessity to maintain a balance, politically as well as psychologically, between the opposing sides. Warning of impending violence, in neutral terms, without finding fault with any particular side, is often very difficult.

Thus far, international NGOs in Macedonia have been involved in activities related to delivering relief and developmental services, creating and supporting citizens' associations, monitoring and reporting on local conditions, creating negotiation and dialogue mechanisms, and monitoring elections. At the same time, many people are under the impression that these NGOs have not been engaged enough in other very important activities, such as collecting and disseminating information in and out of the country; creating channels for expressing grievances; exerting pressure on the governmental agencies and international community; and mediating, negotiating, and implementing agreements between opposing sides. Their participation in these activities could contribute not only to keeping the peace in the country, but also to gaining more respect for themselves within the local community.

Capacities of the NGOs in Relation to the UN, the European Community, and Macedonia

Most Macedonians believe that NGOs in the Republic of Macedonia have a lower capacity than UN and European Community (EC) agencies effectively to warn of a possible crisis and to take appropriate preventive action. Most people, in fact, would rank indigenous NGOs behind international NGOs in this regard.

UN and EC agencies are in the best position to take action that would promote changes in the government. Besides constant monitoring and reporting (provided by the United Nations Protection Forces and the Organization for Security and Cooperation in Europe Mission stationed in Macedonia) and delivering relief and developmental services (by UNICEF, for example), UN and EC agencies in Macedonia have already taken steps toward mediating and negotiating agreements between the opposing sides in the ethnic conflict. By exerting pressure on the government, they have succeeded in changing the government's attitudes. International and indigenous NGOs have never had the same opportunities for action as the UN and EC agencies.

UN and EC agencies are able to be so effective because of the fact that the existence of the Republic of Macedonia, to a considerable extent, depends upon their attitudes toward the country and its efforts in preventing and resolving ethnic conflicts. At the same time, although the international NGOs are, for the most part, regarded as representatives of their home governments, which have significant political power to influence the international community as well as the opposing parties in Macedonia, they still do not have the same opportunities as those enjoyed by the UN and EC agencies. Very often, the success of an NGO depends upon the host government. Even when an NGO provides its own financing, its existence depends on the attitude of the government either toward the proposed project or toward the NGO itself; it needs government approval to operate successfully.

That indigenous NGOs are generally thought to be least able to take effective preventive action can be attributed in part to their inability to overcome attitudes inherited from the former Yugoslav system, in which the people were not expected to criticize public authorities. This constraint, together with difficulties arising from lack of knowledge, weak organization, insufficient resources, and perceived ethnic affiliations, has prevented the indigenous NGOs from working in a more effective manner.

The efficiency of both indigenous and international NGOs could be improved by mutual support. Since international NGOs are not always familiar with the local situation, it is very important that they collaborate with indigenous NGOs. At the same time, international NGOs could help indigenous NGOs by providing training and other professional and financial support in all areas of building civil society and by creating mechanisms for conflict prevention and resolution.

Because ethnic conflict is the most serious threat to peace in Macedonia, collaboration between the international and indigenous NGOs is crucial. These organizations should engage in joint activities whose aim would be to reestablish communication between the ethnic groups, help them understand the needs and fears of the members of the other ethnic group, and dispel stereotypes and misapprehensions about the other ethnic group. Such early action could help prevent the current ethnic tensions from escalating into a serious crisis and could help restore peace and prosperity to the region.

SRI LANKA

CHAPTER SIX

Sri Lanka's Ethnic Conflict and Preventive Action: The Role of NGOs

Neelan Tiruchelvam

IN THE RECENT history of the Indian subcontinent, ethnic violence has become increasingly common. From the Pathan-Bihari clashes in Pakistan to the anti-Sikh riots in New Delhi, the anti-reservation stir in Gujerat, and the Sinhala-Tamil conflict in Sri Lanka, racial violence has left a trail of destruction of property and human life. Indeed, the emotional and psychological scars that remain after such outbreaks are in fact more destructive than the physical damage. The sense of community within a plural society is often shattered by the cruelty, terror, and suffering unleashed by the forces of mob violence.[1]

Ethnic conflict has contributed to some of the most serious and persistent violations of human rights in South Asia. Most of the serious violations relate to disappearances, torture, and extra-judicial killings. Arbitrary and indiscriminate arrests have been linked to ongoing ethnic conflicts.

Competition for scarce resources and economic opportunities has fuelled antagonisms arising from the sharp cleavages of race, caste, tribe, religion, and language. Fragile political institutions have failed adequately to accommodate the demands for power and resource sharing by marginalized ethnic and religious groups. Policies to advance national cohesion have been pursued at the expense of the linguistic and cultural traditions of minority groups, creating additional tensions among them.

Ethnic discontent began manifesting itself in secessionist movements; these actions resulted in repressive responses by the state, posing serious

concerns for social justice and human rights. These problems have been
further compounded by the presence of millions of internally displaced
persons, and the flight of refugees from internal conflict.

Ethnic Issues

In recent years, there has been a growing awareness of the universality and complexities of ethnic problems and the need for concerted action
to devise strategies, programs, and structures for the management of
ethnic conflict. Several multi-ethnic polities have incorporated federal
forms of devolution into constitutional and political orders. In the development of these constitutional models, there has been continuing conflict
between unitary and federal methods, and centralized and decentralized
forms. In India, for example, the federal polity is based on a division into
linguistic states, while in Malaysia, a federation of states is led by local
rulers and includes territories, which were given special concessions.[2]
The former Nigerian model overlapped certain regional and tribal groupings in its demarcation of states. Federal and quasi-federal models of
devolution also have a relevance to strife-ridden societies such as the
Philippines, Pakistan, and Sri Lanka, which have recently enacted new
constitutions or are on the threshold of redesigning their present constitutional framework.[3] Within these societies, each of the diverse ethnic,
tribal, and regional groupings has varying perceptions of federalism
which have tended to condition the conflicts and tensions within federal
or confederal systems.

A growing debate has emerged within each of these societies regarding the need for structural rearrangements to strengthen their federal
character. These efforts have been directed toward the need to redefine
center-state relations in educational and cultural policy, police powers,
resource mobilization and redistribution, and emergency and residual
powers. Such efforts and problems evoke basic issues concerning equitable power sharing among ethnic groups. The failure to address these
issues boldly has accentuated secessionist demands by disaffected ethnic
and other sub-national groups.

Self-determination, often sought by ethnic minorities in the course of
an armed struggle or non-violent political agitation, has been problematic. Nation states become notably defensive in the face of such asser-
tions, and often employ extreme measures of repression in order to

contain ethnic demands which they perceive could result in national dis-integration.[4]

Another focal point of ethnic conflict has been preference policies directed toward disparities in educational, employment, and economic opportunities. These policies are often founded on competing perceptions of deprivation which, in turn, give rise to rival notions of social justice. India, one of the most complex and hierarchically structured societies, has a constitutionally mandated policy of preference toward weak and vulnerable minorities and tribal groups. Policy-makers and judges have had to grapple with issues of bewildering complexity in defining the constitutional limits of such policies, balancing the interests of historically depressed caste and tribal groups with those of economically disadvantaged classes. Preference policies—such as Malaysia's New Economic Policy (1971)—directed in favor of a politically assertive and dominant majority, pose qualitatively different socio-political issues relating to the legitimate limits of preference policies based on proportionality.[5]

The international community must accord highest priority to developing principles and concepts with regard to minority protection, and these must gain universal acceptance and contribute to the peaceful resolution of conflicts. But, given the evolving and changing nature of ethnic identity; the content of ethnic demands; and the shifting balance of power among ethnic groups, most structural arrangements will remain fluid and transient. Thus, these arrangements must continuously be renewed and reconstructed in order to respond to new ethnic challenges and demands.

Ethnic conflicts also pose fundamental issues relating to human rights and social justice, which need to be addressed within the framework of a community's policy on human rights.

Sri Lanka has a diverse population of 19 million. About 74 percent are of Sinhalese origin, 18 percent are Tamil, and 7.6 percent are Indian Muslim. Of the Tamils, 12 percent are Sri Lankan, and 6 percent are recent immigrants called "estate" Tamils.

Collective Violence in Sri Lanka

More than thirteen years have elapsed since one of the cruelest weeks in the troubled history of modern Sri Lanka. The Tamils of Sri Lanka were exposed to collective violence in 1958, 1977, 1981, and 1983; however, the nature of the violence of 1983 was qualitatively different in its intensity, brutality, and organized nature. No other event is so deeply etched in the collective memories of Sri Lanka's victims and survivors; neither time nor space has helped ease the pain and the trauma of all Sri Lankans.

In attacks by mobs in the capital city, between 2,000 and 3,000 defenseless people were brutally murdered, although official records show a death toll of approximately 400. Many were beaten or hacked to death, and several were torched to death. Thousands of homes and buildings were burned or destroyed. Within the city of Colombo, almost 100,000 persons—more than half of the city's Tamil population—were displaced from their homes, many never returning to their neighborhoods or to their work places. An estimated 175,000 refugees and displaced persons fled the country. Hardly a family escaped the death of a relative or the dislocation of family members. Almost everyone suffered great losses of a personal or material nature. In referring to her Tamil identity, one woman who had been victimized by the repeated cycles of violence, exclaimed in despair, "to be a Tamil is to live in fear."[6]

Many observers were particularly disturbed by the organized and systematic nature of the violence. The rampaging Sinhalese mobs had been provided with precise information on the location of Tamil homes and businesses; their leaders often had been armed with lists of voters and detailed addresses of Tamil-owned shops, houses, and factories. Business, entrepreneurial, and professional classes were especially targeted. The objective appeared to be the breaking of the economic backbone of the Tamils. Almost 100 industrial plants, including twenty garment factories, were severely damaged or destroyed. The cost of industrial reconstruction was estimated at Rs.2 billion. This figure did not include the hundreds of shops and small trading establishments destroyed during the rampage.

Equally disturbing was the element of state complicity in the violence. The state not only mishandled the funeral of thirteen soldiers who had been ambushed by the Liberation Tigers of Tamil Eelam (LTTE) on 23 July 1983, but also allowed the inflammatory news to be projected in banner headlines in the newspapers on the following day. In contrast, news of the retaliatory violence of the security forces in Tirunelveli and Kantharmadu, which resulted in an estimated fifty to seventy persons being killed, had been suppressed by the media. Army personnel appeared to have encouraged arson and looting, and in some instances, allegedly participated in the looting. Neither the army nor the police took any meaningful action to prevent the violence or to apprehend the culprits. No curfew was declared for almost two days. Neither the president nor any senior minister made a public appeal for calm and restraint. It was also widely believed that elements within the state and the ruling party had either orchestrated the violence or encouraged the bloodletting. No commission of inquiry was ever appointed to investigate the causes of violence or clear the government of these allegations.[7]

When political leaders finally spoke, four days after the riots, they identified the state with the majority Sinhalese community. President Junius Richard Jayawardene said that the riots had not been a product of urban mobs but rather a mass movement of the Sinhalese people. He spoke of the need politically to "appease" the natural desires and requests of the Sinhalese people. Similarly, none of the senior cabinet ministers who spoke on television, including Lalith Athulathmudali, Minister of National Security, had a word of sympathy for the victims of this terrible outrage, nor did any minister visit the refugee camps to commiserate even briefly with those who had suffered. The president's conduct contrasted sharply with his more conciliatory behavior in the aftermath of the 1981 riots. He was quoted then as saying, "I regret that some members of my party have spoken in Parliament and outside words that encourage violence and murders, rapes and arson that have been committed."[8] The president further promised to resign if his party's members continued to encourage ethnic violence and racial bigotry.

The most disturbing episode took place on 25 July 1983, at Welikade prison, when thirty-five Tamil political detainees were battered and hacked to death with clubs, pipes, and iron rods by fellow prisoners, with the complicity of prison guards. The government conducted a perfunctory magisterial inquiry, but no attempt was made to take legal action against those responsible. More prisoners were killed two days later. The government has yet to pay compensation to the bereaved families and has pleaded immunity to the legal proceedings instituted by the families.[9]

Several scholars have written extensively on the causes and consequences of the 1983 riots, which Spencer, a British anthropologist, has described as "the dark night of the collective soul."[10] How was it possible that an island society renowned for its scenic beauty and the warmth and hospitality of its inhabitants was capable of such collective evil and inhumanity? Some have referred to the competing views of nationalism of the Sinhalese and the Tamils as being a contributory factor in the crisis. Their views of nationalism were antagonistic and incompatible. Others seeking the root causes of the 1983 violence have referred to historical myths that demonized the Tamils. Spencer points out that, in the popular imagination, tigers were believed to be "superhumanly cruel and cunning and like demons ubiquitous," and that ordinary Tamil citizens also became vested with these attributes. The myths remind us, as Voltaire did, that, "if you believe in absurdities you will commit atrocities."[11] Still others have pointed to the propensity for violence in authoritarian political structures, which enthrone the majoritarian principle and provide for the forceful entrenchment of the unitary state. A referendum in 1981, which extended the life of Parliament, further exacerbated the climate of political animosity and of intolerance.[12]

The tragic events of 1983 also contributed to convulsive changes in the politics of the Tamil community and its method of struggle. As Tamil political leaders committed to constitutional means of agitation became marginalized, Tamil militancy became ascendant. Some Tamils even asserted that the violence perpetrated by the victims was on a different moral plane from that of the oppressor. This was a dangerous doctrine, for the violence of the victims soon consumed the victims themselves, who then became possessed by the demons of racial bigotry and intolerance, which had originally characterized the oppressors. These transformations were evident in the fratricidal violence between Tamils and non-Sinhalese Muslims; the massacres at the Kathankudy mosque, in Welikanda and Medirigiya; and the forcible expulsion of Muslims from the Mannar and Jaffna Districts.

More than a decade later, basic problems remain unresolved, and to some extent, are more intractable. In 1993, Prime Minister Ranil Wickremasnghe told the Sri Lanka Aid Consortium, "History has shown us that there are numerous lessons to be drawn from other countries of the world that problems of a minority cannot be resolved by suppressing the minority or by riding roughshod over the heads of the majority. An honorable solution needs a recognizable consensus. We are therefore not relaxing our efforts to find a peaceful solution to the conflict in the North and East based on such a consensus."[13] But, as yet, the Sri Lankan political leadership has not shown the political imagination, the resolve, or the sense of urgency to forge such a consensus.

Early Warning Signals

Although the ethnic minorities in Sri Lanka were unreconciled to constitutional arrangements at the time of transfer of political power in 1948 from Britain to Sri Lankans—which have, since then, singularly failed to establish the foundation of a multi-ethnic polity—few expected that majority rule would quickly be followed by discriminatory legislative measures. The first related to new citizenship laws, which effectively disenfranchised estate Tamils of recent Indian origin. This legislation resulted in the formation of ethnically based Tamil parties to resist discriminatory citizenship laws. They advocated parity with respect to the status of national languages, and urged the creation of a federal constitution.

Ethnic communities were becoming increasingly polarized, and political discourse was becoming politically strident and volatile. The political and ethnic polarization intensified during the run-up to the 1956 general election, when the Sri Lanka Freedom Party was swept into power in all parts of the country except in the north and east. The party's success symbolized the resurgence of the forces of Sinhala Buddhist nationalism, while the Federal Party's success in the north and east represented the emergence of a new form of Tamil linguistic nationalism. Unfortunately, the events of the mid-1950s ensured that the assertion of one form of nationalism was viewed as a denial of the other.[14]

There were two important warnings of the escalating conflict and of likely violence. The first was a monograph by Bertram Farmer, a Cambridge academician and former member of the Land Commission in Sri Lanka. His monograph, *Ceylon: A Divided Nation* (London, 1963), signaled the growing complexities of the conflict and the need for an early resolution. Another significant early warning sign was provided by Colvin R. de Silva, the leading left politician involved in the legislative debates on the Official Languages Act. He warned that the policy of trying to impose the official language of the majority community on the linguistic minority would have dangerous political consequences. He added, "Two languages—one nation; one language—two nations."[15] De Silva accurately predicted that the failure to resolve the language question in a manner satisfactory to the minority would eventually lead to a separatist movement.

These early warnings, however, went unheeded. Sri Lanka did not at that time have a strong NGO which could have responded to this warning in a meaningful way. Professional organizations and religious groups were also reluctant to take a position against the tide of majoritarian sentiment.

The Federal Party continued its non-violent agitation against the discriminatory language legislation, including a *satyagraha* campaign outside Parliament. These non-violent protests led to ugly incidents of mob violence directed against peaceful protestors and progressively escalated into a spate of collective violence directed against the Tamil community in different parts of the island. A state of emergency ensued, during which newspaper censorship was imposed. As a result, little information was available on the scale and intensity of the violence that was being directed against the Tamils. Furthermore, no commission of inquiry was appointed to investigate the first incidents of violence in 1958, particularly those in which the police had failed to intervene. In this regard, an important event was the publication of *Emergency 58*, by Tarzie Vitachchi, a renowned Sri Lankan journalist.[16] This book was informative, not only with regard to current events, but also with regard to the overall context of the deteriorating ethnic relations between the communities.

Local Responses

The initial response to the escalating conflict and the outbreak of violence by civil society institutions was to mobilize humanitarian relief operations. In some instances, local relief organizations worked with religious groups to provide food and other essential items to the refugee camps which had been established for internally displaced persons. The cycles of violence in 1958 and 1977 inevitably led to the migration of populations from the south of Sri Lanka to the north and east, resulting in problems of resettlement. The relief groups were required to provide help to displaced families, including the education of children, and assistance with the re-employment of wage earners. The Sri Lanka Red Cross Society was one of the agencies that provided assistance after the outbreaks of violence in 1956 and in 1977, but it limited its intervention to immediate humanitarian services. The Red Cross Society was also able to mobilize a considerable amount of external assistance to internally displaced persons.

In Sri Lanka in the early 1970s, several important NGOs were founded which progressively acquired the capacity to respond to some of the human rights, political, and humanitarian issues linked to the escalation of the ethnic conflict and subsequent violence. The Civil Rights Movement (CRM), established in 1971 with the objective of protecting and promoting civil rights and liberties, was one of the significant civil society initiatives of this period.[17] It jealously guarded its independence and impartiality, and focused primarily on the exercise and misuse of governmental power. The CRM was also important in conflict prevention during the different phases of the crisis in Sri Lanka, and became directly involved with a number of significant issues. Following are actions undertaken by CRM:

—Protested against security legislation—with respect to the conflict in the north and east—on the grounds that such legislation tended to be too wide and too restrictive of individual rights.[18]

—Protected the freedom of speech of those who articulated minority grievances, including those advocating separatism. On 4 July 1979, the CRM, in referring to a proposal on the advocacy of separatism, drew attention to "grave dangers inherent in using the power of the state to curb the democratic freedom of political debate, for this forces political opponents to resort to other means. A ban on the democratic expression of the demand for Eelam will, far from achieving the stated purpose of curbing violence, in fact create a situation where lawlessness and violence may increase."[19]

—Documented human rights abuses of political dissidents and minorities, including ill-treatment, torture, and death in custody; arbitrary and prolonged detention; and emergency regulations which created the possibility of such human rights abuses occurring, including the admissibility of forced confessions.

—Documented incidents of violence against minorities, their political representatives, and political parties, allegedly by armed forces or police, and urged effective action to maintain law and order.[20]

—Recorded incidents of communal violence against estate Tamils and urged effective action to punish the perpetrators and compensate the victims. A CRM memorandum further recommended the granting of citizenship and electoral rights to estate Tamils and the strengthening of their educational facilities.

—Encouraged the government to adopt international instruments such as the Convention on the Elimination of Racial Discrimination, and the Optional Protocol, relating to the protection of minorities. CRM further urged the signing of twenty-three other international human rights instruments, in the expectation that a more effective protection of individual rights would facilitate better domestic ethnic relations.

—Protested against the collective violence in July 1983, emphasizing, in particular, the complicity of the state in the violence, including the massacre of Tamil prisoners and detainees in the Welikada Prison. The

CRM further instituted legal action on behalf of the families of the victims of the prison massacre.

—Intervened in the process of constitutional reforms in 1977, 1993, and 1994, with a view to protecting individual and minority rights. It also encouraged political negotiations for the resolution of the conflict and urged the cessation of hostilities between both parties involved. It urged both parties to cooperate with the United Nations in resolving the conflict.

In view of its capacity to monitor and document human rights abuses and to retain its moral authority in an increasingly polarized and acrimonious environment, CRM was able to provide effective early warning and to take early action with regard to the ethnic conflicts. It was also effective in maintaining a central focus on the questions of rights and democratic values, and in linking these concerns to questions of constitutional and legal reform. In 1996, CRM remains frustrated, however, by the continuing cycles of violence throughout the country; the impunity granted the state and the lack of accountability of the state with regard to human rights abuses; and the attacks on the defenders of human rights, particularly at the grassroots level. (CRM has been effective in bringing international standards and comparative experience to bear on the resolution of Sri Lanka's ethnic conflicts. CRM received the Carter-Menil award for human rights on 10 December 1990.)

The Movement for Inter-Racial Justice and Equality (MIRJE), another NGO, was established in the aftermath of the 1977 racial violence to promote harmony between ethnic groups. MIRJE has a mixed membership, and has branches in different parts of the country; until 1988, it even had an active branch in Jaffna. Since its founding, MIRJE has continued to note the deteriorating nature of ethnic relations and the need to take effective measures to secure the individual and collective rights for the Tamils. During several fact-finding missions, it documented the incidents of racial violence in 1981 and 1983, thereby ensuring that objective and impartial information was available. It also propagated the concept of a multi-ethnic Sri Lankan society grounded on the bedrock of equality and equal opportunity. It has, more recently, called for a constitutional and political structure that recognizes this reality and gives room to the full expression of the social, cultural, and political aspirations of all ethnic groups. With these objectives in view, MIRJE has engaged in the following activities:

—Published two newspapers, one in Tamil and the other in Sinhala, to ensure that there is balanced reporting on events relating to ethnic conflict and its resolution.

—Engaged in a program of public education through cultural activity, including the organization of peace marches to Jaffna.

—Provided legal assistance to detainees and filed more than 3,000 such applications.

—Framed a model constitution based on the federal form of devolution of power and effective protection of minority rights. It also lobbied for the acceptance of some of the concepts and ideas embodied in this draft.[21]

The International Centre for Ethnic Studies, an NGO with an international mandate and international board of directors, has also made significant contributions to issues relating to internal conflict in Sri Lanka. Established in 1982, the Centre has two offices, one in Colombo and the other in Peradeniya. Each branch has independently developed its own projects and secured its own funding. The Centre has been regarded as an important civil society resource in the ongoing peace efforts and the process of constitutional reform.[22] It has also been active in contributing toward the development of two main policy areas which are critical to ethnic conflict: devolution and bilingualism.

From 1982 to 1987, working against the tide of public opinion in Sri Lanka, the Centre emphasized the need to fashion a plural society and to put into place structural arrangements and policies designed to minimize ethnic conflict. It researched the fates of the victims and survivors of the 1983 riots and made recommendations with regard to the role of education as an instrument of national integration. An important turning point in the work of the Centre was the Indo-Sri Lanka Accord, which recognized that Sri Lanka was a plural, multi-ethnic, and multi-religious society. The Centre has an active media program which focuses on processes of value formation in Sri Lanka and emphasizes respect for diversity, ethnic tolerance, and religious harmony. It has also encouraged the establishment of provincial councils throughout Sri Lanka, partly in response to ethnic grievances and to strengthen democratic participation.

Since 1987, Sri Lanka has been a bilingual society; Sinhala and Tamil are official languages, and English has the status of a linking language. The Centre was effective in drafting legislation to establish an Official Languages Commission to implement the government's language policy.

International Responses

The international community has increasingly become concerned about and involved in the ethnic conflict in Sri Lanka. The International

Committee of the Red Cross (ICRC) has been providing special human-itarian assistance to war-affected areas; the UN High Commissioner for Refugees (UNHCR) has implemented a program of emergency assis-tance to internally displaced persons; the UN Working Group on Disap-pearances has visited Sri Lanka twice and submitted reports; and the Special Representative of the UN Secretary-General visited the country in 1993 to report on conditions of the internally displaced persons. Inter-national NGOs have also been active in documenting human rights abuses, investigating minority grievances, encouraging conflict resolu-tion, and providing humanitarian relief.

The work of Amnesty International has been particularly significant in providing a comprehensive review of emergency laws and security leg-islation, and in reporting incidents of torture, disappearances, extrajudi-cial killings, and arbitrary arrests. Similarly, the International Commis-sion of Jurists, Lawasia, and Asia Watch have investigated different aspects of the ethnic conflict and have published reports which have received considerable world attention. These documentations have been helpful to the donor consortium, in its annual meetings in Paris, and to the UN Human Rights Commission and the Sub-Commission on the Pre-vention of Discrimination and Protection of Minorities. Médecins Sans Frontières has provided medical relief to the north and the east, thereby ensuring that minimal medical services were made available to the war-affected areas. Without the intervention of these organizations over a period of almost two decades, Sri Lanka's humanitarian crisis and its accompanying gross and persistent violation of human rights would have had much more serious consequences than they did.

For many years, domestic human rights organizations in Sri Lanka pressed the government of Sri Lanka to seek the assistance of the ICRC in monitoring the conditions of the detainees and in providing humani-tarian relief.[23] The government resisted this proposal on the somewhat legalistic grounds that the presence of the ICRC in Sri Lanka would signify that Sri Lanka was in a state of civil war. Despite the objections of the Sri Lankan government, the UN Human Rights Commission in 1987 passed a resolution which invited the "Government of Sri Lanka to consider favorably the offer of the services of the ICRC to fulfill its func-tions of protection of humanitarian standards including the provision of assistance and protection to victims of all affected parties."[24]

It was only after 1989 that the ICRC was formally invited to establish an office in Colombo. It now has offices as well in Batticaloa, Jaffna,

Amparai, Anuradhapura, Kandy, Mannar, Trincomalee, and Vavuniya. Following are a number of activities with which the ICRC has been involved:

—It has visited detainees in places of detention across the country, including prisons, detention camps, police stations, and military camps. In 1993, the ICRC visited 483 places of detention. Delegates conducted investigations on the physical and psychological treatment of the detainees. Whenever necessary, they accompanied released detainees back to their homes. The ICRC has also sought access to persons in the custody of the LTTE; however, in view of the ICRC mandate, it could submit confidential reports only to the government. They were not otherwise available to the local human rights community.

—The ICRC has been active in tracing missing persons, particularly in connection with the situation in the north and east of the country, and in Colombo. The organization has maintained a register of detainees.

—It has helped to provide security to the civilian population—including displaced persons—in the conflict zone, by keeping them under observation. The ICRC delegates bring to the attention of authorities any problems related to the safety and living conditions of these people.

—The ICRC has ensured the protection of vessels and road convoys transporting essential items to the north. In 1993, the ICRC transported by ship and road convoys a monthly average of 9,500 tons of goods, supplied by Colombo to the northern Sri Lankans. The ICRC also transported medical supplies to Jaffna hospital.

—The ICRC has provided continued protection to the Jaffna teaching hospital and has monitored a safety zone around it to ensure that, in the event of fighting, the sick and the war wounded would have access to medical care, and to ensure that the fighting does not spread to the hospital area. The ICRC has also made certain that the hospital has been stocked with adequate medical supplies.

—The ICRC has been used as an important intermediary between the government and the LTTE, communicating confidential messages between the two sides. This intermediary role was important in establishing the initial contacts and the modalities of conflict resolution regarding peace talks between the LTTE and the Sri Lankan government. The ICRC played a cautious role in this regard in order to avoid any implication that it was moving outside its traditional humanitarian mandate.[25]

The role of UNHCR in Sri Lanka's ethnic conflict was slightly more complex and controversial than that of the ICRC. The traditional mandate of UNHCR has been limited to concerns involving refugees who are outside their countries of origin. But in Sri Lanka the organization was able to develop a program which focused on the needs of internally displaced persons. This program was established in 1990 to provide emergency relief in the Mannar district for refugees, displaced persons, and other victims of the conflict. Bill Clarence, who was Resident Representative of the UNHCR in Sri Lanka, pointed out that "the situation on the ground in northern Sri Lanka at that time was extremely complicated, and the raw humanitarian imperative which it imposed required that broad common sense should prevail. The resulting program helped clear some of the institutional inhibitions against UNHCR involvement with internally displaced persons and paved the way for a significantly protective role in areas of conflict."[26]

The UNHCR initiatives included the following:

—It established an open relief center in Pesalai, on Mannar Island, which provided basic necessities such as shelter, food, and medical care for displaced persons. They were free to move into and out of the center at will.

—It implemented a rehabilitation program for refugees repatriated from south India. This program raised questions as to the voluntary nature of the repatriation process since the UNHCR was not able always to verify whether the consent of the repatriates had been obtained freely.

—It oversaw the administration of reception centers, transit centers, and transit camps for repatriates returning to Sri Lanka. In addition, the UNHCR also endeavored to negotiate with the LTTE to open up safe passage from Jaffna to the south of Sri Lanka, but these efforts proved unsuccessful.

The work of the UNHCR provided an interesting case study of an inter-governmental humanitarian organization's being compelled by humanitarian imperatives to undertake relief functions and responsibilities which other humanitarian organizations were unwilling or unable to carry out. Its work in Sri Lanka often posed contradictions between the protective and operational functions of the UNHCR and exposed the agency to the criticism that its activities were compromising an obligation to protect the fundamental right to asylum. It also exposed the agency to the criticism that it was taking on extra-mandatory functions, when its existing programs were underfunded. Several other NGOs, including Médecins Sans Frontières, Save the Children Fund, CARE, Oxfam, and the Quaker Peace and Services, performed essential relief functions.[27] However, they were not institutionally capable of performing the UNHCR functions, nor were they capable of maintaining the complex relationships with the military, the government, and the LTTE that a UN agency could sustain.[28]

The documentation of human rights abuses was an important task of both human rights organizations and NGOs in response to the consequences of ethnic conflict. The quality of human rights documentation in Sri Lanka was extraordinarily high, particularly in the areas affected by the conflict. Domestic NGOs such as the CRM, the MIRJE, and the Law and Society Trust have endeavored to ensure the accuracy and objectivity of their human rights reports. Since 1993, these organizations have also cooperated to produce an *Annual Status of Human Rights Report*, which covers concerns involving both civil and political rights, socio-economic rights, minorities, and internally displaced persons. The reports of the local NGOs have also assisted the fact-finding missions undertaken from time to time by international NGOs such as Amnesty International, the International Commission of Jurists, and Asia Watch. Similarly, the UN Working Group on Disappearances has also made frequent references to the documentation of local human rights organizations.

Conclusion

Sri Lanka's ethnic conflict remains one of the most protracted and intractable in Asia. The hope of peace and reconciliation has too often been overtaken by the despair of death, displacement, and destruction. Neither side has been able to mobilize the resolve, the generosity of spirit, and the political imagination necessary to overcome the legacy of distrust. NGOs have to struggle against difficult odds to respond effectively to the consequences of the conflict.

Sri Lanka remains an important case study on the complementary roles of domestic and international NGOs and inter-governmental organizations in responding to the needs of civilians affected by conflict. There has been a conscious effort to coordinate relief operations, to share information and resources, and to maintain the greatest independence possible in the management of relief efforts. These tasks, however, have never been free of complexity. As a result, several international and some domestic relief agencies have had to fend off charges of partisanship and have experienced threats and overt expressions of hostility because of perceptions of their partiality.

The state's attitude toward these NGOs and relief agencies has been ambivalent. On the one hand, the state has been dependent on international relief agencies to deliver food and medicine and to assist with routine governmental functions, such as the delivery of mail or of examination papers, to areas outside the state's control. Government spokesmen point out that the international community has a presence in Sri Lanka, in relation to human rights and humanitarian issues, which is significantly more than what has been possible in other parts of South Asia. On the other hand, the government is very sensitive to any public criticism of its humanitarian, and even its human rights record, by any of the relief agencies or international NGOs operating in Sri Lanka. Occasionally, domestic human rights groups, peace activists, and NGOs advocating alternative developmental visions, face similar hostility. Even international relief agencies with impeccable humanitarian credentials have at times been targeted by the media and by hardline political groups. Despite these constraints, NGOs have continued to respond to pressing humanitarian needs and important human rights concerns. Inter-governmental organizations have been compelled by realities on the ground to modify and extend their traditional mandates.

The case of Sri Lanka also reveals efforts to draw a distinction between the humanitarian and human rights aspects of the conflict, on the one hand, and the political aspects of the conflict, on the other. The international community has been permitted to intervene on the issues relating to humanitarian relief, displacement, human rights, and reconstruction. The international community has not, however, been encouraged to help facilitate political contacts between the LTTE and the government or to address issues relating to a durable political solution. Humanitarian issues are inextricably linked to the political resolution of the conflict. NGOs are an important component of Sri Lanka's civil society, which needs to renew its resolve and reassess its strategies in responding to new challenges and demands. The continuing involvement of NGOs remains critical to the alleviation of human suffering and to the process of peace and reconciliation in Sri Lanka.

Notes

1. See Veena Das (ed.), *Mirrors of Violence: Communities, Riots and Survivors in South Asia* (Delhi, 1990).

2. See B.H. Shafruddin and Ifthikar A.M.Z. Fadzli, *Between Centre and State: Federalism* (Kuala Lumpur, 1988).

3. See Yash Ghai, *Decentralization and Accommodation of Ethnic Diversity* (Colombo, 1995).

4. Law & Society Trust, Special Issue on Self-Determination, *Fortnightly Review,* IV (1993), 1–27.

5. See Neelan Tiruchelvam and Radhika Coomaraswamy, *The Role of the Judiciary in Plural Societies* (London, 1987).

6. See Valli Kanapathipilla, "The Survivor's Experience," in Das (ed.), *Mirrors of Violence,* 321–344.

7. See Sunil Bastian, "Political Economy of Ethnic Violence in Sri Lanka, the July 1983 Riots," in Das, *Mirrors of Violence,* 286–304.

8. See Stanley J. Tambiah, *Sri Lanka, Ethnic Fratricide and the Dismantling of Democracy* (Chicago, 1986), 20.

9. See Tambiah, *Sri Lanka,* 16, 24–25.

10. See Jonathan Spencer, "Introduction, the Power of the Past," in Spencer (ed.), *Sri Lanka: History and the Roots of Conflict* (London, 1990), 192.

11. See Jonathan Spencer, "Popular Perceptions of the Violence: A Provincial View," in James Manor (ed.), *Sri Lanka: In Change and Crisis* (London, 1984), 192.

12. See Gananath Obeyesekere, "Political Violence and the Future of Democracy in Sri Lanka," in Committee for Rational Development (ed.), *Sri Lanka: The Ethnic Conflict, Myths, Realities and Perspectives* (New Delhi, 1984).

13. Speech by Ranil Wickramasinghe, Prime Minister of Sri Lanka, at the Sri Lanka Aid Consortium Meeting, Paris, 1993.

14. See, on this period, A. Jeyaratnam Wilson, *Politics in Sri Lanka 1947–1973* (London, 1977).

15. See Second Reading of the Official Language Bill, 14 June 1956, Parliamentary Debate (Hansard), column 1914.

16. See Tarzie Vitachchi, *Emergency 58* (London 1958).

17. See Civil Rights Movement, *21 Years of CRM—An Annotated List of Documents of the Civil Rights Movement of Sri Lanka 1971–1992* (Colombo, 1994), 5.

18. See Civil Rights Memorandum on 21 May 1978 on the Proscription of Liberation Tigers of Tamil Eelam and Other Similar Organizations law.

19. See Civil Rights Movement of Sri Lanka, CRM Statement, 1/7/79, "Freedom of Speech and the Cry for the Eelam," (1993), in *21 Years of CRM—An Annotated List of Documents of the Civil Rights Movement of Sri Lanka 1971–1972* (4 July 1979), 27.

20. See the Statements of Civil Rights Movement on the Alarming Incidents of 31 May 1981, in Jaffna and on the Events in Jaffna Since May 1981.

21. For a selection of interventions by MIRJE on the ethnic conflict from 1977–1988, see Kumar Rupasinghe and Berth Verstappen, *Ethnic Conflict and Human Rights in Sri Lanka: An Annotated Bibliography* (London, 1989), 534.

22. See "Annual Report: Colombo," International Centre for Ethnic Studies (1983–1995).

23. See statement of the Civil Rights Movement on 1 October 1987, "Island-Wide Violence After the Peace Accord."

24. See UN Human Rights Commission Resolutions 1987/61 (12 March 1987).

25. The Norwegian Red Cross Society and the headquarters of the International Federation of the Red Cross and Red Crescent Societies (IFRC) in Geneva suspended assistance of 4.2 million rupees to the Sri Lankan Red Cross Society, unless the Ministry of Social Services intervened and put a stop to alleged misappropriation and corruption in the SLRC. The Ministry then appointed an interim panel of administration, although the Minister had no legal authority to do so. Members of the former Board of Governors took over the SLRC following a court case in which an interim injunction was issued against the interim panel of administration. As a result, an amendment has been proposed to the Voluntary Social Service Organizations (Registration and Supervision) Act No. 31 of 1980, which would validate the actions of the minister and permit similar interference in any case in which there is evidence to support any allegation of fraud or misappropriation by any voluntary organization.

26. See Bill Clarence, "A Personal View from the Field—UNHCR's Role in Ethnic Conflict," in Law & Society Trust, *Fortnightly Review,* IV (May, 1994).

27. The Government appointed a Commission of Inquiry called the Wanasundera Commission to inquire into the activities of NGOs. The Commission recommended that all NGOs be required to seek registration and file financial accounts with the Department of Social Services. Emergency Regulations were framed to require that all NGOs receiving assistance in excess of 50,000 rupees per year register with the Director of Social Services and, if in excess of 100,000 rupees, to submit a statement of accounts to the Director. With the end of the all-island state of emergency at the end of 1994, these Regulations have lapsed.

28. See Law & Society Trust, *Sri Lanka, State of Human Rights 1994* (Colombo, 1995), chapters on The Internally Displaced and Refugees and Repatriation, 228–268.

NIGERIA

Before "Things Fall Apart" in Nigeria: The Role of Non-Governmental Human Rights Organizations in Conflict Prevention

Melissa E. Crow and Clement Nwankwo

THE CLOSED TRIALS of some fifty alleged coup plotters, including former Head of State General Olusegun Obasanjo and former Deputy Head of State Major-General Shehu Musa Yar'Adua, in June 1995, riveted the attention of the international community on the progressive disintegration of the rule of law in Nigeria. The accused, who included active and retired military personnel, as well as civilians, were tried by a seven-man military tribunal headed by Brigadier-General Patrick Aziza. Their trials were devoid of many due process guarantees required under international law, including access to independent and freely chosen legal counsel and the right of appeal to a higher court. Critics of the regime of General Sani Abacha, who seized power in a 1993 military coup, claim that the government fabricated the coup to perpetuate its tenure. Whether or not such claims are justified, the aftermath of the so-called coup attempt and the execution subsequently of Ken Saro-Wiwa and eight other Ogoni activists in November, 1995, highlighted the Abacha regime's apparent indifference to international human rights standards and generated much concern, both locally and internationally, about the future of the Nigerian federation.

There is a pressing need for new strategies to halt the continuing downward spiral of repression in Nigeria. NGOs, particularly those that focus on human rights, have played an important role in focusing attention on the flagrant abuses perpetrated by the Abacha regime. They have

167

highlighted the shortcomings of the international community in addressing the current political crisis, and they have formulated proactive recommendations intended to promote an accountable, rights-respecting
government.

Human rights violations often lead to the exacerbation of tensions
within a society; consequently, human rights NGOs have an important
role to play in the realm of conflict prevention—particularly in the area
of early warning. However, the mandates of most NGOs do not encompass conflict prevention per se. In the context of the crisis in Nigeria, this
chapter draws on the experience of Human Rights Watch/Africa and the
Lagos-based Constitutional Rights Project, as well as the work of other
local and international human rights NGOs, to explore linkages between
human rights and conflict prevention.

The Current Crisis

Although the specter of the Biafran war hovers in the background of
the army purge (another occurred in 1996) that followed the alleged coup
attempt, the possibility of a comparable conflict along ethnic lines seems
remote in 1996—even if some or all of the accused were actually conspiring to overthrow the Abacha government. The impetus behind the
Biafran civil war (1967–1970) was an early 1966 coup attempt, sus-
pected by northern Nigerians to have been orchestrated by Igbo officers
from eastern Nigeria seeking to assume a position of dominance in
national politics. The murders of some notable northern politicians
during the coup strengthened such fears. The subsequent counter-coup in
mid-1966, led by northern officers, targeted Igbo officers. The ensuing
violence spread to several northern cities, where thousands of Igbo were
killed. In early 1967, in response to the government's failure to stop the
violence, the Igbo, under the leadership of Lieutenant-Colonel
Odumegwu Ojukwu, declared their intention to secede, making the
eastern region a separate country. The ensuing war, in which close to
1 million Igbo were killed, was intended to preserve the country's unity—
and to keep control of its rich oil resources in national hands. In 1995,
the ethnic affiliations of the alleged coup plotters were more diverse,
although the majority were Yoruba from the southwest.

The recent "coup attempt" also brings to mind the events of 22 April
1990. On that date, a group of middle-ranking military officers

announced on national radio that they had overthrown the military government of General Ibrahim Babangida and declared that they had expelled the country's five northernmost states. These states were asked to reapply if they wanted to resume membership in the Nigerian federation. The perpetrators of the 1990 coup claimed that they had acted to prevent the northern Hausa-Fulani from dominating the government. Although the coup plot—and, consequently, the expulsion of the northern states—failed, it exposed the delicate balance and tensions existing among different sections of the country and the possibility that this balance might one day be upset.

Even if the 1995 "coup" plot was intended as an excuse to quell opposition, it illuminates the high level of tension and factionalization that have come to characterize the Nigerian military. Should a major crisis erupt in Nigeria, the first shots may very well be fired within the barracks. Whether the cleavages within the military would occur along ethnic, religious, or other lines remains to be seen.

The cursory form of justice meted out to the alleged coup plotters of 1995 is consistent with the repressive tactics that have become the hallmark of the Abacha regime. Through a series of draconian decrees promulgated in 1994, the Abacha government severely restricted freedom of the press, crippled trade unions, and emasculated the judiciary. Human rights advocates, pro-democracy activists, and outspoken journalists have been detained without charge for prolonged periods. Extrajudicial executions by security and law enforcement officials are commonplace, particularly in the case of armed robbery suspects. These trends continue, notwithstanding Abacha's announcement on 27 June 1995 that he was lifting a ban on political activity. These tactics have doomed Nigeria's once vibrant civil society and generated increasing skepticism in Nigeria and internationally about the country's promised transition back to democracy.

In addition to resorting to direct repression of its opponents, the Abacha regime has intermittently manipulated ethnic tensions in an apparent effort to foment unrest and thereby justify its continued dominance. In the wake of the annulment of the June 1993 elections, which were presumed to have been won by Chief Moshood Abiola, and again during the oil workers' strike in the summer of 1994, government officials used the print and broadcast media to pit other ethnic groups against the Yoruba, who generally supported Abiola, in an effort to undermine any unified threat to the northern-dominated power structure. Notably, former Minister of Information Uche Chukwumerije accused the Yoruba of planning to bomb the northern cities of Abuja and Kaduna and to blow up the north-south oil pipeline a few kilometers from Kaduna. This accusation was followed by propaganda alleging that Yoruba were conspiring with foreigners to wage a guerrilla war against the federation, which led to the mass exodus of most Igbo and some Hausa- Fulani from the southwest. Meanwhile, the state-owned Nigerian Television Authority broadcast gory pictures of the Biafran war, in order to create the impression that Abiola's supporters were calling for hostilities.

Although government-initiated ethnic propaganda later died down, the government has played an active role in perpetuating communal tensions. For example, the Nigerian government has publicly claimed that outbreaks of violence in Ogoniland prior to May 1994 were the result of ethnic clashes between the Ogoni and neighboring ethnic groups, including the Andoni, the Okrika, and the Ndoki.[1] Evidence now available shows that some attacks attributed to rural minority communities were, in fact, carried out by army troops masquerading as members of these communities. Moreover, clashes continue between Christians and Muslims in the north, with only minimal efforts by the government to prosecute the perpetrators.

The Role of Human Rights NGOs

Despite severe constraints on their activities, Nigerian human rights groups continue to thrive as a result of the courage and commitment of local activists. All of them advocate an expeditious transition to civilian rule and the need for an accountable government, although they employ diverse strategies to achieve their goals. The Constitutional Rights Project and the Civil Liberties Organisation are engaged in fact-finding and documentation of human rights abuses throughout the country, litigation in national courts intended to protect the rights of individuals and groups, and filing petitions with international bodies. The Committee for the Defense of Human Rights engages in human rights litigation, publishes leaflets to generate increased awareness of human rights developments, and organizes symposia and rallies to promote human rights and democracy. Both the Lagos-based Legal Research and Resources Development Center and the Port Harcourt Institute for Human Rights and Humanitarian Law have established networks of paralegals who are involved in human rights education. Women's groups such as the International Federation of Women Lawyers (FIDA) undertake litigation, education, and community organizing throughout the country. The Campaign for Democracy and the Democratic Alternative are involved in community organizing and political consciousness-raising, which is intended to result in sustained mass pro-democracy action.[2]

By virtue of their constant interaction with grassroots communities, their familiarity with local politics and culture, and their on-site location, Nigerian human rights NGOs are in touch with the nation's heartbeat. Notwithstanding periodic disagreements about appropriate strategies and perpetual competition for limited funds, Nigeria's leading human rights activists generally support each other's efforts. Together, they are among those actors best equipped to monitor continuously repressive acts by the authorities and gauge the level of civil discontent. Prevailing constraints on press freedom in Nigeria make the research and documentation efforts of local human rights groups essential to facilitating the flow of information regarding abuses perpetrated by the government.[3]

For several years prior to the annulment of the 1993 election, for example, Nigerian human rights groups had warned that Babangida, who had announced his plan to relinquish power to a "new breed" of Nigerian politicians shortly after he took power in 1985, had no real intention of doing so.[4] Elections originally scheduled for 1990 were postponed to 1992, then to 1993. Having refused to register independent political parties, Babangida established two political parties, drew up their manifestos, provided them with offices, furnished funds, and repeatedly banned and unbanned certain categories of politicians. Warnings from human rights groups that these were not the signs of a government ready to relinquish power were ignored by politicians, who continued to participate in the electoral process, and viewed by government authorities as "subversive." Babangida's decision to suspend and then annul the election results in an attempt to cling to power gave rise to protests, both locally and internationally. Soldiers killed more than 150 people in the course of riots in Lagos and other southern cities. Only then did the United States, Great Britain, and other foreign governments cut off non-humanitarian aid and curtail military cooperation.

International human rights NGOs effectively supplement the efforts of local human rights NGOs by continuously monitoring and documenting abuses—based on first-hand investigations as well as the information provided by a range of Nigerian human rights activists, by channeling information to the press and the international community, and by proposing constructive recommendations for policy-makers. Cases of direct government repression have continually been the focus of reports by international human rights NGOs. By documenting in painstaking detail the nature of abuses and citing relevant provisions of international treaties, international human rights NGOs have traditionally tried to promote accountability by "shaming" abusive governments into compliance with their international obligations.

In addition to highlighting instances of direct repression by government actors, human rights NGOs—both local and international—have a vital role to play in investigating and documenting the involvement of government agents in communal violence. The latter is exceptionally problematic because, while the government is quick to use ethnic strife as an excuse for remaining in power, the government's direct involvement is not readily apparent. In a fact-finding mission to southeastern Nigeria in early 1995, Human Rights Watch/Africa uncovered evidence of involvement of Nigerian government troops in the Ogoni-Andoni disturbances (1993). Two soldiers interviewed by Human Rights Watch/Africa described their participation in military operations that took advantage of tensions between the Ogoni and the Andoni to launch attacks on Ogoniland from Andoni territory. Residents of the Ogoni village of Kaa told Human Rights Watch/Africa that they had seen soldiers attacking their village in August 1993, along with Andoni fighters.[5]

Human rights NGOs have also documented the Nigerian government's role in perpetuating tensions between Christian Igbo and Muslim Hausa-Fulani in the northern part of the country by engaging in discriminatory practices and by failing to prosecute the perpetrators of abuses. For reasons dating as far back as British colonial rule, when Britain relied on traditional rulers to ensure compliance with its authority, the government provides residences, vehicles, and salaries to traditional rulers throughout the country. Government authorities seek the views of traditional rulers on many political matters. Ethnic groups whose leaders are not recognized by the government resent the government's denial of material and other benefits to their groups. In the north, the traditional rulers are generally Muslims whom other Muslims view as spiritual, as well as political, leaders. Regardless of their ethnicity, those who live in a traditional ruler's area of influence are expected to honor him by, for example, paying him visits and bringing him gifts. Many Christians within the jurisdiction of Muslim rulers resent having to pay homage to a religious leader in a supposedly secular state.[6] Moreover, the predilections of traditional rulers may be reinforced by the judgments of area courts, where fluid procedures, poor working conditions, and scarce resources render poorly qualified judges subject to bribery.[7]

Through interviews with Christian and Muslim leaders in 1995, the Constitutional Rights Project established that other sources of tension included the authorities' reluctance to grant Christian leaders certificates of occupancy for lands on which churches were to be built. Admissions policies favored Muslims in state-run educational institutions. The same source documented a series of Muslim-Christian clashes in the north. In September 1994, Muslims attacked and killed some Christian residents of Potiskum in Yobe State and, reportedly, demolished several churches. By 1996, the perpetrators had not been brought to justice.

Additional clashes occurred in late May 1995, at the Sabon Gari market in Kano, and were reportedly sparked by an argument between a Christian Igbo and a Muslim Hausa over a tip for a parked car. In mid-July, a commission of inquiry reported that seventeen people had been killed and property worth over $2 million had been destroyed in the disturbances. The chairman of the commission of inquiry recommended the establishment of a special tribunal to try the fifty-four people who were arrested for their role in the disturbances—a step which had the potential to defuse prevailing tensions. Until that time, however, the recommendations of such commissions had either gone unheeded or proven ineffective in curbing religious tensions.[8]

By late 1995, the signs of a burgeoning Islamist movement were becoming increasingly visible in the north. Decaying social infrastructure, a judiciary incapable of delivering justice, a declining economy, and the general social malaise in the country provide a fertile breeding ground for those who promise change in the name of religion. In late December 1994, self-proclaimed Islamists claimed responsibility for beheading Gideon Akaluka, a Christian trader detained in a Kano prison as a result of allegations that he had desecrated the Qu'ran. The prison authorities appear to have collaborated with the Islamists by permitting Akaluka's removal. In an interview with the Constitutional Rights Project in March 1995, the Kano State Deputy Commissioner of Police refused to comment on the incident, claiming that the matter was under investigation. Seven months later, no arrests had been made.

Beyond Documentation: Advocacy, Information Sharing, and Coalition-Building

In an attempt to support the work of Nigerian human rights and pro-democracy groups, international human rights NGOs use documentation regarding abuses by officials to encourage third-party governments to use diplomacy, military assistance, and/or economic leverage to demand accountability by implementing appropriate policy recommendations. To date, the efforts of the international community to promote human rights and democracy in Nigeria have been largely ineffectual. Both the European Union and the United States government have made strong public declarations condemning the Abacha government and adopted certain coercive measures, including suspension of aid and military cooperation, visa restrictions on government officials, and a case-by-case review, with a presumption of denial, for all export license applications for defense equipment. However, the practical impact of these steps has been minimal.

Notwithstanding the existing provision for case-by-case review, for example, the British government issued thirty export licenses for military equipment in 1994.[9] The president of the British Board of Trade described all of this equipment as "non-lethal," although he refused to disclose its precise nature.[10] In mid-1995, moreover, Britain was reportedly completing delivery of eighty Vickers tanks pursuant to a contract executed in 1991; when the new provisions were implemented, forty-six tanks had reportedly already been delivered.[11] The British Foreign and Commonwealth Office does not deny that weapons shipments have taken place since December 1993, pursuant to export licenses granted prior to the imposition of restrictions.

International human rights NGOs constantly struggle to formulate creative and realistic policy recommendations that are devoid of "loopholes," such as those mentioned above. Recommendations proposed by Human Rights Watch/Africa to the governments of the United States, the European Union, the Commonwealth countries, and the Organization of African Unity have included:

—Instituting an embargo on the purchase of Nigerian oil;

—Banning new investment in Nigeria;

—Banning exports to Nigeria of new technology and spare parts for the energy sector such as oil drilling and refining supplies and equipment;

—Freezing all foreign assets of members of the Nigerian government who are responsible for serious human rights violations;

—Imposing embargoes on all arms transfers and deliveries, including those pursuant to contracts signed prior to the imposition of the embargoes;

—Suspending all non-essential high-level official visits to and from Nigeria;

—Publicly naming those members of the Nigerian government and the Nigerian military and security forces and their families to whom visas are denied;

—Using their leverage at the World Bank, the African Development Bank, and other international financial institutions to block all non-"basic human needs" loans and disbursements to Nigeria;

—Publicly protesting the detention of political prisoners and making efforts to visit prisoners in detention;

—Urging their embassies to support the efforts of Nigerian human rights groups by meeting regularly with local human rights activists, issuing statements condemning human rights abuses, and providing project assistance.

Notwithstanding the defeat of a resolution on Nigeria at the 1995 session of the United Nations Commission on Human Rights, the UN is also potentially an effective forum for shaming the Nigerian government into compliance with its international obligations. UN officials appear to have taken a particular interest in Nigeria since the announcement of the convictions of the alleged coup plotters. Both José Ayala Lasso, UN High Commissioner for Human Rights, and Bacre Waly Ndiaye, UN Special Rapporteur on Extrajudicial, Summary, or Arbitrary Executions, issued appeals for clemency. In an effort to capitalize on this momentum, the International Human Rights Law Group, based in Washington, D.C., embarked on a joint initiative with the Nigerian Civil Liberties Organisation. It was intended to convince the UN High Commissioner for Human Rights to undertake a mission to Nigeria. In addition to supporting the Law Group initiative, Human Rights Watch/Africa called upon the UN Security Council to take the following steps in the wake of the hangings of Ken Saro-Wiwa and eight other Ogoni activists:

—Impose an oil embargo on Nigeria;

—Impose a mandatory arms embargo on Nigeria and prohibit any arms deliveries or sales, including pursuant to pre-existing contracts;

—Order member states to freeze the assets of Nigerian officials and their immediate families;

—Order the dismissal of all non-essential Nigerian peacekeepers from UN peacekeeping operations.

Besides advocating steps intended to shame the Nigerian government, international human rights NGOs seek to facilitate "constructive engagement" by well-placed corporate actors in the Nigerian political crisis. Because oil accounts for an estimated 96 percent of Nigeria's annual foreign exchange earnings and 80 percent of the federal government's revenue, the principal multinational oil companies operating in Nigeria—Shell, Elf, Agip, Chevron, and Mobil—are particularly influential. By virtue of their participation in joint ventures in which the government is a principal stakeholder, they are well placed in the course of their business dealings with local, state, and federal authorities to convey their concern about Nigeria's rapidly deteriorating human rights record. Because the Nigerian security forces have often employed grossly abusive measures to quell protests by residents of oil-producing areas against the activities of the multinational oil companies, the oil companies have a particular responsibility to address abuses perpetrated in this context.

Human Rights Watch/Africa initially called on these companies to adhere to certain basic human rights principles in the course of their business operations. These included:

—Appointing responsible high-ranking corporate officials to monitor the use of force by the Nigerian military in the oil-producing areas and to denounce the use of excessive force;

—Publicly and privately calling upon the Nigerian government to restrain the use of armed force in the oil-producing areas;

—Urging the Nigerian government to allow nonviolent freedom of association and expression, particularly with respect to grievances directed against the oil industry;

—Urging the Nigerian government to cease arbitrary detention of peaceful protestors and to release all individuals held for the nonviolent expression of their political beliefs;

—Protesting the Abacha government's dissolution of the governing bodies of the oil workers' unions and detention of oil union leaders without charge or trial, and pressing the government for their reinstatement.

Several months later, following the executions of the Ogoni activists, Human Rights Watch/Africa called upon the multinational oil companies to condemn the hangings and the rapidly deteriorating human rights situation in Nigeria. In an open letter to the CEOs of Royal Dutch Shell, Elf, and Agip, Human Rights Watch/Africa called upon them to state publicly and privately that the regime's contempt for the rule of law cast doubt on their companies' willingness to pursue a $4 billion liquified natural gas project at Bonny, in conjunction with the Nigerian National Petroleum Corporation. When the multinational oil companies failed to implement any of the above-mentioned recommendations, Human Rights Watch/Africa called upon them to suspend their operations in Nigeria until the Nigerian government made substantial progress in promoting human rights and facilitating a transition to democracy.

In addition to human rights monitoring and advocacy, international human rights NGOs can make a valuable contribution to preventive action by sharing information with other NGOs that have different mandates. One such group is TransAfrica, which, in 1995, launched a campaign to mobilize U.S. public opinion in support of Nigerian democracy. TransAfrica sought to generate public awareness through a variety of initiatives, including frequent vigils outside the Nigerian embassy. TransAfrica was among the first Washington, D.C.-based NGOs to advocate an embargo on Nigerian oil.

In order to facilitate the flow of information among groups, Amnesty International convenes monthly meetings in Washington, D.C. of a coalition of NGOs working on Nigeria. The participating NGOs, which include Amnesty International, Human Rights Watch/Africa, TransAfrica, the International Human Rights Law Group, the Washington Office on Africa, Greenpeace, the Sierra Club, Nonviolence International, the Nigerian Democratic Movement, the Nigerian Democratic Awareness Committee, and the Africa Faith and Justice Network, focus on human rights, democratization, environmental protection, conflict resolution, and public education. To date, the coalition has organized protests outside the Nigerian Embassy and the offices of U.S. oil companies operating in Nigeria, briefed members of Congressional delegations to Nigeria, coordinated press conferences, and provided a forum for visiting Nigerian speakers.

The London office of Human Rights Watch has organized a similar coalition of London-based NGOs working on Nigeria. The Body Shop, a private company, has convened coalitions of German and Dutch NGOs targeted primarily toward generating increased awareness of the plight of the Ogoni people. Due to differences of mandate among the participating organizations, the primary purpose of the coalition meetings is to exchange information. Human Rights Watch/Africa has urged the participating groups to undertake campaigns intended to encourage member states of the European Union to incorporate certain "politically binding" measures—including suspension of aid and military cooperation, visa restrictions, and case-by-case review, with a presumption of denial, for all export licenses for defense equipment—into a legally binding common position, in accordance with Article J.2 of the Treaty of Maastricht. The adoption of a legally binding common position would not only recognize the strong commitment of member states, but also require them to adopt stronger implementing mechanisms. Moreover, a member state that violated the position could be sued by another member state in the European Court.

The Link between Human Rights and Conflict Prevention

As evidenced by the foregoing case study, international human rights NGOs, working with local human rights activists, have established an impressive track record for revealing the facts, monitoring and documenting ongoing abuses, analyzing trends, and formulating appropriate policy recommendations. These recommendations, which are directed toward governments, intergovernmental organizations, influential private actors, and other international NGOs with different concerns, are intended to curb future abuses. They may also serve to reduce the possibility of violence. However, prevention of human rights violations and prevention of violent conflict are in many ways distinctly different.

Whereas the standards for assessing a government's human rights performance are enumerated, albeit ambiguously in some cases, in various international declarations and treaties, no such detailed standards exist for conflict prevention.[12] A downward cycle of repression perpetrated by an abusive government does not always mean that conflict is a foregone conclusion. Moreover, unlike gross human rights abuse, conflict itself is not always an affront to international standards. Conflict in the form of resistance to tyranny, for example, is contemplated in the preamble to the Universal Declaration of Human Rights. In this sense, recourse to violence to halt genocide will involve conflict; measures to prevent such conflict should previously have addressed the gross human rights abuses that caused the conflict.

While Chapter VII of the United Nations Charter gives the Security Council the authority to "determine the existence of any threat to the peace, breach of the peace, or act of aggression" and to make recommendations to maintain or restore international peace and security, there are no existing guidelines to determine when outside intervention is appropriate and what form such intervention should take. With respect to conflict prevention in Africa, the Organization of African Unity's Mechanism for Conflict Prevention, Management, and Resolution would appear to be appropriately placed to make such determinations—assuming that sufficient resources are forthcoming and that governmental delegates succeed in remaining impartial. This mechanism, established in 1993, is empowered to mount and deploy observation and monitoring missions, both civilian and military, for the purposes of conflict prevention, peace-making, and peace-building.[13]

Another key difference is that conflict prevention is inherently preemptive and often political, requiring active intervention to dissuade key actors from resorting to violence. Both aspects of conflict prevention are often problematic for human rights monitors. Because of the inherent difficulty of predicting the future actions and reactions of government actors under indeterminate circumstances, human rights monitors focus on past and current infringements of human rights as their primary means to press for change or preempt a worsening situation in the future. Given the political, social, and cultural particularities of different situations, drawing unfounded comparisons between governments is inadvisable.

Despite these caveats, human rights NGOs—both local and international—still have a crucial role to play in catalyzing a transition to an accountable, rights-respecting government in Nigeria and elsewhere.

The impact of human rights monitoring, documentation, and advocacy at the local level can be magnified by the complementary work of international human rights NGOs to shame abusive governments, channel information to the press and key actors in the international community, and formulate constructive recommendations for policy-makers. Efforts to enlist the influence of significant corporate actors—in the Nigerian context, multinational oil companies—on behalf of human rights are particularly significant in view of these companies' bargaining power vis-à-vis their host governments. The trend toward coalition-building in the United States and the European Union represents a particularly encouraging attempt to prevent the duplication of efforts, maximize scarce resources, and ensure that ripening conflicts are approached holistically. Finally, the long-term success of any solution to the Nigerian and other political crises will depend on the willingness of governmental and opposition actors to uphold basic human rights standards. In this regard, the work of human rights NGOs will give negotiators a head start in outlining the "rules of the game."

Notes

1. Like other indigenous communities in the Niger Delta, the source of over 90 percent of Nigeria's oil, the Ogoni contend that multinational oil companies, in concert with the Nigerian government, have ravaged their land and contaminated their rivers, while providing little, if any, tangible benefit in return. Human Rights Watch/Africa, "The Ogoni Crisis: A Case-Study of Military Repression in South-eastern Nigeria," *A Human Rights Watch Short Report* (July 1995), 7–11.

2. For a comprehensive survey of the strategies employed by Nigerian NGOs, see Claude E. Welch, Jr., *Protecting Human Rights in Africa: Roles and Strategies of Non-Governmental Organizations* (Philadelphia, 1995).

3. Decrees 6, 7, and 8 imposed six-month bans on *The Punch, The Concord,* and *The Guardian,* independent publications which had criticized the government. Although the ban on *The Guardian* was lifted after the publisher apologized, the government renewed the bans on *The Punch* and *The Concord* in 1995. Other publications have also been intermittently banned. Moreover, local journalists often practice self-censorship in a purported effort to "defuse tension."

4. George Klay Kieh Jr. and Pita Ogaba Agbese, "From Politics Back to the Barracks in Nigeria: A Theoretical Explanation," *Journal of Peace Research,* XXX (1993), 414.

5. Human Rights Watch/Africa, "The Ogoni Crisis," 12–14.

6. Human Rights Watch/Africa, "Nigeria: Threats to a New Democracy," A Human Rights Watch Short Report (June 1993), 11.

7. For more information on the area courts, which handle about 80 percent of the court cases in northern Nigeria, see Anselm Chidi Odinkalu, *Justice Denied: The Area Courts System in the Northern States of Nigeria* (Lagos, 1992).

8. See Babatunde Olugboji, "Religious Uprising: Deadly, Divisive, Destructive," *Constitutional Rights Journal,* V (1995), 4–12 [published in Lagos by the Constitutional Rights Project].

9. *Official Report of the House of Commons,* 27 January 1995, Col. 397.

10. *Official Report of the House of Commons,* 10 May 1995, Cols. 517–518.

11. "Secret arms exports evade ban," *Observer* [London], 21 May 1995.

12. In the case of Nigeria, these include the Universal Declaration of Human Rights, the African Charter on Human and People's Rights, the International Covenant on Civil and Political Rights, the Convention on the Elimination of All Forms of Discrimination Against Women, and the Convention on the Elimination of All Forms of Racial Discrimination.

13. Declaration of the Assembly of Heads of State and Government on the Establishment Within the OAU of a Mechanism for Conflict Prevention, Management and Resolution, (July 1993), 8.

THE SUDAN

Sovereignty and Humanitarian Responsibility: A Challenge for NGOs in Africa and the Sudan

Francis M. Deng

THE SUDAN has been at war with itself since 1955, with a decade of precarious peace from 1972 to 1983. Although the configuration of the conflict situations is complex, the war has largely been between successive governments in Khartoum, dominated by the Arab-Muslim North, and rebel movements in the more indigenous South, whose modern leadership is predominantly Christian.

During the first phase of the war, from 1955 to 1972, the objective of the southern liberation struggle was secession from the North, although the then Southern Sudan Liberation Movement, with its military wing, the Anyanya, settled in 1972 for regional autonomy. With the resumption of hostilities in 1983, the Sudan People's Liberation Movement and its military wing, the Sudan People's Liberation Army (SPLM/SPLA), although southern-based, embraced elements from the North, especially in the non-Arab regions of the Nuba and the Ingassana bordering the South. Commensurately, the SPLM/SPLA postulated the liberation of the whole country from Arab-Islamic domination, the goal being to create a "new Sudan" free from any discrimination based on race, ethnicity, religion, culture, or gender. The feasibility of this project, at least in the short run, has been questioned, and there is indeed reason to wonder whether it was ever seriously intended, or presented only as a ploy to widen support and minimize resistance from national, regional, and international forces opposed to secession, which remained the ultimate objective. As the war has lingered on, the goal of creating a new Sudan has become even more remote as the Islamic fundamentalists who seized power through a military coup on 30 June 1989 have tightened their grip on the country. The Movement has increasingly embraced the call for self-determination, not only for the South, but also for the marginalized regions of the North.

The war has inflicted a devastating blow on the country in general and the South in particular. It is estimated that at least 1.3 million southerners have died. Several million people have been displaced internally; about 1 million have moved to the North in search of security, where they live under precarious conditions, dispersed throughout the North or clustered in the camps for displaced persons in the desolate outskirts of the capital city of Khartoum. Half a million have fled to the neighboring countries of Kenya, Uganda, and Ethiopia.

As the war escalated, with the declaration of the Islamic *jihad* (holy war) by the present regime in the North, the North, too, suffered a heavy death toll. In material terms, the war in 1995/6 was costing the government about $1 million a day. Despite Sudan's wealth of natural resources, including oil reserves, and the vast agricultural lands that gave the country a reputation in the 1970s as a potential breadbasket for North Africa and the Middle East, war has stifled its development potential. Inflation has rocketed and the Sudanese pound has plunged to an all-time low, from an exchange rate of one Sudanese pound to 2.5 U.S. dollars in the 1970s, to the 1996 rate of $1 to nearly 1200 Sudanese pounds.

The war-ravaged South and neighboring areas of the North have been surviving on international relief assistance, with access often made difficult by the warring parties, the government, and the various factions of the rebel movement. The case of the Sudan is one in which national sovereignty in the traditional sense has been challenged severely: The government neither discharges its responsibilities toward its citizens nor encourages the international community to provide them with needed protection and assistance out of humanitarian concern.

Sudan's civil war and the humanitarian crisis which it has generated illustrate many of the priorities facing African countries and the international community. Conditions on the African continent pose severe policy challenges: conflict management, human rights protection, democratic participation, and sustainable development. Although the order of priority of these issues is obviously debatable, there is a logic to the sequence. Since a situation of conflict, especially one involving mass violence and a breakdown of order, often implies gross violations of human rights, denial of democratic liberties, and frustration of socio-economic development, conflict management can claim a rightful place on the top of the list, even though it is more accurate to emphasize the interconnectedness of these policy areas and the agglutination of the values involved. In the context of conflicts, humanitarian emergencies call for immediate responses and, in most cases—certainly in the case of the Southern Sudan—NGOs have been in the forefront of those responses. With the end of the Cold War, the humanitarian agenda has become the main basis of international involvement in conflict situations worldwide. This has given the NGO community additional resources and added leverage to make a difference, not only in providing relief assistance, but also in promoting protection and lasting solutions through a quest for a just peace.

Policy Overview

Over the past several years, the intensification of internal conflicts around the world has resulted in unprecedented humanitarian tragedies and, in some cases, has led to partial and even total collapse of states. Although the crisis is global, the genocidal carnage in Rwanda, the collapse of Somalia and Liberia as states, and the civil wars raging in the Sudan, and, until recently, Angola and Mozambique, clearly demonstrate that Africa has been the region most devastated by internal conflicts and their catastrophic humanitarian consequences. Millions of innocent lives have been lost in Africa's civil wars. About 20 million of the world's 25 million to 30 million internally displaced persons and 7 million of the 20 million refugees worldwide are Africans.

Sources of Conflict

The main sources of conflicts in Africa are now recognized to be inherent in the traumatic evolution associated with state-formation and nation building, complicated by colonial intervention and post-colonial policies and responses. The colonial state incorporated racial, ethnic, cultural, linguistic, and religious groups that might previously have interacted, but had not experienced their relationship within a centralized nation state. Identity groups with broad regional affinities were broken up and distributed among the new states, while the diverse groups that were included within the new borders were encouraged to retain their separate identities rather than to assimilate into an integrated national identity.

The centralization of the political process, management of resources, and the distribution of vital services, in addition to the introduction of the welfare state, replaced the autonomy and self-reliance of the indigenous population with dependency on the state. Given the limitation of the resources available to the new nations, social services, employment, and development were unevenly distributed along regional, ethnic, and other preferential lines, creating disparities and envy.

Once control of state institutions and resources passed on to the national elites at independence, conflict over power, wealth, employment opportunities, and development became unavoidable. This change, in turn, led to gross violations of human rights, denial of civil liberties, disruption of previous patterns of economic and social life, and a consequential frustration of political and economic development.

Although most African countries have more or less consolidated national unity within the colonial borders, those torn apart by civil wars are still struggling against the arbitrariness of the colonial borders. The result of these internal conflicts is that the ethnic pieces that had been put together by the colonial glue began to pull apart and reassert their autonomy or independence after the end of the Cold War.

Crisis of Identity

In most of these situations, the politics of identity comes into direct conflict with the demands of nation building. On the one hand, individual and group identities and loyalties often rotate around such descent-oriented institutions as the family, the clan, the tribe (or ethnicity), language, and their correlative religious and regional affiliations. On the other hand, forging national unity requires transcending these contexts and developing an overarching framework. The crisis of national identity emanates not only from the conflict between the exclusive and the inclusive notions of identity, but also from the tendency of the dominant, hegemonic groups to impose their identity as the nationally uniting framework. This inevitably provides a basis for discrimination, national integration, or both. As Stedman has observed, "Conflict in Africa arises from problems basic to all populations: the tugs and pulls of different identities, the differential distribution of resources and access to power, and competing definitions of what is right, fair, and just."[1]

The myths of superiority associated with the dominance of the hegemonic groups nearly always run against the counter-myths of self-esteem and defensive assertiveness of the disadvantaged minorities or politically weaker groups. Studies of relatively isolated societies indicate that virtually all groups and individuals in their own specific cultural contexts not only demand respect as human beings, but ethnocentrically assume that they represent the ideal model. As has been observed, ethnocentrism essentially means that "One's own group is the center of everything and all others are scaled and rated with reference to it. Folkways correspond to it to cover both the inner and the outer relation. Each group nourishes its own pride and vanity, boasts itself superior, exalts its own divinities, and looks with contempt on outsiders. Each group thinks its own folkways the only right ones, and if it observes that other groups have other folkways, these excite its scorn."[2]

It is only when members of different cultures come into contact and begin to interact with others and are adversely affected by the competition and conflict entailed in that interaction because of their relative military, economic, or other weakness that they begin to see themselves in a less favorable light. The new hierarchy may become internalized and accepted as reality, or it may provoke an embittered and violent reaction that may take the form of armed rebellion or insidious criminal behavior. "In a political environment lacking an overriding consensus on values and issues," Rothchild warns, "adversarial politics . . . can go beyond healthy competition and contribute to intense and highly destructive conflicts."[3]

The larger the gap in the participational and distributional patterns based on racially, ethnically, or religiously determined forms of identity, the more likely the breakdown of civil order and the conversion of political confrontation into violent conflict. When the conflict turns violent, the issues at stake become transformed into a fundamental contest for state power. The objectives may vary in degree from a demand for autonomy to a major restructuring of the national framework, either to be captured by the demand-making group or to be more equitably reshaped. When the conflict escalates into a contest for the "soul" of the nation, it may turn into an intractable "zero-sum" confrontation. The critical issue is whether the underlying sense of injustice, real or perceived, can be remedied in a timely manner that avoids the zero-sum level of violence.

In this sense, internal conflicts, while destructive and therefore objectionable, also offer opportunities for addressing the fundamental problems that are the source of tension, violence, and instability. Conflict resolution then becomes a means of negotiating a new social contract to the benefit and satisfaction of all concerned.

The normative bases for such a contract must be the promotion of the dignity of the human being, both as an individual and as a member of a group. More than a value goal, the pursuit of human dignity is also a pragmatic political reality. Fundamental principles of human dignity provide a framework for understanding people's motivation to react, both individually and collectively, to what they perceive as gross injustices and violations of their fundamental human rights and democratic freedoms. While there is considerable variation in the institutional dimensions of these norms, the principles involved are universal and have become largely adopted by the international community and enshrined in the International Bill of Rights, composed of the Universal Declaration of Human Rights, the International Covenant on Civil and Political Rights, the International Covenant on Economic, Social, and Cultural Rights, and a wide array of other human rights instruments. This represents the corpus of human rights law recognizing the inherent dignity and equality of all human beings and setting a common standard for their rights.[4]

The demand for human dignity is therefore not a utopian slogan; it is operationally or functionally translatable into a quest for recognition and respect for human beings, both as individuals and as members of identifiable groups. It is, moreover, a demand for freedom; equitable participation in political, economic, social, and cultural life; and a fair share in the distribution of national wealth, services, employment opportunities, and resources for development. Human dignity demands, at the minimum, equal treatment with full rights and duties of citizenship.

Responsibilities of Sovereignty

Since conflict management, political stability, economic growth, equitable distribution, and social welfare are functions of governments, the responsibility for failed policies and their tragic humanitarian consequences must rest with the states concerned. And although accountability for such responsibility rests with the citizens of the countries themselves, when a people are oppressed and denied democratic participation in their own government, and when their civil liberties and fundamental human rights are violated, then their power to hold their governments accountable becomes limited. To the extent that the international community is the ultimate guarantor of the universal standards that safeguard the dignity of all human beings, it has a corresponding responsibility to provide innocent victims of internal conflicts and gross violations of human rights with protection and assistance.

Resort to external sources of protection and assistance, however, runs against the notion of national sovereignty. The more deficient the performance of a government and the more vulnerable to external scrutiny, the more likely it is to plead sovereignty as a barricade. This defensive reaction by targeted or targetable governments in turn challenges the determination of the international community to act affirmatively against the abuse of national sovereignty. Unless driven by strategic or ideological reasons, the political will of the major actors of the international community becomes significantly challenged and constrained. Indeed, post-Cold War developments and the reduction of geostrategic motivations as bases for international action, multilateral or unilateral, explain the ambivalence now confronting the international community. Moreover, the war is not being won by those governments that are attempting to barricade themselves against international scrutiny.

Responsible sovereignty must first and foremost ensure for its citizens peace, security, and stability through a system of law and order that enjoys broad-based support and, therefore, has legitimacy. This accomplishment, in turn, requires postulating guiding principles, of which human dignity, defined as a broad-based democratic shaping and sharing of values, is paramount. Within the framework of universal values, a major objective of responsible sovereignty should be conflict management through a system of just and fair distribution of power, wealth, and other material, cultural, spiritual, moral, and symbolic values. Conflicts which degenerate into widespread violence essentially reflect a breakdown of public order and the legal system designed to protect it. A normative approach to this crisis must address the concept of law as an instrument of control, the degree to which it lives up to the overriding goals of human dignity—at least to the pragmatic extent of ensuring functional legitimacy—and the rights and wrongs involved in the confrontation leading to the breakdown of the system, all of which ultimately depend on a system of international accountability.

The proper response to the dilemmas of sovereignty is to reaffirm the sovereign state's responsibility and accountability to both domestic and external constituencies as interconnected principles of the national and international orders. The conceptual framework of such a normative code is anchored in the assumption that in order to be legitimate, sovereignty must demonstrate responsibility, which means, at the very least, providing for the basic needs of a people. Most governments, under normal circumstances, do, in fact, discharge that responsibility; when they cannot do so for reasons of incapacity, they legitimately call upon the international community for assistance. But under those exceptional circumstances when governments fail to discharge this responsibility and fail to call for help, leaving masses of its citizens threatened and suffering, the international community should step in to provide the needed remedies.

The desirable and normal situation is one in which a system of law and order is responsive to a nation's needs for justice, democratic freedoms, and general welfare. When things fall apart to the degree that peace, security, and stability cannot be guaranteed, and the prevailing order becomes challenged by a rebellion with a significant degree of legitimacy and effectiveness, then the authority of those entrusted with sovereignty is subject to question. In between these two extremes lie the many cases where internal conflict is endemic, societal needs and demands are unmet, and government is seen as a private function. While law and order are overriding objectives, they cannot be seen as concepts of value-free control and authority, but rather as elements of an exercise of power legitimized by the pursuit of the common and overriding objectives of a community or the nation as a whole.

International intervention becomes a compelling imperative when there is a widespread breakdown of order, a collapse of the state capacity to manage the situation, and the exposure of masses of innocent civilians to severe suffering and death. The current isolationist tendency among the major Western countries, however, reflects the international community's move away from interventionist policies of the past, as the end of great power rivalry and the rise of budgetary constraints make it harder for Western governments to pursue activist policies outside their national borders. Although often driven by humanitarian concerns to deliver needed assistance, and occasionally taking military action to facilitate that mission, the international community generally fails to address the political dimensions which are often at the root of the crises. Increasingly, the message to Africa is that, while the international community is prepared to assist, the primary responsibility must fall on the Africans themselves.

The irony, indeed the paradox, of strategic withdrawal and isolationism, as contrasted with increased humanitarian intervention in crisis situations, was dramatically demonstrated in Rwanda. The United Nations withdrew at precisely the time of the country's greatest need for humanitarian intervention in the face of genocide, and then, as though to compensate for this gross failure to meet an urgent humanitarian challenge, the international community returned with a massive emergency assistance program, especially for the refugee and internally displaced populations, costing hundreds of millions of U.S. dollars.[5] What was particularly striking was that humanitarian operations were being conspicuously conducted by expatriates, well-equipped with vehicles, communications systems, and other supplies in an atmosphere in which the newly established Rwandan government lacked the basic needs—authority, infrastructure, and resources—for running a state. The inevitable outcome was for the Rwandan government to respond ambivalently to international humanitarian operations to a degree that began to threaten the continuation of relief assistance programs.

Tensions notwithstanding, developments worldwide show that a broad system of collaboration among international agencies, intergovernmental organizations, and NGOs, national and international, is the appropriate response to the multifaceted challenges of humanitarian emergencies. In this collaborative map, the role of the NGOs which operate at the grassroots level is particularly appropriate to helping states undergoing identity crises. By their presence and activities, NGOs provide both protection and assistance and can even help generate a process of sustainable development by utilizing indigenous resources, values, and institutions.

The fact that the more powerful countries of the West are withdrawing strategically, but becoming more involved in humanitarian emergencies through NGOs, means that the NGO community is being empowered beyond its conventional capacity. This is both an asset and a responsibility, especially as international humanitarian emergencies always engender enormous tensions and dilemmas caused by domestic failure and the need for outside intervention.

The Sudanese Context

The civil war in the Sudan is, ironically, the result of the country's promise as a microcosm of Africa and a bridge or crossroads between the continent and the Middle East. The racial, ethnic, cultural, and religious diversities in the Sudan's composition are divided North and South. The

North—two-thirds of the country in land and population—is inhabited by indigenous tribal groups, the dominant among whom intermarried with incoming Arab traders, and, over a period preceding Islam but heightened by the advent of Islam in the seventh century, produced a genetically mixed African-Arab racial and cultural identity. The resulting racial characteristics look very similar to those of the African groups in the continent immediately below the Sahara: Ethiopia, Eritrea, Djibouti, and Somalia in the East; Chad, Niger, and Mali in the center; and Senegal to the west. Indeed, the Arabic phrase, *Bilad el Sudan*, from which the Sudan derives its name, means "Land of the Blacks," and refers to all of those sub-Saharan territories.

Conflict of Identities

Unlike the situation in the above-mentioned countries, where people identify themselves as Africans even if they are Muslims, in the Sudan, Islam, the Arabic language, and Arabism as a combined racial, ethnic, linguistic, cultural, and nationalist concept are closely intertwined. Northern Sudanese Muslims therefore see themselves simply as Arabs despite the visible African element in their skin color and physical features. There are, however, non-Arab communities in the North which, although large in numbers proportional to the Arabized tribes, have been partially assimilated by their conversion to Islam and adoption of Arabic as the language of communication with the other tribes.[6]

It is in the South, the remaining third of the country in land and population, that the African identity in its racial and cultural composition has withstood assimilation into Arabism and Islam. Northern incursions southward met with strong resistance dating back to the hostile encounters of the slave trade during the eighteenth and nineteenth centuries.

The British colonial policy of administering the Sudanese North and the South separately reinforced Arabism and Islam in the North, encouraged southern development along indigenous African lines, and introduced Christian missionary education and the rudiments of Western culture as elements of modernization in the South. Interaction between the two sets of people was strongly discouraged.

While British administration invested considerably in the political, economic, social, and cultural development of the North, the South remained isolated, secluded, and undeveloped. The principal objective of colonial rule in the region was the establishment and maintenance of law and order. The separate administration of the North and the South left open the option that the South might eventually be annexed to one of the East African colonies or be an independent state. Suddenly, in 1947, only nine years before independence on 1 January 1956, the British reversed the policy of separate development, but they had neither the time nor the political will to put in place constitutional arrangements that would ensure protection for the South within a united Sudan.

The preoccupying concern among the northerners since independence has been to correct the divisive effect of the separatist policies of the colonial administration, which pursued the assimilation of the South through Arabization and Islamization. For the South, northern domination has been tantamount to replacing British colonialism with internal Arab "colonialism." Southern resistance first took the form of a mutiny in 1955 by an army battalion, then took the form of a political call for a federal arrangement, and finally intensified into an armed struggle for secession, or at least the right of self-determination.[7]

The political impasse created by the situation in the South prompted the military to take over in 1958, only two years after independence, with the aim of pursuing strategies of Arabization and Islamization vigorously and unhampered by parliamentary democracy. The ruthlessness with which these assimilation policies were pursued in the South aggravated the simmering conflict, which became a full-fledged civil war in the 1960s. The effect of that war led to a popular uprising that overthrew the military regime in 1964. Oppressive policies toward the South were temporarily relaxed. An official conference of the contending parties rejected separation or self-determination but mandated a twelve-man committee to formulate an appropriate constitutional arrangement that would reconcile southern demands with the preservation of national unity. It recommended regional autonomy for the South. Parliamentary democracy, however, was restored before the committee's recommendations could be implemented by the interim government. With the return of democracy, the traditional political parties assumed control and resumed the assimilation policies with a vengeance. As violence escalated, the differences between the North and the South became sharper, and the level of political instability rose.

This vicious cycle was broken in 1969, when another military junta, this time under the leadership of Jaafar Muhammed Nimeiri, seized power in alliance with the Communist Party, which believed in autonomy for the South (provided the region first accepted socialism, something southerners resisted). After displaying an ambivalent attitude toward the rebels following the abortive coup of 1971, when the leftist elements in the government tried to take over power from within, Nimeiri's regime eventually negotiated with the Southern Sudan Liberation Movement (SSLM) and, in 1972, concluded the Addis Ababa Agreement, which, based on the recommendations of the committee, granted the South regional autonomy with a democratic parliamentary system.[8]

The regime, however, remained under pressure from the conservative and radical Islamic elements, in particular, the sectarian parties and the Muslim Brothers (*Ikhwan el Muslimeen*), a radical rightist religious group, with whom Nimeiri eventually entered into an uneasy alliance. Nimeiri also underwent a personal conversion, becoming a born-again Muslim, even though he still hoped that through religious reforms he could pull the rug from under the feet of the sectarian opposition leaders. He also hoped to remove the anomaly of liberal democracy in the South, which was incongruous within the national system of an authoritarian presidency. Nimeiri gradually eroded the South's autonomy, moving relentlessly toward imposing Islamic law, the *Shari'a,* and establishing an Islamic state. Eventually, in 1983, he unilaterally abrogated the Addis Ababa Agreement by dividing the South into three regions and ordering the transfer of southern troops to the North. This triggered the formation of the Sudan People's Liberation Movement (SPLM) and its military wing, the Sudan People's Liberation Army (SPLA), under the leadership of John Garang de Mabior. To the surprise of most people, the declared objective of the Movement was not secession but the creation of a new, secular, democratic, and pluralistic Sudan. Within only two years of the resumption of hostilities, a popular uprising, the *intifada*, largely fueled by the military situation in the South, led to Nimeiri's own demise in 1985. Most northerners expected the SPLM/SPLA to put down its arms and ride the democratic wave. But the SPLM seemed genuinely committed to the creation of the new Sudan, which posed an even greater threat to the Arab-Islamic establishment of the North than secession.

After Nimeiri's overthrow, the Muslim Brothers reorganized themselves into a broader-based political party, the National Islamic Front (NIF), which won the third largest number of seats in the parliamentary elections of 1986. The Front's Islamic national agenda was endorsed and significantly reinforced when General Omar Hassan al-Bashir, in alliance with the NIF, seized power in 1989, in the name of the Revolution for National Salvation. The SPLM/SPLA condemned the coup as an

Islamist move engineered by the NIF.[9] The SPLM agreed, however, to participate with the government in peace talks, which, while raising no controversies on such generalities as preservation of the unity of the country, adoption of a federal system of government, and correction of the disparities in economic and social development among the regions, broke down on the characterization of the problem as "southern" rather than "national," the implication being a fundamental disagreement on the objective of restructuring a new Sudan.[10] Further talks, which have been sponsored by various mediators over the years, have raised issues of detail such as pluralistic democracy, separation of religion and state, and the right of self-determination, all of which have been severely contentious. As a result, no appreciable progress has so far been made on the peace front between North and South.[11] The Sudan's conflict has escalated into a crisis of national identity with far-reaching implications for the future of the country.

The current struggle over national identity is reflected at two principal levels: One has to do with the configuration of Sudanese identity in the light of historical processes that have left the peoples with layers of civilizations, racial characteristics, and cultural traditions; the second concerns the repercussions for unity in a pluralistic modern nation state in which the conflict between the two sets of identities that give the country its geopolitical significance now threatens the nation with disintegration.

The crisis of national identity manifests itself in two corresponding sets of discrepancies: One is the gap between self-perceptions of identity—what people claim to be, and the reality of what they are as determined by objective factors. The other is the gap between how individual groups perceive themselves or are perceived objectively and how the national framework is defined.

What makes the identity crisis in the Sudan particularly acute is the fact that the policies of the various governments since independence have tried to fashion the entire country on the basis of their Arab-Islamic identity. The South, with a bitter historical memory and a colonial legacy of separate development in the modern context, is decidedly resistant to being racially, culturally, and religiously assimilated into the Arab-Islamic mold of the North. It is, however, not the mere fact of integration of African and Arab elements to which the South is opposed; rather, it is the political domination of the South by the North and the imposition of the North's racial, cultural, linguistic, and religious elements of identity on the whole country, which the South uncompromisingly opposes. Conflict over identity "takes the form of opposition by the non-Muslims and/or non-Arabs to the adoption of: (1) Islam as the state religion and the basis of the constitution and public laws of the Sudan; (2) Arabic as the official and national language of the Sudan; and (3) Arabism and Islam as determinative factors in national self-identification and in foreign relations."[12]

Unlike the case of Nigeria, where the political weight of numbers in the Muslim North and the economic, educational, and bureaucratic power of the South balance each other and give the "federal character" a balancing advantage, in the Sudan, the North is the beneficiary of all political, economic, social, and cultural power and development, and the South is relegated to the lowest spectrum of the scale. The scale was tilted even more when the National Islamic Front, led by Hassan al-Turabi, the party most committed to the Arab-Islamic agenda, and which had been extending its basis of support into all the political, economic, social, and cultural fields of life, allied itself in 1989 with sympathizers in the army and, in the name of the "Revolution for National Salvation," overthrew the democratically elected government of Sadiq al-Mahdi. Since then, the national government's unwavering pursuit of the Arab-Islamic agenda has become clear.

The fundamentalists and the secularists represent the competing counterparts of parallel identities which have now come into intensive contact within a unitary state system. As El-Affendi noted, "What we are witnessing is the clash of two antagonistic cultural outlooks, both of which are experiencing a revival."[13]

Humanitarian Dimensions

The war in the South has been the main cause of humanitarian emergencies associated, in particular, with the conditions of the displaced and their survival needs. Since the Islamic coup of 1989, war-related atrocities and the clash of Islamic laws with the universal human rights standards have made the Sudan the object of severe scrutiny by the international community on both humanitarian and human rights grounds.

A drought-related famine in the western and the eastern parts of the country in the early 1980s affected mostly the marginalized populations of those regions who, though Muslims, were predominantly non-Arab. A significant feature of that emergency was the reticence of the then military regime of Nimeiri to admit that there was a famine. The authorities did not identify fully with the affected populations and did not provide relief assistance.

News leaked, however, and the international media followed. Despite the enormity of the highly publicized wars in nearby Ethiopia and Eritrea, and the plight of the many refugees from these countries, the world discovered that there was a much greater emergency in the Sudan. Gradually, the media, the NGO community, and eventually some neighboring governments began to pressure the Sudan to the point where, eventually, Nimeiri found himself forced to invite the international community to assist. The response of the international community, coordinated by the United Nations, was massive and on an unprecedented scale.

At the time the international community became involved in the emergency situation in the North, the war in the South was generating a famine there. Both sides in the conflict used food as a weapon. The rebels prevented food from reaching southern towns under government control, on the grounds that relief supplies would be used for the army, could provide cover for weapons, and would attract people to the towns. The government prevented food from reaching the areas held by the rebels for reasons of sovereignty and pride; they also sought to deplete what they saw as the popular base of support for the rebel movement. Indeed, the prime minister at the time was alleged to have argued that the food distributed to the civilian population in the South was "killing my people"—the soldiers.

Shortly after coming to power, al-Bashir made a similar statement. He complained that the international community was not giving the Sudan adequate support to help the country provide for the refugees from Eritrea and Ethiopia. An international representative, while agreeing with the president, pointed to the scarcity of the available resources and noted that the international community was providing assistance to hundreds of thousands of "your people," the southern Sudanese refugees in Gambela, Ethiopia. The president is reported to have said, "Those are not my people."[14]

The politics and actions of the respective parties left the starving people of the South in a vacuum of moral leadership; they were uprooted, unprotected, and without care. Worse, the government recruited, trained, and armed tribal militias to fight the rebel forces. Indeed, much of the destruction of human life and property in rural areas in the late 1980s came from the southern and northern tribal militias, the so-called "friendly forces."

In response to the humanitarian tragedy in the South, the international community pressured the parties into accepting emergency assistance through what became known as Operation Lifeline Sudan, first negotiated by the United Nations with the government of the Sudan in 1989, and then agreed to by the rebel forces of the SPLM. This agreement enabled the United Nations and a wide array of NGOs to provide food, medicine, and needed relief to displaced populations throughout the country. Both sides also agreed on zones of peace, or "corridors of tranquility," in the areas of conflict to enable the passage of humanitarian relief assistance. Although the parties have continued to obstruct access to needy populations, Operation Lifeline Sudan has been extended several times over the last several years. Indeed, the people of the war-stricken regions have been dependent on international relief assistance delivered by humanitarian agencies, intergovernmental and non-governmental, for their survival needs. It can be argued that, except for the towns under government control, the South is considerably autonomous, if not independent, and that a significant portion of responsibilities normally associated with sovereignty has already devolved to both the local population and the international relief organizations. Accordingly, it is in this area of humanitarian intervention that the greatest erosion of sovereignty takes place today, mostly with the consent of the states, but at times through forceful enforcement. Although the narrow concept of sovereignty remains a major obstacle to assisting and protecting victims of internal conflicts, it is no longer insurmountable.

Nevertheless, mechanisms and procedures of implementation of the wide array of human rights and humanitarian standards remain undeveloped and grossly inadequate. Furthermore, the more assertive that the international community has been, the more defensively vulnerable governments have reacted against the erosion of state sovereignty. The Islamic regime in the Sudan has been one of the most defensive in its assertion of sovereignty and cultural relativity with respect to human rights, even as the human rights situation in the country continues to deteriorate and attract intense international scrutiny, culminating in the appointment by the UN Commission on Human Rights of Professor Gasper Biro of Hungary as Special Rapporteur on the human rights situation in the Sudan.

The fact that the situation of the internally displaced in the Sudan remains grave has been highlighted by a recent report to the General Assembly by Biro.[15] His report expresses serious concern about the government's indiscriminate aerial bombardments of civilian targets in the South, especially of places where there are concentrations of internally displaced persons. It describes the deteriorating health and food situation in some camps, resulting from the government's refusal to grant access to international relief efforts in such areas and the looting of convoys by the different factions of the SPLA. The report draws attention in particular to the 800,000 children affected by the war in the South, including unaccompanied minors and those forcibly conscripted by all parties. It expresses alarm at reports regarding the forcible return of displaced persons to areas under SPLA control or outside Khartoum. Nevertheless, Biro expressed his conviction that southerners and Nuba in the North were ready to return to their homes as soon as the necessary political and security conditions permitted them to do so. He called upon the government to "cease immediately the deliberate and indiscriminate aerial bombardments of civilian targets" and to "give free access to regional and international humanitarian and human rights organizations throughout the country, in particular in the Nuba mountains and the towns of southern Sudan."

Biro also urged the international community "to address the continued interference by all parties in the distribution of humanitarian aid and relief that has direct and immediate effects on the civilian population in the war zones." He specifically called upon the government and the other parties involved in the armed conflict in central and the Southern Sudan to agree to a cease-fire, to intensify their efforts to come to a peaceful solution, and to address the problem of displacement and create appropriate conditions for the displaced persons and refugees to return to their homes. While the government contested the specific findings of the Special Rapporteur, there can be no doubt that, in 1995, the situation of human rights and humanitarian crisis remained grave, especially in the war zone.

Of all African countries, the Sudan is the country in which the conflict between the universality and the relativity of human rights standards has been most pronounced. This is largely because the Sudan applies *shari'a* law, with Islamic penalties involving amputation of limbs for theft, flogging for consumption or possession of alcohol, stoning to death for adultery, and similar punishments which the Special Rapporteur has declared to be in conflict with the provisions of relevant international human rights instruments to which the Sudan is a party. In his report to the Commission on Human Rights, Biro drew attention to two main components of the Sudanese penal code which he said were "radically opposed to provisions of the international conventions to which the Sudan is a party."[16]

The government of the Sudan saw the criticism of the Special Rapporteur as totally inappropriate and unacceptable. Their position was that these laws were not only reflective of Sudanese cultural values, but were the dictates of Islamic Law; as such, they were God-given, and therefore would prevail over any inconsistent and purportedly universal standards.

Dilemmas of Emergency Operations

Although international humanitarian intervention has increasingly become accepted as overriding sovereignty in its narrow classical sense, foreign relief operations raise serious problems. Evaluations of the drought-related relief operations and Operation Lifeline Sudan conducted by independent researchers revealed four sets of dilemmas resulting from these interventions, from which both the international community and the recipient countries have much to learn.[17]

The first dilemma related directly to the inherent externality of the emergency operations, which meant that the country had failed and needed foreign intervention. That in itself created a situation injurious to national pride, particularly on the part of those who were not directly affected by the famine—the urban population, the intellectuals, and the middle class. One professor spoke with outrage, "We should have been left alone."[18] The number of relief workers operating in the country, representing governmental organizations and NGOs, was overwhelming; it was like an invasion. Their cars and walkie-talkies were conspicuous. Humanitarian help had turned into humiliation. Their presence was greatly resented by much of the population. Considering that these relief workers were living much better than even the country's well established middle class, it is easy to understand the local response.

The failure of the government to discharge its responsibility to its citizens, which led to this external involvement, created ambivalent feelings of needing help and resenting it at the same time. The foreign donors and relief workers were equally outraged: They had come to help because the country had failed to provide for its citizens and yet, they were regarded as intruders and treated with hostility. Feelings ran high on both sides.

The second dilemma had to do with the limited degree to which external assistance made use of the country's existing structures, institutions, and resources, and the resourcefulness of its people. The external assumption was that the Sudanese were incapable of managing their own problems. Thus, the emergency operations were seen as an exercise not aimed at enhancing the capacity of the country to manage its own future emergencies.

Third, literally hundreds of NGOs wanted to operate independently or autonomously (but needed to be coordinated). Quite apart from not wanting to be coordinated by local government officials as a matter of principle, the NGOs viewed coordination as an undesirable impediment to their work, since speed and results were the objectives of their operations.

Fourth, the emergency operations were externally focused. In the end, observers wondered whether what had been done had ultimately strengthened or weakened the nation's capacity. Some experts argued that, while lives had been saved, relief operations had also been a source of weakness since they encouraged dependency on the part of those receiving assistance.

Does this conclusion argue against external assistance? Of course not. What it means however, is that prevention, as the old saying goes, is better than a cure. Putting one's house in order is the best way of protecting one's sovereignty. During emergency operations, all sides must realize the complexities and dilemmas involved and work hard to provide needed relief while minimizing negative consequences.

Africans are increasingly being told by the international community that, given the scarcity of resources in the world and the tendency toward isolationism on the part of the wealthier industrialized countries of the West, they will have to rely on themselves primarily and that, whatever help they can expect from the outside world will be targeted selectively. This limited help will naturally be motivated by the values of those who are coming to assist. Accordingly, the degree to which a country lives up to the values of human rights, humanitarianism, democracy, and the market economy will determine the degree to which it will receive support from the outside. But this promise, too, poses a paradox because the situations of greatest humanitarian need are those in which governments are neglectful of their victim population.

Africans are responding to this challenge, not only because they are being told to shape up, but also because they have begun to scrutinize their own performance and are sharpening their own sense of responsibility, especially in the area of conflict prevention, management, and resolution. In this sense, preventive action is becoming more of a common ground. In both preventive and remedial areas of action, the NGO community can do much, especially in building the capacity of local populations to become self-reliant.

Indigenous Resources for Conflict Management

Self-reliance essentially means making use of the existing human and material resources of the country. The zero-sum nature of identity conflicts implies that a nation is not making adequate use of its indigenous resources as represented by its ethnic and cultural diversity. Governments and the international community have managed conflict ineffectively because of this gap in nation building. Accordingly, those who work with people at the grassroots level, among whom NGOs are often the best qualified, need particularly to be sensitized to these values and their relevance for conflict prevention, management, and resolution.

Although conflict is normal in the sense that it occurs along with human interactions, people are more apt than not to cooperate and harmonize their incompatible or potentially conflictual positions. Intrastate conflict, in fact, signifies a breakdown in the regulated pattern of life. In the normal course of events, society is structured around accepted fundamental values and norms which guide behavior and regulate relations in order to avoid a destructive collision of interests or positions. If people observe the principles of the normative code, which they generally do, the normal pattern is one of relative cooperation and mutual accommodation, even in a competitive framework.

The extent to which members in a community or group live together in peace depends in large measure on the cohesiveness of their culture and the effectiveness of its normative code. Culture in this context may be defined as "a set of shared and enduring meanings, values, and beliefs that characterize national, ethnic, or other groups and orient their behavior."[19] As Deutsch has observed, "Social interaction takes place in a social environment—in a family, a group, a community, a nation, a civilization—that has developed techniques, symbols, categories, rules and values that are relevant to human interactions. Hence, to understand the events that occur in social interactions one must comprehend the interplay of these events with the broader socio-cultural context in which they occur."[20]

The traditional African approach to conflict resolution emanates from the kinship orientation of the society, with its emphasis on living together amicably as members of the kingroup or community. The process of decision-making begins on the family level, and only if the family elders fail to reach a settlement does the case then move upwards until it reaches territorial leadership.[21]

In the context of the modern nation state, the roles of the elders or chiefs and warrior age-sets have been assumed by the state, whose power ultimately rests on a monopoly of force. The division of functions between the chiefs and elders as peacemakers and young men as warriors has been replaced by the concentration of all sources of power in the state—the government. Since the state is seen as the only beneficiary of institutionalized hegemony, contestation for state power is concomitantly intensified, if need be, by force. Warfare, as a youthful cultural expression, is replaced by rebellion as a way of stating demands.

Rather than utilize indigenous values and institutions as effective building blocks, African states have tended to dismiss them as relics of an outmoded system, without substituting functional alternatives that can be as effective in maintaining civil order at the communal level. Both to prevent civil disorders of massive dimensions and to help reconstruct collapsed states and societies, it is imperative to develop a deeper understanding of such cultural resources, to adapt them to the modern context, and to design ways of applying them in their adapted form. No society can have a viable future without building on the roots of its past, from which it derives the resilience to resist destructive winds of change.

Sharing the Responsibility

Because the major Western countries are becoming increasingly isolationist, it is now widely recognized that sharing the responsibilities of sovereignty should begin on the sub-regional and regional level. The role played by the Economic Community of West African States (ECOWAS) in Liberia, the Southern African Development Community (SADC) in Lesotho and Mozambique, the Inter-Governmental Authority for Drought and Development (IGADD) in the Sudan and Somalia, and the Arab-Maghrib Union (UMA) in the Western Sahara indicate an emerging trend of sub-regional responsibility and accountability. The important thing about these initiatives is that they have been predicated on the premise of the interconnection of the security situations of the various countries in the region. It is therefore in their collective interest to work for regional peace, security, stability, and development. Such regional responses offer a potential that can grow to encompass a wide range of contexts requiring cooperation, from the search for peace to regional economic arrangements, which, in themselves, could be effective preventive measures against famine.

Although emphasizing the primary responsibility of sub-regional and regional organizations, it would be a major strategic mistake to absolve the international community of its regional responsibilities. As the Secretary-General of the Organization of African Unity has repeatedly stated, Africa is a part of the international community, and has the right to expect from the international community both the privileges and obligations of membership. Africa's continued involvement in the international system, both as a source of support and an obligation, is inherently in the interest of global order. If that order is to be stable and sustainable, global peace and security must be comprehensive. The interdependency of the now dominant market economy; the uncontrollable flow of information; the universalizing quest for democracy and respect for fundamental rights and liberties; the massive exodus across national borders in search of physical security and the necessities of a relatively decent life; the concomitant spread of diseases, drug trafficking, arms trade, and crimes of poverty; and the globalizing environmental concerns that are becoming both physical and human are bound to generate a response marked as much by isolationist withdrawal as by increased awareness of the universal characteristics of the challenge. But the outcome cannot be taken for granted. Enlightened self-interest is required to realize that the threat to international peace and security as a ground for collective or cooperative action must be seen as truly indivisible in the long run. The old cliché of being in one boat is acquiring a new reality and demanding a pragmatic realism in a globalizing self-interest alongside the altruistic motivation of humanitarian idealism.

Ultimately, the solutions to the problems of lasting peace and stability must be found internally. The values of respect and tolerance for others and of sharing power and resources equitably or fairly must be inculcated and sanctioned by the international community. Preventive measures should therefore include: defining national identity to be equitably accommodating to all the contending groups; developing principles of constitutionalism or constitutive management of power that creatively and flexibly balance the dynamics of diversity in unity to promote national consensus and collective purpose; designing a system of distribution or allocation of economic opportunities and resources that is particularly sensitive to the needs of minorities and disadvantaged groups and induces them to see unity as a source of security and not deprivation; and, through all these measures, challenging every group to recognize that it has a distinctive contribution to make to the process of nation building by utilizing its own cultural values, institutional structures, and a self-propelling sense of purpose within a national framework of diversified unity and equitable pluralism. Where conditions make such a uniting sense of national identity impractical or too costly, the residual alternative, which should be internationally supported, is to allow the right of self-determination, including the option of partition.

Conclusion

The internecine conflict that has raged intermittently in the Sudan for the last four decades is undoubtedly one of the most ferocious in the world. The humanitarian tragedies emanating from the civil war are also among the most devastating. The crisis is further compounded by the fact that the Sudan suffers from one of the worst crises of national identity, involving extreme cleavages.

Although the case of the Sudan is clearly extreme, it illustrates problems of a much more generic and global nature, and the humanitarian challenges that they pose for the international community. The most critical one posed with respect to the masses of people who fall victim to humanitarian tragedies and gross violations of human rights as a result of internal conflicts or natural disasters is where to place responsibility for meeting their pressing and most compelling needs for protection, assistance, and transition toward sustainable development. While the fundamental assumption is that a national government has the primary responsibility for taking care of its citizens, if the country is severely divided, then the government itself is likely to be a party to the conflict. In other cases, the state has collapsed and there is no government to assume the necessary responsibilities of sovereignty. An affected population nearly always finds itself caught in between and forced to identify with one party or the other. Often, it is not even a matter of choice, but of belonging to either of the parties on the basis of race, ethnicity, religion, culture, or political ideology. Since the victims of internal conflicts are often members of the groups challenging the status quo and, therefore, the government, there is an inherent tension between the responsibility of a government toward its citizens and the tendency to identify groups with the adversary. This often results in the government's denying them the protection and assistance that they expect from their government. Whom can they count upon to provide them with their fundamental needs for protection, assistance, reconstruction, and development?

Questions arise concerning both national and international responsibility: To whom is a government accountable for failure to discharge its responsibility toward its citizens? To argue that it is the people of a country would be to give an obvious, but only partial answer. The mere fact that a government that has failed dismally remains in power indicates the limits of national accountability. The alternative leverage can only be external. But to whom among the external actors or sources of influence, persuasive or coercive, can a people turn for remedies?

Any effort to address these issues in the context of both the assumed national sovereignty and international concern must build on a number of basic assumptions. The first is that, although the state is under pressure from above and below, it will continue to be a central factor in national and international affairs. The framework of the state is part of global interdependence that has both international and national dimensions. The global dimension embraces sub-regional, regional, and international contexts, while the national envisages internal structures: central, provincial, district, and local. Humanitarian and human rights problems emanating from internal conflicts need to be analyzed and responded to at those multiple levels—the global, regional/continental, sub-regional, state, and local levels.

The second is that the national framework is dominated by the laws, policies, and actions of the central government which, while pertinent to the maintenance of law and order, favor the status quo. Citizens are therefore forced to choose between conformity and various forms and degrees of opposition, sometimes culminating in armed rebellion. Rather than being seen by the government as citizens to be protected, civilians who sympathize or are otherwise identified with an opposition become perceived as adversaries. For those falling into the cracks of the national identity crisis, the only alternative source of protection, relief assistance, and rehabilitation has to be the international community, both intergovernmental and non-governmental.

The third assumption is that the existing international legal and institutional frameworks for making available these alternative sources are fundamentally constrained by the state-orientation of the international system and its commitment to national sovereignty. This presents something of a dilemma. On the one hand, the cooperation of states is needed to move the international system to respond to the call of the needy within the framework of national sovereignty. On the other hand, the mere fact that the international community is needed implies the failure of national sovereignty and the exclusive reliance on states for the welfare of their citizens.

The fourth logically flows from the third: As long as the international system remains state-oriented, any policies and strategies to help a population within the framework of national sovereignty must first aim at winning the cooperation of the national government. But where a government refuses to cooperate, thereby exposing large numbers of citizens to suffering and maybe death, the international community, or intergovernmental or non-governmental actors must make it clear that such a result threatens global order and will not be tolerated. The challenge is to persuade states to live up to their responsibilities.

The linkage of sovereignty, responsibility, and accountability encourages good governance by promising to set well-defined standards for gauging state performance and, by definition, holds decision-makers with authority and effective control accountable. This process provides an objective yardstick for evaluating one's own national performance and the performance of others in the hierarchy of authority and control in the global system. Given such a yardstick, a wide variety of observers and actors, governmental and non-governmental, national and international, can contribute to the monitoring of a crisis situation, signaling early warning, and indicting deserving culprits to be accountable to their own domestic constituencies or to the international community, as appropriate.

The international community will have to articulate specific legal standards to which all governments are expected to adhere and which have sufficiently broad legitimacy to motivate enforcement activities. These legal principles could be supplemented with a code accessible to policy-makers.

Since the masses of the people who are directly and acutely affected by internal conflicts usually live in local communities that are often remote and isolated from the central government and, certainly from outside sources of protection and assistance, it is the NGOs, international and local, with whom they usually come in close contact. The protection and assistance that these organizations offer necessarily depend on the degree to which they are non-partisan or neutral, yet they must also apportion rights and wrongs in any conflict. How to convey their judgment to the contending parties in a tactful way is critical. Human rights and humanitarian concerns must be closely linked, and so must protection and assistance. There is much more to human dignity than being sheltered and fed. Political and civil rights must inevitably figure into the early warning equation of NGOs.

The basic guiding principle of sovereignty and responsibility, it should be reiterated, is to assume that under normal circumstances, governments strive to ensure a just system of law and order, democratic freedoms, respect for fundamental rights, and general welfare. If they are unable to provide adequate protection and assistance for their people, they should invite or welcome foreign assistance and international cooperation to supplement their own efforts. A controversy arises in exceptional cases when a state has collapsed or a government is unwilling to invite or permit international involvement, while the level of human suffering or the threat of genocide dictates otherwise. This is often the case in civil conflicts characterized by racial, ethnic, or religious crises of national identity in which the conflicting parties perceive the affected population as part of "the enemy." It is essentially to fill the vacuum of moral responsibility created by such cleavages that international intervention becomes a moral imperative. Providing protection and assistance for the affected population becomes a responsibility shared by both international humanitarian agencies, governmental and non-governmental, with the latter often assuming the lion's share of on-the-ground operations that focus on assistance, but with protective implications.

As the necessity for this international role emanates largely from the failure of the national authorities to discharge their responsibilities of sovereignty, it is important to develop more effective ways of "sharing" those responsibilities. More specifically, in the case of the Sudan, it is vitally important for the Sudanese, both the government and the people, to realize that their country has, in this regard, failed dismally, thus posing difficult, continuing challenges for both intergovernmental organizations and NGOs.

Notes

1. Stephen John Stedman, "Conflict and Conflict Resolution in Africa: A Conceptual Framework," in Francis M. Deng and I. William Zartman (eds.), *Conflict Resolution in Africa* (Washington, D.C., 1991), 367–368.

2. William Graham Sumner, *Folkways: A Study of the Sociological Importance of Usages* (New York, 1906), 12–13.

3. Donald Rothchild, "Regime Management of Conflict in West Africa," in I. William Zartman (ed.), *Governance as Conflict Management in West Africa* (Washington, D.C.), forthcoming.

4. "Universal Declaration of Human Rights," A/810 (United Nations, 10 December 1948); "International Covenant on Economic, Social and Cultural Rights," A/6316 (United Nations, 16 December 1966); and "International Covenant on Civil and Political Rights," A/6316 (United Nations, 16 December 1966). See Frank Newman and David Weissbrodt, *International Human Rights: Law, Policy and Process* (Cincinnati, 1990), 11–15, 16–24, 25–41.

5. "The Endless Wait for Justice," *World Press Review* (March 1995), 12. In this article, Shahryar Khan, the UN Secretary-General's special representative in Kigali, is reported as saying: "The world has spent $700 million on emergency aid to Rwanda—milk, power, and jerrycans. By contrast, the Justice Ministry has received two payments—$27,000 from the Germans and $1 million from the Belgians—and two typewriters."

6. In the Sudan, unlike other African countries with a Muslim population, Islam is closely associated with the Arabic language, culture, and race, perhaps because of the historical association with the Arab world and in particular with Egypt. For the contrasting models of Islam in sub-Saharan and northern Africa, see Omar H. Kokole, "The Islamic Factor in African-Arab Relations," *Third World Quarterly*, VI (1984), 687–701. According to the author, while African countries south of the Sahara underwent Islamization, North Africa experienced two processes: Islamization and Arabization. "With time the North Africans came to see themselves as 'Arabs.'" 688.

7. For a background on the conflict and a history of the first phase of the war, see Mohamed Omer Beshir, *The Southern Sudan: Background to Conflict* (London, 1968). See also Dunstan M. Wai, *The Southern Sudan: A Problem of National Integration* (London, 1973); idem., *The African-Arab Conflict in the Sudan* (New York, 1981). For a southern point of view, see William Deng and Joseph Oduho, *The Problem of the Southern Sudan* (Oxford, 1962); Oliver Albino, *The Sudan: A Southern Viewpoint* (London, 1970).

8. For a detailed account of the Addis Ababa Agreement, see Ministry of Foreign Affairs, *Peace and Unity in the Sudan: An African Achievement* (Khartoum, 1973); Beshir, *Southern Sudan*. For the negotiations that led to the agreement, see Wai, *African-Arab Conflict in the Sudan*; Hizkias Assefa, *Mediation of Civil Wars: Approaches and Strategies—The Sudan Conflict* (Boulder, CO, 1987); Abel Alier, *Southern Sudan: Too Many Agreements Dishonored* (Exeter, Eng., 1990).

9. For the reaction of the SPLM/SPLA, see John Garang de Mabior, "Statement to the Sudanese People on the Current Situation in the Sudan," General Headquarters, SPLM/SPLA, 10 August 1989.

10. Between 9 September and 21 October 1989, the government convened a National Dialogue Conference on Peace Issues, whose principal recommendation for solving the country's problems of regional, ethnic, cultural, and religious diversity was a federal constitution. The government endorsed the recommendations of the

conference and the SPLM-SPLA acknowledged them, along with recommendations from other sources, as useful bases for constitutional talks. For the official report on the conference, see Steering Committee for National Dialogue on Peace Issues, *Final Report and Recommendations* (Khartoum, 1989), the so-called *Red Book*. The report was officially endorsed and reissued as "The Government's Peace Programme for Negotiations with the SPLM-SPLA" in November 1989, with an "Introduction" by Colonel Mohamed al-Amin Khalifa, a member of the Revolutionary Command Council for National Salvation and Chairman of the National Dialogue.

11. The latest initiative by the countries of the Inter-Governmental Authority for Drought and Development, IGADD, shows a more sustained commitment to the search for a just and lasting solution, but even that seems to have reached a dead end as the parties remain committed to seemingly unbridgeable positions on the critical issues of secularism and self-determination. For more on the IGADD peace initiative, see the *Sudan Democratic Gazette: A Newsletter for Democratic Pluralism* (May to November 1994), 48–54.

12. Peter Nyot Kok, "The Sudanese Conflict: Unity or Creative Deconstruction," unpublished paper.

13. Abdelwahab el-Affendi, "Discovering the South: Sudanese Dilemmas for Islam in Africa," *African Affairs,* LXXXIX (1990), 371.

14. Evidence of Roger Winter, in a meeting sponsored by the U.S. State Department on Refugees and Displaced Persons in the Horn of Africa, Washington, D.C., 17 October 1995. In the summary report on the meeting, Winter is reported to have said that the "government of Sudan views the African population in the South as 'not our people.'" (unpublished draft, 3).

15. Report to the General Assembly #A/49/539.

16. "Situation of Human Rights in the Sudan," Report of The Special Rapporteur, Gaspar Biro, submitted in accordance with Commission on Human Rights resolution 1993/60, E/CM 4/1994/49 (1 February 1994), para. 59, 15.

17. For an appraisal of these emergency operations, see Francis M. Deng and Larry Minear, *Challenges of Famine Relief* (Washington, D.C., 1992).

18. Deng and Minear, *Challenges of Famine Relief,* 37.

19. Guy Olivier Faure and Jeffrey Z. Rubin (eds.), *Culture and Negotiation: The Resolution of Water Disputes* (Newbury Park, CA, 1993), 3.

20. Morton Deutsch, "Subjective Features of Conflict Resolution: Psychological, Social and Cultural Influences," in Raimo Väyrynen (ed.), *New Directions in Conflict Theory: Conflict Resolution and Conflict Transformation* (London, 1991). For more on the system, see National Democratic Institute for International Affairs, *Democracies in Regions of Crisis* (Washington, D.C., 1990).

21. This was the essence of the answer given by President Sir Ketumile Masire of Botswana to the question of whether and how his country had made use of any traditional cultural values in building its model of democracy and development, which has been highly acclaimed.

RWANDA

CHAPTER NINE

Making Noise Effectively: Lessons from the Rwandan Catastrophe

Alison L. Des Forges

AT A CONFERENCE on averting catastrophes like the genocide in Rwanda, an academic linked with the French Ministry of Defense provoked unintended laughter when he asserted that preventive diplomacy was certainly not a new idea—that France had relied on it for years to keep order in certain African nations; it was just that they had not called it that. Less disingenuous than it might seem at first, his analysis has the merit of putting into perspective current efforts at averting crises.

The call for NGOs to play a role in preventive diplomacy has come as states show themselves increasingly less willing or less able to avert massive man-made crises. Even France, slow to relinquish its own special form of "preventive diplomacy," has apparently been so shaken by the Rwandan experience that it may bow out of further interventions. The United States, bitterly disappointed in Somalia, views future involvement in Africa with great skepticism. Other industrialized nations are preoccupied with their own shrinking economies, and are increasingly reluctant to seek a major role in those parts of the world thought to be chronically troublesome. The apparent failure of states to resolve complex humanitarian emergency situations has encouraged experts, both inside and outside governments, to investigate other kinds of initiatives, ideally by non-governmental actors.

The impetus for NGOs to intervene in critical situations results also from changes in the nature of the conflicts. Many more wars are now taking place within rather than between states, and—most important— are causing vastly increased suffering to civilian populations. In light of these changes, it is hardly surprising that NGOs, ordinarily closer to the people than are state hierarchies, increasingly seek to avert, limit, and end conflicts. This is true not just of local NGOs, which are struggling to contribute to the creation of a responsible "civil society," but also of international organizations. Even those foreign groups that once eschewed politics and narrowly defined their objective as promoting economic development have come to realize that no economic gains will last—much less increase—without minimal guarantees of peace, political participation, and human rights. Many chastened funders and experts ask what is left now of the many "model projects" that used to dot the Rwandan hillsides. In addition, foreign personnel often respond to pleas for help from endangered local partners, whether out of genuine collegiality or a simple sense of responsibility. If even developmental NGOs now understand the need to avert crises in order to ensure that their long-term goals are met, humanitarian NGOs recognize all the more that doing everything possible now to avert catastrophes helps to reduce the loss of lives and resources in the future.

The Rwandan crisis illustrates some of the possibilities as well as some of the limits for early intervention by NGOs. The crisis divides naturally into four phases: the first, from its beginning in 1990 to the signing of the Arusha Accords on 4 August 1993; the second, the phase of active preparation for the genocide, from August 1993 to April 1994; the third, the genocide itself, from 6 April to 4 July 1994; and the fourth, from the end of the genocide to 1996.

On 1 October 1990, a small guerrilla force of the Rwandan Patriotic Front (RPF) invaded Rwanda from across the Ugandan frontier, purportedly to oblige the Rwandan government to permit the return of Rwandan Tutsi, who had been in exile for decades. In a revolution at the end of the colonial era (1960), the Hutu, who constituted about 85 percent of the population, had overthrown the Tutsi aristocracy and driven many thousands into exile in neighboring countries.

In addition to bringing home the refugees, the RPF hoped to end the political monopoly of Juvenal Habyarimana, a Hutu general who had seized power in 1973 from Hutu politicians accused of corruption and regionalism. At the start, Habyarimana had enjoyed considerable popularity both at home and abroad, but after nearly twenty years in control, he was losing support. Rwanda's economy was faltering; the country had been stricken by a drought and crippled by the sudden and drastic fall in the world market price for coffee, Rwanda's chief export and source of foreign exchange. The economic decline produced domestic discontent and resulted in strict international fiscal controls. As Habyarimana's regime grew more corrupt and repressive, a domestic opposition took root, encouraged by the general move toward multi-party government throughout Africa and supported by foreign donors who hoped that a more open political system would improve economic performance.

In this increasingly unfavorable context, Habyarimana seized upon the RPF invasion as an opportunity to mobilize renewed support among the Hutu population. Central to his effort was a campaign to vilify Tutsi residents within the country as well as those moderate Hutu willing to work with the Tutsi for reform. Habyarimana accused these people of being *ibyitso*, or accomplices of the invaders and, within days of the invasion, he had arrested about 8,000 of them. Many were tortured and held in deplorable conditions for months. Two weeks later, the strategists of hate stepped up their campaign by launching several days of attacks against Tutsi residents in the northwestern commune of Kibirira. About 300 people were slaughtered and many thousands more driven from their homes. Even as late as 1 October 1990, extremists were willing to slaughter civilians to win the war against the RPF and to intimidate and destroy the domestic political opposition. Their grim determination would lead to the genocide of 1994.[1]

The first Rwandan human rights organization, the Association Rwandaise des Droits de l'Homme (ARDHO), was founded on the eve of the October invasion. Composed largely of lawyers and magistrates, it focused at first on denouncing the campaign of arrests. But as the state continued to slaughter and harass Tutsi and members of the political opposition, other human rights organizations—Association Rwandaise pour la Défense des Droits de la Personne et des Libertés Publiques (ADL), Ligue Chrétienne de Défense des Droits de l'Homme au Rwanda (LICHREDHOR), and Association des Volontaires pour la Paix (AVP)— were created, and joined in the struggle against government abuses. In cooperation with a Belgium-based organization of Rwandan exiles, they made contact with several international NGOs and church-based groups that began sending missions to examine the local situation.[2]

By the end of 1991, several leading international human rights associations as well as other organizations had published reports about abuses by the Habyarimana government, but with no apparent effect either on the behavior of the government or the attitudes of the international community, which, in general, continued to support his regime.

Rwandan human rights groups, encouraged by foreign donors to collaborate more effectively, formed a coalition known as the Comité de Liaison des Associations de Défense des Droits de l'Homme au Rwanda (CLADHO) in September 1992. They then turned the tables on the foreigners by pushing them, too, to operate in a more cohesive fashion. At the end of 1991, Rwandan human rights activists badgered and cajoled international human rights organizations to mount a joint inquiry into abuses in Rwanda, an idea originally proposed by Belgian lawyer Eric Gillet during a mission to Rwanda in August 1991. The activists argued that a group investigation carried out jointly by several organizations and several nationalities would have greater credibility than a series of smaller missions. The international organizations hesitated, perhaps from reluctance to depart from past practice or from concerns about territoriality. But in the end, only one major association, Amnesty International, refused the request.

By late November 1992, Rwandan persistence paid off with the agreement of four associations to organize the inquiry: Human Rights Watch, the International Federation of Human Rights Leagues, the International Center for Human Rights and Democratic Development, and the Interafrican Union of Human and Peoples' Rights. The organizers then moved rapidly, selecting participants, defining the terms of their mandate, and putting the investigators in the field by the first week of January 1993. The Rwandan government, anxious to preserve its still favorable image within the international community, openly welcomed the commission but, at the same time, punished and sought to intimidate those willing to assist in the investigation. In the worst such case, officials incited an attack that resulted in the death of the father of a young man who had helped the commission locate a mass grave.

The commission required no administration beyond that already existing within the sponsoring NGOs. Financed by two Belgian coalitions of NGOs that worked primarily in development, it demonstrated the possibilities of collaboration between such groups and NGOs specializing in human rights. The commission cost about $65,000, a modest sum for a two-week mission that gathered substantial amounts of data and excavated mass graves. The team of ten, including experts in different disciplines from eight nations, rapidly produced a report that was published six weeks after it left Rwanda. Commission members had been told that massacres that had begun just before their arrival had been interrupted during their stay but would resume when they left. In fact, the massacres did begin again just hours after their departure, lending great urgency to their publication of the results of the investigation.[3]

The report concluded that President Habyarimana and members of his government had engaged in acts of genocide by massacring Tutsi simply because they were Tutsi. It called for an end to violence and insisted that the Rwandan government dissolve the militia groups that were playing an increasingly important role in the killings. It further recommended that donor nations condition future aid upon a halt to the slaughter and other abuses, and upon the prosecution of those accused of the crimes.

Since the beginning of the war, most local NGOs had focused on documenting the abuses of the Rwandan government. The commission, however, also reported on human rights violations by the RPF and underscored the problems faced by some 350,000 people displaced by the war.

The commission attracted considerable attention when it presented its report in Brussels and in Paris in March 1993. It was able to provide several European television stations with dramatic film footage of mass graves. But the attention was also due to the credibility and visibility of an international undertaking jointly backed by major human rights organizations.

As Rwandan activists had foreseen, such a commission had greater impact than did the sum of the parts that had created it. Members of the commission who presented its results to European and North American governments noted that they had been received more quickly and at higher levels than during previous visits when they had represented only their individual organizations. In many cases, the officials had already read the commission's report and accepted its conclusions.

The Belgian government recalled its ambassador for discussions concerning the abuses, while the United States expressed grave concern about the extent of the violations documented in the report. Because of the human rights violations involved, as well as for several other reasons, the United States cut funds allocated to Rwanda and redirected much of its remaining aid through NGOs rather than through the government itself. The European Parliament and the Assemblée Paritaire ACP-CEE, the legislative body of the European Economic Community, condemned and called for a halt to the abuses described in the report. The United Nations Human Rights Commission declined to consider the report in open session, supposedly because it already had too many African nations on its list of violators. However, its Special Rapporteur on Extra-judicial, Summary, and Arbitrary Executions conducted his own inquiry, and published a report that confirmed most of the findings of the international commission and warned of the need for corrective action to avert further loss of life.[4]

The report of the commission reinforced the increasingly effective work being done by NGOs to publicize violence in Rwanda. In the preceding year, for example, as the four human rights groups constituting CLADHO became more experienced, they succeeded in getting more information published and in attracting more attention from the local diplomatic community. Activists were even able to persuade members of several embassies to accompany them into the field, where attacks on Tutsi were taking place. They and other local NGOs and church groups had issued declarations (13 March 1992; 17 September 1992; 16 November 1992; 8 December 1992; and 29 January 1993), both on their own and in cooperation with international humanitarian or developmental NGOs, documenting the violence within the country.

Information reported from embassies to their home governments, combined with the report of the international commission, provided European and North American governments with a clear, well-documented account of violence against Tutsi and others. These accounts focused on documenting past and current abuses rather than on warning of future catastrophe, but they made clear that the violence was certainly not going to diminish without strong pressure on the extremists who were then directing Rwandan government policy.[5]

Because foreign governments were taking the commission's March 1993 report seriously, the Rwandan government was obliged to take it seriously as well. It issued a statement admitting that grave human rights violations had taken place, although it disavowed any deliberate intent to kill Tutsi. In an attempt to improve its image, the government also surreptitiously sponsored the publication of a document contesting the commission report, purportedly by a group of new local human rights NGOs. It sent a delegation to Europe to present its findings to the press and government officials. In the months immediately following the publication of the international commission's report, the violence against Tutsi and Hutu of the political opposition diminished markedly, probably because the Habyarimana regime wished to avoid further international criticism.[6]

The one government that refused publicly to credit the information provided by the international commission was France. A firm supporter of

Habyarimana for years, France had replaced Belgium, the former colonial power, as the chief patron of his regime. France kept hundreds of troops in Rwanda, supposedly to protect French citizens and to train Rwandan troops, and quickly responded to the Rwandan cry for help when the RPF invaded. In fact, some of the French soldiers "advised" the Rwandans in a way indistinguishable from commanding them, even in battle.

France also served as one of the chief arms suppliers for the Rwandan government. In February 1993, the RPF violated a cease-fire, asserting the need to force the Rwandan government to halt the massacres of Tutsi that had begun with the departure of the international commission. In response, France significantly increased its military aid, including sending heavy weaponry, other arms, and more soldiers. Unwilling to call into question the virtues of its client, France dismissed the international commission report as "mere rumor."[7]

In private, however, the leading adviser on African affairs to French President François Mitterand agreed that the Habyarimana government had committed serious human rights abuses and that a way had to be found to end the war.[8]

With the RPF attack in February 1993, hundreds of thousands of people fled their homes in the northern part of Rwanda. What had been a serious but still manageable problem of assisting 350,000 internally displaced persons now swelled to a far more critical one of caring for about 1 million people, or one-seventh of the total population of Rwanda. The International Red Cross warned of impending disaster.

In the face of the renewed war and build-up of arms, the Rwandan government's abuses, a collapsing economy, and the crushing burden of feeding the displaced, the donor nations redoubled their efforts to end the conflict. Even France joined the other donor nations and the World Bank to issue an ultimatum requiring the Rwandan government to sign a peace treaty with the RPF or face a complete cancellation of foreign assistance.

The Rwandan government and the RPF signed the Arusha Accords on 4 August 1993, bringing to an end the first phase of the Rwandan crisis. The major foreign players relaxed, prepared to enjoy the fruits of their strenuous efforts to negotiate a settlement: They equated signing the Accords with averting the impending crisis.[9]

Almost immediately, it became clear that Habyarimana would do his best to avoid implementing the agreement. He maneuvered skillfully to create divisions in two of the major political parties opposed to him, a task facilitated by personality conflicts and opportunism among politicians in those parties. He then parlayed this division into a series of delays for installing the transitional government provided for in the Accords. The RPF and other political parties also occasionally created obstacles to implementing the Accords. But it was the Habyarimana forces who profited from the delays, using the time to consolidate opposition to the Accords and to organize their striking force for grassroots violence.

As the slow process of implementing the Accords dragged on, the president of neighboring Burundi was assassinated, an event that heightened fears and hatreds in Rwanda. A near twin to Rwanda in its demographics and colonial experience, Burundi had nonetheless experienced a very different political history since independence. Until June 1993, the Tutsi minority had retained control of the political, military, and economic systems, but then had apparently acceded to a peaceful handover of authority following the free and fair election of Melchior Ndadaye, a Hutu, as president. The illusion of a peaceful transition was shattered on 21 October 1993, when a group of extremist Tutsi soldiers removed Ndadaye from his residence and killed him in cold blood at their military camp. In the weeks immediately after, Hutu killed thousands of Tutsi, both to avenge Ndadaye and to assert their determination to retain the political control won in the election. The army responded by brutal repression, killing both Hutu who had participated in the massacres and others clearly innocent of such crimes. In the face of a death toll in the tens of thousands, the international community did nothing. In Rwanda, Hutu and Tutsi alike viewed the carnage across the border as a warning of what could happen to them should people of the other group launch a slaughter. In addition, Rwandans of both groups took note of the international reluctance to intervene to protect civilians from massive attack. Hard-line Hutu used the example of the Tutsi betrayal of Ndadaye to persuade waverers that Tutsi could not be trusted to participate in a democratic sharing of power.

The United Nations moved with its accustomed slowness to assemble and send the peacekeeping force that was to help implement the Accords. Its presence was essential to installing the transitional government. Although the UN had supposedly begun organizing for the force sometime before the Accords were signed, UN troops did not begin dribbling into Rwanda until late November 1993, thus affording hard-liners considerable time to foment opposition to the Accords.[10]

The force was not only late in coming, but was also weak, both in its mandate and in its numbers. Several key provisions of the Accords which delegated responsibility to the peacekeepers were diluted before the Security Council finally authorized the force on 5 October. A provision in the Accords that mandated the force to "guarantee overall security of the country" was reduced in scale, and then in authority, to permit it only to "contribute to the security of the city of Kigali inter alia within a weapons-secure area established by the parties in and around the city." The Accords provided that the force would "assist in tracking of arms caches and neutralization of armed gangs throughout the country" and would "assist in the recovery of all weapons distributed to, or illegally acquired by, the civilians." In the final mandate, these provisions were completely eliminated. A provision for assisting with the providing of security for civilians was, in an intermediate version, transformed into a responsibility for monitoring the security situation through "verification and control" of the gendarmerie and communal police. In the final version, however, it became merely a mandate to "investigate and report on incidents regarding the activities of the gendarmerie and police." Similarly, although some UN experts had initially recommended a force of 8,000 troops, the Security Council approved only about 2,500. In addition, because of budgetary constraints, the force would never be fully equipped and, despite repeated requests from the field, lacked such essentials as armored personnel carriers and ammunition.[11]

Apparently many of the major players in the Security Council were anticipating an easy success with a Rwandan peacekeeping force, one that could help remove the disgrace of the Somali operation. They hoped to obtain success relatively inexpensively as well, a strategy which would, in the end, prove fatal for some of the peacekeepers as well as for untold numbers of Rwandans.

Just after the Arusha Accords were signed, a group of persons close to Habyarimana, including his wife, organized a private radio station, Radio Television Libre des Mille Collines (RTLM), and put it under the direction of Ferdinand Nahimana, formerly head of the national radio. (He had been responsible for false news reports that had incited Hutu to massacre Tutsi in March 1992.) In August 1993, RTLM began broadcasts that vilified the RPF and those people within Rwanda thought to support them. The broadcasts became increasingly virulent after the October assassination of Ndadaye. As the crescendo of hate broadcasts peaked through the final months of 1993 and early 1994, RTLM began identifying individuals as traitors to the country and calling for them to be destroyed. Diplomats were well aware of the RTLM incitements to violence and reported on them to their home governments.[12]

Militia attached to the political parties of Habyarimana and his supporters attacked Tutsi in a number of communities after Ndadaye's assassination, in one case killing thirty-seven people. That the militia were
undergoing military training at several remote military camps was
common knowledge. In rural areas, guns were distributed to supporters
of the regime, while in the capital, young men armed with grenades
strolled the streets. Unidentified assailants tried to kill several judges and
a leading human rights activist in September and November 1993.

In a series of statements, press releases, and letters to authorities,
Rwandan and international NGOs decried current violence as well as the
preparations for further killings. On 8 December 1993, for example,
CLADHO wrote to the diplomatic representatives in Kigali and to the
head of the UN peacekeeping force. After describing some of the
instances of violence that had recently taken place, they asked specifically that the militia be disarmed and that the media that incited people
to violence be curbed. The Conseil de Concertation des Organisations
d'Appui aux Initiatives de Base (CCOAIB), a coalition of Rwandan
NGOs for development, repeated these requests in a 17 December press
release. On 28 December, the Bishop of Nyundo and the clergy of his
diocese asked authorities to explain why arms were being distributed to
some parts of the population. Throughout violent street demonstrations
in January 1994, and following the assassination of two important politicians and further killings in the capital at the end of February, local and
international NGOs multiplied their statements of concern and warnings.
The last in the series of these public calls for help came at the end of
March, just days before the beginning of the genocide.[13]

Seeing that their warnings were not attracting a great deal of attention,
Rwandan and international NGOs discussed sending a second international commission to emphasize the seriousness of the situation. The
strategy of using a multinational group of NGO representatives to signal
a crisis had already been adopted in Burundi, where local NGOs had
appealed for an international NGO inquiry into the assassination of President Ndadaye and the massacres that had followed. The two organizations most involved in the original Rwandan commission, Human Rights
Watch and the International Federation of Human Rights Leagues, had
led a commission to Burundi in November 1993 and January 1994.
Struggling to complete the publication of the Burundi report, these organizations agreed in principle to another mission to Rwanda but were
unable to carry it out before the genocide began. Thus, throughout the

second phase of the crisis, there was no central focus to dramatize NGO warnings. Nor was there any catastrophic event like the displacement of hundreds of thousands of people, which had predisposed the press and public to pay attention during the first phase. It is harder to attract notice for impending catastrophes than for disasters currently unfolding, particularly when those predicting a future crisis cannot provide a specific starting date. Finally, Rwanda was no longer in the limelight. The international community seemed to believe that Rwanda's problem had apparently been solved by the Arusha Accords, and those interested in Africa were looking at Burundi, or even more, at South Africa, where elections were about to take place.

While NGOs felt that their warnings were going unheeded, they did not know that their message was being reinforced and amplified for policymakers through information from confidential, official sources. Jacques-Roger Booh-Booh, the Special Representative of the UN Secretary-General, arrived to take up his post in Kigali at the end of October, just after the assassination of the president of Burundi. Almost immediately, he reported to the Secretary-General that the forces opposed to implementing the Arusha Accords were strong, well organized, and well armed.

On 11 January 1994, General Romeo Dallaire, the Canadian commanding officer of the UN forces in Rwanda, telegraphed a more detailed warning to his superiors in New York. He had been informed about a possible resumption of "hostilities," should the current political blockage end and the transitional government actually be installed. As observers had often commented, the killing of Tutsi and moderate Hutu accompanied deadlines for political action with such regularity as to be virtually predictable. Dallaire had obtained his information from a Rwandan military officer who had been involved in training the militia but who had decided that he could no longer participate, given that their real purpose was to kill Tutsi rather than to oppose a RPF advance, as he had once supposed. He described to Dallaire both the training of the militia and the location of caches of arms. He informed Dallaire that militia groups stationed throughout the capital city would be able to kill 1,000 Tutsi every twenty minutes. Based on the credibility of the person who had brought the informant to him and on his own verification of some of the information, Dallaire asked permission to conduct a raid, remove the arms, and arrange protection for the informant. General Maurice Baril, his superior in New York, refused permission on both counts, apparently within hours of receipt of the telegram. It appears that the proposed action was immediately deemed to be beyond the mandate and was not even submitted to the Security Council for consideration.[14]

Dallaire knew that arms were continuing to flow into the capital in violation of the Arusha Accords. He intercepted one delivery of munitions from France in late January, and soon after, prohibited two other planes that were bearing arms from landing at Kigali airport. In February and March, Dallaire tried at least three more times to get permission from his superiors to confiscate arms, but was turned down each time. As tension increased following the assassinations and violence in February, Dallaire asked that his original force of some 2,500 troops be supplemented by an additional 150 soldiers, a request that he repeated in mid-March. Again the answer was "no."[15]

Others both inside and outside the UN understood the reality of the threat. At the end of January, the Special Representative of the Secretary-General told a group of African diplomats that militia were being trained and arms distributed widely throughout the country. Several weeks later, a Belgian officer with the UN troops complained to the press that the restrictive mandate made it impossible to confiscate the stockpiles of arms that were being built up.

Leo Delcroix, the Belgian Minister of Defense, was kept well informed by Belgian military intelligence in Kigali. One dispatch, dated 2 March 1994, reported that Habyarimana's political party had just finished drawing up a plan to "exterminate the Tutsi on all the hills of Rwanda." Other dispatches revealed efforts to draw up lists of all the Tutsi in Kigali and to establish a system of communication involving telephones and such methods as calls and whistles in order to keep all units within the city in touch with each other.[16] Presumably, U.S. authorities were informed of the disturbing information known to their UN and Belgian colleagues. Whether drawing on this information or other sources, a CIA expert produced, in January 1994, three scenarios of possible outcomes if current developments were to continue unchecked. The worst of the three predicted violence that would take half a million lives. The document was circulated within some U.S. government channels but was not widely distributed otherwise.[17] The final warning of what was to come took place on the evening of 4 April. At a celebration for the Senegalese national holiday, Colonel Theoneste Bagosora, a highly placed official at the Defense Ministry, told other guests that the Arusha Accords were finished and that the Tutsi would soon be completely eliminated from Rwanda.[18]

At the time, NGOs could not have known to what extent their warnings had been confirmed and expanded by confidential information. Had they known what government officials knew, they would have understood that they were needed less to provide warnings than to pressure policy-makers to act responsibly in face of the warnings. Judging from what happened once the genocide began, however, it is reasonable to conclude that even armed with full knowledge and prepared to collaborate to the maximum in lobbying efforts, NGOs would have, at that time, fallen short of obtaining significant changes in the policy of individual donor nations or of the UN as a whole.

For the UN and the nations determining its policy to have acted more vigorously to avert tragedy would have required both a capacity and a will that did not exist during this second phase of the crisis. Because the UN peacekeeping force was small, poorly equipped, and burdened with a mandate so limited that it could do little other than react to events, enlarging this capacity, either in material terms or in terms of mandate, would have required considerable will. That will was as absent in the early months of 1994 as it had been in October 1993, when the force had been created. The major actors were preoccupied with events elsewhere in the world. Rwanda was not a priority issue for any of them, except perhaps for France, and because of France's prior links with the Habyarimana regime, it was ill placed to advocate forceful intervention. Unwilling to act, policy-makers found many excuses for ignoring warnings: The warnings had not been substantiated, they were too vague, or they were not credible.

As the delays for installing the transitional government continued and the warnings of potential violence multiplied, various foreign officials began to take notice. Delcroix was sufficiently worried after a visit to Rwanda in March to appeal to UN authorities to enlarge the mandate for its peacekeepers.[19] Rather than take such a positive action, however, decision-makers at the UN decided instead to threaten the parties with the withdrawal of the peacekeepers on 5 April, the expiration of their mandate, unless progress was made in installing the transitional government. It is hard to see how carrying out the threat would have improved the situation, but, in fact, it was not carried out. The mandate was renewed, although for a shorter term of four months, despite the fact that there had been no real movement in the political situation. A last "solemn appeal" by the diplomats resident in Kigali and the Secretary-General to implement the peace accords failed. Clearly, the situation had gone too far for threats or appeals to have any effect.

The early warnings were to no avail: The genocide began after the plane crash on 6 April 1994. In the midst of catastrophe, members of both local and international NGOs in Rwanda scrambled to save lives, those of others as well as their own. Many fled the country. They did continue to gather and disseminate data obtained through brief and anxiety-laden telephone conversations with colleagues, clergy, or friends who remained behind, but they were generally—though inadequately— supplanted by journalists as sources of information. In part to correct the distortions introduced by poor journalism, personnel of NGOs assumed new importance as analysts and interpreters of the situation. Not all of them excelled in this role: Some were too traumatized to speak convincingly; others, foreigners who been in the country only briefly or who had served largely in technical capacities, were not possessed of a broad or sophisticated view of Rwandan society. Several, however, helped to shape the attitudes of the press, the public, and policy-makers.

Journalists initially depicted the killing in Rwanda as a savage tribal war based on age-old antagonisms—one more round in a bitter conflict that would no doubt continue indefinitely. Whether from ignorance, laziness, or lack of time, they wrote from their personal predispositions rather than from accurate data. NGO representatives invested hours of persistent, if not patient, effort in educating journalists and trying, through them, to teach the public that the tragedy in Rwanda was a genocide that demanded international action.

Profound analysis, however, was not always to the taste of the journalists. One NGO representative took an hour from a crowded schedule to discuss the Rwandan situation in depth with a journalist from a national TV news program. The next day the journalist telephoned to apologize for having dropped the entire segment. They had, she said, just gotten in the most wonderful film of a decapitation from Rwanda and had used that instead. Press coverage that maximized the sensational aspects of the slaughter, in most instances, had the undesirable effect of so sickening and discouraging the public as to diminish any sentiment for intervention. NGO representatives were more certain of sending the appropriate message when they published their own articles or opinion pieces.

Policy-makers, of course, had access to other sources of information and should have understood better what was happening in Rwanda. But a substantial number of the Security Council members, perhaps misled by faulty reporting within the UN bureaucracy, accepted the slaughter as simply a revival of the war between the RPF and the Rwandan government. Drawing from inaccurate information, spooked by ghosts of other African catastrophes—particularly that of Somalia—afraid of further losses after the killing of ten Belgian peacekeepers, and unwilling to commit further resources to what appeared a hopeless situation, members of the Security Council voted on 21 April to withdraw most of the peacekeepers, leaving only a token force in place.

In the midst of this rush to desert Rwanda, Monique Mujyawamariya, a native Rwandan already well known outside Rwanda, served as a most effective lobbyist for the contrary policy. Already established authorities on Rwanda by virtue of several years of detailed reporting on human rights abuses there, Mujyawamariya and representatives of Human Rights Watch presented their interpretation of the situation to leading diplomats at the UN as well as to the U.S. National Security Advisor and his staff, to high-ranking officials at the State Department, and to influential members of Congress. In Europe, Mujyawamariya joined with representatives of other Rwandan and international NGOs in making the rounds of European officials.

Beginning in mid-April, several NGOs that had had no prior formal links—including Human Rights Watch, Amnesty International, the U.S. Committee for Refugees, Refugees International, Doctors without Borders, and Oxfam—exchanged information and coordinated strategies for lobbying. In Europe, the important coalition of NGOs for development, known as EUROSTEP, disseminated information and facilitated collaboration among its members in lobbying for action in Rwanda. Human Rights Watch also circulated a memo among European colleagues proposing a strategy to increase public attention to the genocide and to maximize simultaneous pressure on a number of governments for a coherent and effective policy.

NGOs like Human Rights Watch and Amnesty International were the first to call the Rwandan tragedy "genocide." They were influential in obliging numerous governments to admit that genocide was taking place. Together with the press, they ridiculed the U.S. government's refusal to use the term and pushed government officials toward accepting not just the word but also the moral and legal obligations implied by the term. At an emergency meeting of the UN Human Rights Commission at the end of May 1994, Rwandan and international NGOs were permitted to take the floor. Through their concrete and impassioned pleas, they introduced a sense of the reality of the Rwandan horror into two days of otherwise arid rhetoric by professional diplomats. Through these presentations and behind-the-scenes lobbying, they also were influential in securing the commission's decision to appoint a special rapporteur to investigate whether, in fact, genocide was taking place. His report, submitted the following month, concluded that there had been a genocide in Rwanda and called for an international tribunal to judge its perpetrators.

As the casualties mounted to 100,000, and as the first massive outpouring of refugees to Tanzania indicated that the catastrophe could destabilize the entire region, policy-makers began to reconsider their decision to pull out. At this point, representatives of NGOs redoubled their lobbying efforts and contacts with the press to attempt to shape the size of the new peacekeeping force and its mandate. Once a moderately satisfactory decision had been adopted by the Security Council, NGOs still had weeks of work before the necessary steps were taken to send the troops on their way. Human Rights Watch, for example, played a major role in publicizing the delays in the American delivery of fifty armored personnel carriers thought to be essential for transporting the troops within Rwanda.[20]

With the victory of the RPF and the establishment of the new government of Rwanda in July 1994, the third phase of the Rwandan crisis—the genocide—was ended. Even before that point, officials of several governments as well as NGO leaders began calling for an international tribunal to try those accused of organizing the genocide. Although everyone seemed to feel that it was an excellent idea, few have given it the financial or political support it needs to operate efficiently. NGOs specializing in human rights have been the most vociferous in demanding aid for the tribunal, but other NGOs have also insisted on the importance of bringing the guilty to justice. In the future, NGOs may have a role to play in insisting that national governments deliver indicted persons to the tribunal for trial or in obliging national governments themselves to bring to trial accused persons who have sought refuge on their territories.

International NGOs have continued to monitor activities of the authorities of the former Rwandan government now in refugee camps in Zaire, Tanzania, or Burundi. They have documented arms flows to the region and other preparations for renewed war. They have also reported on human rights violations by the new government, arguing that continued insecurity in Rwanda makes the return of the refugees unlikely and thus prolongs instability in the region. Several observers have called for the creation of a new NGO international commission to examine charges of killings and other serious human rights abuses against the current government.

Overwhelmed by the loss of life in the Rwandan genocide, government officials and NGOs alike have stressed the importance of trying to use early warning and preventive diplomacy more effectively in neighboring Burundi, where massive slaughter of civilians has occurred in the past and threatens to happen again in the near future. Such a catastrophe could well spill over national borders into Rwanda and Zaire, putting at risk millions of persons. Local NGOs summoned an international NGO commission to report on the 1993 violence and to make proposals for interrupting the cycle of killing. With a strong insistence on ending the impunity given to killers, the commission recommended international aid to the Burundian judicial system, some of which has been delivered. The Security Council sent its own commission of inquiry to Burundi in late 1995, aiming to gather material needed for prosecuting those responsible for earlier violence. In addition, national governments, the UN, and a number of NGOs have sent missions to Burundi, each hoping to ease the tensions. Despite all this international attention, the situation has not improved. Although Burundi has not known large-scale slaughter since 1993, hundreds of its citizens are killed each month.

In the first days of 1996, the Secretary-General appealed to the Security Council to create a rapid response force to be stationed in Zaire, ready to move into Burundi should massive killings begin there. The Security Council showed no more enthusiasm for the proposal this time than it did when the idea had first been proposed some months before. Although the risk of greater slaughter is well known to government officials and NGOs concerned about the region, the Burundian crisis has received little coverage in the press and is consequently little known by the general U.S. public. Were there widespread pressure for halting the killing and averting disaster, officials would certainly be more ready to intervene in a more decisive fashion than they were during the previous crises.

During a meeting in April 1994 with U.S. National Security Advisor Anthony Lake, the Human Rights Watch representative asked what NGOs could do to be more effective in taking action to halt the genocide. His answer was: "Make more noise." That should be the central lesson of the Rwandan crisis for NGOs.

In the first phase of the Rwandan crisis, NGOs made noise on their own and through the international commission, with sufficient volume to reach not just officials but also the press and the general public in Europe. Coinciding with the resumption of open warfare and the displacement of hundreds of thousands of persons, NGOs' warnings helped to spur policy-makers toward a new determination to end the war and halt violence against civilians.

In the second phase, NGOs multiplied their warnings of imminent disaster, but because they lacked any special focus, such as an international commission, to highlight their information, the impact of their warnings was dissipated. They received little attention from the press or the public. At this stage, however, policy-makers knew enough from their own sources not to need NGO warnings. Despite knowing about the risk of a massive slaughter of civilians, however, the major players took no steps toward action. They had designed a peacekeeping force that was not strong enough to deal with a resumption of hostilities, and they had saddled it with a mandate that restricted it from taking any meaningful initiatives. The same interests—or lack of interests—that had led them to settle on this half-hearted attempt to keep the peace still prevailed in early 1994. NGO warnings would have been most useful in obliging policy-makers to act, but to win such a major change in policy would have required widespread press attention and public pressure—exactly what was lacking.

In the third phase, through lobbying and contacts with the press, NGOs were instrumental in changing the interpretation of the Rwandan catastrophe from that of another round of tribal civil war to that of genocide. Certainly this change was fundamental to the decision to send UN troops back to Rwanda. Extensive public interest would have been particularly helpful in persuading political leaders to act more rapidly to halt the genocide. Unfortunately, many of the NGOs interested in Rwanda, like Human Rights Watch, lacked the kind of popular constituency needed to mobilize broad-based pressure on decision-makers. Others with a larger outreach, mostly the humanitarian NGOs, used their resources to raise money for the victims rather than to organize the letter-writing and telephoning campaigns that would have influenced government leaders.

In the fourth phase, NGOs are active in 1996 in trying to ensure that justice is achieved, an indirect but perhaps ultimately effective means of deterring others who may consider launching a massive campaign of slaughter of civilians. Having emerged with enhanced credibility from the first phases of the crisis in Rwanda, NGOs are being looked to for information on the current situation, both in Rwanda and in the refugee camps.

Whether their future warnings—if they are needed—will have any greater impact than those delivered in the past will depend on how well they make noise. From the Rwandan experience, NGOs should learn that:

— an international group speaks with a louder voice than a group from a single nation;

— collaboration between and among organizations—even across national borders—can be successfully organized on a temporary basis with relatively little cost;

— NGOs without large constituencies should seek to enlist mass-based organizations in advocating action in crises.

Information alone is not enough to move governments to act. They must see an interest in acting, and that interest is best brought home to them by a combination of well-informed NGOs, the press, and a concerned and organized public.

Notes

1. Human Rights Watch/Africa, "Rwanda: Talking Peace and Waging War, Human Rights Since the October 1990 Invasion," *News from Africa Watch* (27 February 1992).

2. Association Rwandaise pour la Défense des Droits de la Personne et des Libertés Publiques, *Rapport sur les Droits de l'Homme au Rwanda* (Kigali, 1992), 12–38, 57–58.

3. Africa Watch, Federation Internationale des Droits de l'Homme, Centre International des Droits de la Personne et du Developpement Democratique, Union Interafricaine des Droits de l'Homme et des Peuples, *Report of the International Commission of Investigation on Human Rights Violations in Rwanda since 1 October 1990* (Paris, 1993).

4. Human Rights Watch/Africa, "Beyond the Rhetoric, Continuing Human Rights Abuses in Rwanda," *News from Africa Watch* (June 1993).

5. Association Rwandaise pour la Défense des Droits de la Personne et des Libertés Publiques, *Rapport sur les Droits de l'Homme au Rwanda* (Kigali, 1993), 159–164.

6. Human Rights Watch, "Beyond the Rhetoric," 20–22.

7. Stephen Smith, "France-Rwanda: levirat colonial et abandon dans la r(gion des Grands Lacs," in Andre Guichaoua (ed.), *Les Crises Politiques au Burundi et au Rwanda* (Lille, 1995), 447–453; Human Rights Watch Arms Project, "Arming Rwanda, the Arms Trade and Human Rights Abuses in the Rwandan War" (January 1994).

8. Interviewed at Human Rights Watch, Washington, D.C., January 1994.

9. Alison Des Forges, "Face au Genocide: Une Réponse Désastreuse des Etats-Unis et des Nations Unies," in Guichaoua, *Les crises politiques,* 455–464.

10. Des Forges, "Face au Genocide," 455–464.

11. Compare articles B1, 3, and 4 of the Arusha Accords with articles 3a and 3h of the Security Council Resolution 872 of 5 October 1993; information from General Romeo Dallaire, Force Commander.

12. Colette Braeckman and Thierry Fiorilli, "Rwanda: le genocide se tramait et la Belgique savait . . .," *Le Soir* (10–12 November 1995).

13. Documents in the possession of the author.

14. Document in the possession of the author. "Falende VN-bureaukratie werd blauwhelmen fataal," *De Morgen* (7 November 1995), 6.

15. "Falende VN-bureaukratie werd blauwhelmen fataal"; information from General Romeo Dallaire.

16. Documents in the possession of the author.

17. Information from a highly placed U.S. official.

18. Braeckman and Fiorilli, "Rwanda: le genocide se tramait." Newspaper accounts report that this incident took place on 5 April; eyewitnesses indicate that it actually happened on 4 April.

19. Colette Braeckman, *Rwanda, Histoire d'un genocide* (Brussels, 1994), 207.

20. Des Forges, "Face au genocide," 458–461.

BURUNDI

CHAPTER TEN

Humanitarian Assistance and Conflict Prevention in Burundi

Richard A. Sollom and Darren Kew

MORE THAN HALFWAY through the 1990s, enthusiasm has waned over the capability of both NGOs and international organizations to address international systemic failures like the collapsing state of Burundi. As with their governmental counterparts, NGOs and international organizations initially found themselves approaching new problems with tools and perspectives shaped in the Cold War era. NGOs have generally adapted quickly—thus far achieving mixed results—while the United Nations and regional organizations have suffered both deserved and undeserved blame for setbacks in Somalia, Rwanda, Bosnia, and elsewhere. The United Nations now finds itself fighting for its financial life, and NGOs are soul-searching over their own roles in the conundrum of collapsing states and complex humanitarian emergencies.

We explore the role of NGOs and international organizations in Burundi since 1993, when the political assassination of President Melchior Ndadaye unleashed a devastating civil war. NGOs have increasingly assumed a quasi-governmental role in executing conflict prevention and resolution initiatives in Burundi, where recent tumultuous

The Council on Foreign Relations, with whom Kew was associated, takes no institutional position on policy issues, and this article is the sole responsibility of the authors. This paper benefited greatly from comments by Fabienne Hara, Barry Hume, and Charles Petrie.

events have posed complicated problems for NGOs and international organizations alike. We ask how a new partnership among NGOs and international organizations can provide an effective future mechanism capable of preventing violent ethnopolitical conflict, either in Burundi or elsewhere.

Through their attempts worldwide to fill the vacuum left by retrenching or collapsing governments, NGOs and international organizations increasingly find themselves in quasi-governmental roles. In practice, these organizations exercise significant de facto political authority in the host country. They participate in political negotiations, facilitate peace processes, and often unwittingly contribute to the resumption of conflict. They provide access to important international resources, bring a variety of pressures to bear on the parties to a conflict as well as on foreign governments, and are often viewed by the parties as partial to their rivals, or even as being political rivals themselves. Yet, neither governments nor NGOs have been willing to address the full implication of their new status.

While recent history has demonstrated that NGOs and international organizations have an important role to play in conflict prevention and resolution, no one has defined the parameters of that role. How must these organizations be held accountable, to whom and by whom? Do their funders decide their mission and mandate, do their staffs, or do the populations that ostensibly benefit from their work? From what sources do these organizations draw their legitimacy to pursue their agendas? On what do they base their claimed rights and prerogatives? What body of laws should regulate their conduct? Who decides when they should become involved and when they should terminate their initiatives?

Recent events in Burundi raise these questions more than they answer them. Conflict prevention and resolution efforts for the country, both internally and externally, however, provide a perspective on how organizations are beginning to address these overarching questions of governance.

The Ndadaye Assassination

A brief examination of the events since the assassination of Ndadaye in 1993, and the role that NGOs and international organizations have played since that time, illustrates the challenges of governance facing both domestic interests and the international community. The development of partnerships to coordinate conflict-prevention and peacebuilding efforts in Burundi may provide a model for a more coherent and efficient strategy toward political crises globally.

The people of Burundi ushered in a period of optimism on 1 June 1993, when 65 percent of the voters elected Ndadaye as president of their tiny East African country. This election marked not only the first time that a Hutu had held the office of president in a country long dominated by Tutsi political control, but also the first democratic election held in Burundi since it gained formal independence in 1962.

Yet, five months after the presidential election, the Burundi military (under Tutsi control) assassinated Ndadaye as well as the two highest-ranking members of Parliament who would have succeeded him. The assassination left Burundi without effective government and unleashed a three-week wave of killing outside the capital. Casualties numbered more than 50,000 among both Hutu and Tutsi ethnic groups; more than 280,000 people became displaced throughout most of the central and northern provinces of the country, and nearly 670,000 refugees fled across national borders to Rwanda, Tanzania, and Zaire.

The assassination marked the beginning of a period of great chaos in Burundi. In the succeeding months, internal civil unrest and political upheaval, coupled with the external influences of unpredictable movements of refugee populations, generated extraordinary instability. While the international community mobilized to assist the affected populace, the humanitarian challenges proved daunting. To this day, neither political moderates in Burundi nor the international community has managed to end the cycle of violence and the resulting civil war.

The Aftermath of the Assassination

Nearly three months elapsed before the National Assembly elected Cyprien Ntayamira, a Hutu member of the Front pour la démocratie au Burundi (FRODEBU) as Ndadaye's successor on 13 January 1994. Opposition leaders protested and organized strikes and demonstrations. When Ntayamira's government dissolved the Tutsi-dominated Constitutional Court on 29 January, Tutsi opposition leaders again took their grievances to the streets, resulting in violent protest and killings. The tumult subsided only in February, when FRODEBU leaders granted key ministerial posts to the opposition.

Response from the international community focused on providing humanitarian relief to the 1 million Burundians who had been dispersed and displaced within and outside their country. The predominantly Hutu populations who had hidden within rural areas of Burundi were referred to as "dispersed," and those largely Tutsi groups who had sought refuge in schools, in public buildings, and near military posts were referred to as "displaced." The Tutsi-dominated military protected the latter group, whereas the dispersed Hutu had no such security.

Governments, humanitarian NGOs, and UN agencies mobilized to assist the affected groups. Relief programs were mounted immediately to deliver emergency medical care for the wounded, led principally by the International Committee of the Red Cross (ICRC). Shortly thereafter, food aid programs were organized to assist the displaced who had been unable to grow their own crops, and the dispersed who had missed the planting season. The number of food aid recipients grew rapidly to more than 600,000 in early 1994, and reached 800,000 in May 1994. In response to the growing crisis, the number of NGOs in Burundi expanded from about ten to more than thirty.

Burundi again fell into a political tailspin when the plane carrying President Juvénal Habyarimana of Rwanda and President Ntayamira of Burundi was shot down on 6 April 1994. Burundi was once again left without effective leadership. The subsequent protracted political crisis was not resolved until 10 September 1994, when most political parties in Burundi signed a power-sharing agreement that granted opposition parties a check on the FRODEBU government. Known as the "Convention on Government," the agreement, in effect, amended the Constitution and established the following:

— Political institutions based on consensus, and the restoration of the state based on peace, security, trust, and the rule of law;
— The sharing of central and local government, each side being awarded a percentage of ministerial, diplomatic, and provincial posts;
— A government of twenty-five members whom the president appointed (55 percent from the presidential majority, FRODEBU, and the rest from the Tutsi opposition);
— The appointment of a prime minister representing the opposition, who countersigned all presidential decisions—thereby weakening the presidency;

— A ten-member National Security Council (equally divided between FRODEBU and the opposition parties) that deliberated on any matter it deemed important. This body assumed broad powers and consequently diminished the power of the National Assembly.[1]

The significant concessions granted to the opposition by the signing of the Convention incensed extremist Hutu factions. Léonard Nyangoma, leader of the Conseil national pour la défense de la démocratie (CNDD), declared war on the Tutsi-dominated army. Violence broke out in Kamenge and Kimana (predominantly Hutu suburbs of Bujumbura), where Tutsi military fought with Hutu militias for two days, killing at least sixty people.

The Tutsi-dominated Burundian military forcibly returned and executed scores of Rwandan Hutu refugees who had sought safety in Burundi during the summer months. But it was not until unknown assassins killed José Lopez Herera, a field officer for the United Nations High Commissioner for Refugees (UNHCR), along with a local leader in Kirundo, that the acute ethnic tensions throughout Burundi received worldwide attention. International humanitarian assistance increased in the following months, helping to stabilize the humanitarian situation. Nevertheless, violent unrest in Cibitoke Province, which borders Zaire and Rwanda, broke out between Hutu militias and the Burundian armed forces. Hundreds were killed, and tens of thousands of Hutu fled to Zaire by mid-October.

The National Assembly, by a vote of sixty-eight to one, elected Sylvestre Ntibantunganya (a Hutu who had been serving as interim president since the death of Ntayamira in April 1994) as Ntayamira's successor. The new president was officially sworn into office on 1 October 1994. Two days later, Anatole Kanyenkiko, a Tutsi, was confirmed as prime minister and formed a government of national unity. The situation in Burundi stabilized, but remained precarious.

In December, hundreds marched through the capital to protest the election of Jean Minani as the new speaker of the National Assembly; leaders of the Union pour le progrés national (UPRONA) accused Minani of inciting violence following the 1993 coup attempt. The government imposed a dusk-to-dawn curfew to quell rising violence in the capital. Despite the curfew, dozens of Hutu were killed in Bwiza, a predominantly Hutu suburb of Bujumbura. The crisis was resolved when the president announced that Minani would relinquish his post. Léonce

Ngendakumana, the Secretary-General of FRODEBU, was subsequently appointed speaker on 12 January 1995.

At the end of January, Charles Mukasi, UPRONA's chairman, called for strikes in Bujumbura and the overthrow of the government. In a strong show of disapproval, the UN Security Council immediately denounced his call to arms. One week later, a Burundian newspaper owned by Jean-Baptiste Bagaza, a former military-backed president, issued a statement threatening the lives of U.S. Ambassador Robert Krueger and UN Special Representative of the Secretary-General (SRSG) Ahmedou Ould Abdallah, and called for their immediate departures. A second round of strikes paralyzed the capital in mid-February, and the daily death toll rose.

In the meantime, the Organization of African Unity (OAU) and UNHCR co-hosted an important four-day regional conference on humanitarian assistance to central African refugees, returnees, and displaced persons. It was a strange irony that the participants at this conference bore live witness to very inhuman acts. Although housed in a secure facility in the center of the capital, the conference delegates were surrounded by the sounds of unrest—from the daily indiscriminate killing of Bujumbura townspeople by exploding grenades in the market to the nightly crackling of machine gun fire. Violence abounded.

As security worsened, Prime Minister Kanyenkiko resigned under pressure. Strikes brought on by a Tutsi-supported "ville morte" campaign continued, which paralyzed the capital. Two days following the close of the UNHCR-OAU conference in Bujumbura, UPRONA called off the seven-day strike when opposition leaders agreed on a new prime minister, Antoine Nduwayo, a Tutsi member of UPRONA, who took office on 23 February 1995.

Nduwayo immediately initiated a pacification program which called on all politicians to travel to the provinces and preach peace and reconciliation. Many villagers believed, however, that the politicians should be pacifying themselves, and the campaign yielded negligible results. In fact, violence throughout the country intensified during the spring of 1995, often inspired by political elites. In March, two prominent politicians, including Ernest Kabushemeye, the Minister for Energy and Mines, and Colonel Lucien Sakubu, former mayor of Bujumbura, were brutally assassinated. One week later, Hutu guerrillas mercilessly ambushed a caravan, killing three Belgian residents (including a four-year-old girl and her mother) and thirteen Burundians. A spate of reprisal killings of Hutu and Tutsi ensued in and around Bujumbura. In the worst violence since 1993, Tutsi military and militia massacred at least 150 people in the two predominantly Hutu neighborhoods remaining in Bujumbura. The UNHCR estimated that 23,500 fled the capital toward Zaire over the next two-day period.

In the northeast, 16,000 Burundians and 8,000 Rwandan Hutu refugees fled to Tanzania to escape military attacks during the same month. At the end of March 1995, Burundi's military killed twelve Rwandan Hutu refugees at Majuri camp (home to 30,000 refugees) in Ngozi province. At the same time, other Burundian military slaughtered up to 400 Burundian Hutu in nearby Muyinga Province—the single greatest massacre since the crisis had begun in October 1993. These two events incited an entire camp population of 40,000 Rwandan refugees to flee their first country of asylum for the safety of neighboring Tanzania. Following the initial cross-border movement, Tanzania closed its border with Burundi, leaving thousands of stranded Rwandan refugees in limbo. Some 8,700 eventually returned to northern Burundi on 2 April 1995. Two days later, in the same area, Tutsi militia attacked five UN World Food Program (WFP) trucks and allowed displaced Tutsi to unload the food onto Burundian army vehicles.

In April 1995, President Ntibantunganya appealed to the international community to augment diminishing food aid for the country's refugees and displaced persons. Killings throughout the country in the spring continued unabated. On 8 May 1995, a Greek expatriate aid worker with Catholic Relief Services (CRS) was killed in northern Kirundo Province. In protest, twenty-one Burundi-based international aid organizations suspended all but essential humanitarian assistance. One month later, residents from Bujumbura halted a twenty-five-truck WFP convoy transporting food to Hutu refugees in Zaire. They falsely accused the UN officials of trafficking arms to the refugees.

The reaffirmation by Burundi's president and prime minister of their commitment to the Convention on Government in June and their continued program on pacification could not dissipate violence throughout the country. Ntibantunganya announced a "non-state of emergency" in June 1995 to restore public order. His plans included extending the curfew nationwide, censoring the media, banning all political meetings, requiring internal travel permits, and establishing military governance in several provinces.

In spite of his steadfast attempts at governance, Ntibantunganya suffered a series of setbacks that further compromised his already circumscribed ability to govern. First, Foreign Minister Jean-Marie Ngende-hayo resigned, citing his disenchantment with a government unable to effect meaningful change. Second, in a very public display of frustration and no-confidence, the president's own political party accused him of appeasing the opposition—on the one hand by signing the Convention on Government and ceding political power to the Tutsi opposition, and, on the other hand, by granting the Tutsi-dominated military increased powers of governance through his proposed emergency plans. Third, following a fierce four-day debate on the president's emergency measures, the National Assembly rejected them. And one month later, nearly one-fourth of all sixty-five FRODEBU National Assembly members fled to Zaire after receiving death threats. Fourth, adding to the public message of no-confidence, UPRONA called for the dissolution of the National Assembly, accusing the government of obstructing efforts at peace. Finally, in June 1995, Tutsi military attacked a French aid convoy, killing one Burundian aid worker and injuring four others. In response to these killings, UN aid agencies suspended humanitarian operations, leaving Burundi not only without internal governance but also without external support.

Although humanitarian operations came to a halt, diplomatic efforts continued. Indeed, the international community dispatched a series of delegations to Burundi to bolster the middle ground against attacks from extremists on both sides trying to derail the coalition government. Both UN Secretary-General Boutros Boutros-Ghali and UN Special Rapporteur for Human Rights on Burundi Paulo Pinheiro visited in July.[2] In addition, the European Union (EU) and the OAU both sent delegations to the country, which resulted in EU member states' agreeing to pay to increase the number of OAU military observers in Burundi from forty-seven to sixty-five. Unfortunately, due to its restrictive mandate, the OAU Military Observation Mission to Burundi (MIOB) has since done little to quell violence and mainly serves as a symbolic gesture of support from the international community.

After two years of adept mediation to strengthen constitutional government among political parties in Burundi, Ould Abdallah resigned from his post in October 1995. His immediate successor, Moroccan diplomat Aziz Hasbi, did not remain long because of unmet demands on the United Nations, and he was quickly replaced by retired Canadian diplomat Marc Faguy, the UN Special Representative to Burundi in 1996. The EU, meanwhile, dispatched Aldo Aiello, its own special envoy.

Increased International Attention

Burundi came under increased scrutiny in the fall of 1995, when delegates from the International Commission of Inquiry, which the UN Secretary-General had proposed during his July 1995 mission to Burundi, arrived to investigate the October 1993 coup attempt and subsequent massacres.[3] The Commission's work was hampered by a lack of sufficient investigators and funding, and by travel difficulties because of security concerns. Its main objective, which proved difficult, was to obtain the requisite evidence related to the coup and presidential assassination.

Robert Krueger, the outspoken U.S. Ambassador, charged the Burundian military with the massacre of hundreds of Hutu civilians in the summer of 1995. He had lodged similar protests against the military in the past, which led to numerous death threats from the pro-Tutsi press. On this occasion, Gabriel Sinarinzi, UPRONA minister of the interior, protested vigorously against the allegations, while Paul Munyembari (FRODEBU), the new minister for foreign affairs, supported the ambassador's claims. Other ministers were more reticent in stating their position, and the government ground to a halt by September. To overcome the political impasse, the president and prime minister coordinated a dramatic reshuffling of cabinet posts and fired the two outspoken ministers. The precarious constitutional governance of Burundi withstood these changes, but the president's already weakened position vis-à-vis the opposition diminished even further.

By the fall of 1995, civil unrest throughout the country amounted to civil war. Fighting was most intense in the north, where, in some areas (for example, Cibitoke Province), the military prevented journalists and aid workers from entering. As a result, military attacks against Hutu militias as well as civilian and refugee populations went largely unreported. In a major victory in October 1995, the Burundi military captured a Hutu militia stronghold in Kibira forest, which borders Rwanda. About 2,500 Hutu fled to nearby Zaire and untold numbers were killed. In addition, the military massacred 253 Burundian civilians in the northern province of Ngozi—refuge to tens of thousands of Rwandan Hutu as well.

On the humanitarian front, NGOs providing relief to the Hutu refugees were increasingly pulled into the conflict. The Tutsi viewed many humanitarian agencies as being biased toward the Hutu, although many were giving aid to displaced Burundian Tutsi populations to safeguard their neutrality. Humanitarian organizations and their staff nonetheless continued to be targeted. In November 1995, ICRC trucks were ambushed, and a month later the NGO offices of ICRC, Oxfam, and Action internationale contre la faim (AICF) were all attacked.

Despite a mass exodus of Hutu from Bujumbura in March and April 1995, civil war continued in the capital throughout the summer and fall. The military launched a major attack on remaining Hutu settlements in Bujumbura in early December. The stepped-up operation included the use of helicopters and heavy artillery. Thousands of civilian Hutu fled to Zaire. In response, Hutu militias went on the offensive, targeting strategic electricity and water supply stations in Bujumbura in late 1995 and early 1996. The president managed to survive a three-day "ville morte" campaign in January designed by Tutsi to oust him. In the meantime, the number of political casualties continued to mount. Tutsi criminal gangs (for example, *sans échec* and *sans défaite*) were responsible for the assassinations of three FRODEBU politicians in December, and the governor of Ngozi was also assassinated. A second provincial governor resigned, citing his inability to prevent the military from killing innocent civilians.

As the spiraling civil war continued throughout the country, 30,000 Rwandan refugees fled Ntamba camp in late January 1996. While Tanzanian officials permitted some 14,000 refugees to enter Tanzania, others were turned back after the border was closed. In December 1995, 4,000 women (including the wives of the current president and prime minister and the wives of former presidents Pierre Buyoya and Ndadaye) flocked to the streets in the capital to demonstrate for peace.

To address the increased possibility of a protracted civil war in Burundi, the UN, the OAU, and the EU dispatched a series of delegations. Attracting the most attention, however, was a November 1995 summit in Cairo, to which none of these organizations was invited. Former U.S. President Carter convened heads of state from Burundi, Rwanda, Tanzania, Uganda, and Zaire to tackle the formidable humanitarian challenges that these states faced. A follow-up summit with the same heads of state took place in Tunis in March 1996, when regional leaders pledged mutual support and cooperation aimed at fostering an environment in which the current 1.7 million refugees could return home. The Tunis meeting also confirmed what the United Nations, the United States, and other governments had already determined—that former Tanzanian President Julius Nyerere had universal acceptance among both Burundians and the international community as the lead mediator for peace. Doing his best publicly to lower expectations of the outcome, Nyerere, in April 1996, began cautious discussions involving key Burundian parties to the conflict with the debilitating exception of the CNDD.

Pinheiro arrived in Burundi in December 1995, and argued that international inaction was tantamount to complicity in Burundi's ongoing civil war and attendant massacres. He proposed limited sanctions against Burundi, but the United Nations ignored his recommendations. Boutros-Ghali revived a 1995 proposal to place stand-by forces in Zaire in case genocidal violence broke out, which critics saw as a move in part to avoid future accusations of blame for failing to act, as in Rwanda.[4] Predictably, the Hutu government supported such intervention, while the Tutsi military and opposition regarded any initiatives involving foreign troops as an act of aggression against them.[5] The government also rejected another proposal to dispatch UN guards to protect aid agencies and UN personnel in Burundi. Nevertheless, a five-person UN delegation arrived in February 1996 to assess the feasibility of troop deployment.

Belgium later proposed the establishment of a "Eurocorps" to be stationed in Tanzania or Kenya, but EU member states were slow to respond. They did, however, agree to fund the deployment of UN human rights monitors to Burundi—a long-overdue, but welcome, initiative.[6]

Burundi in Early 1996

President Ntibantunganya presided over a frail coalition government. To achieve national stability, he agreed to a power-sharing agreement that effectively weakened the executive and legislative branches. Despite continued compromise, he was proving ineffectual in combating increasing civil unrest, and appeared to be held hostage by the military—the de facto power holder in Burundi. In turn, the 14,000-strong, predominantly Tutsi military remained under constant and growing attack by Hutu militias that operated inside and outside the country. Although it is highly unlikely that the military can ever win, they have vowed never to lose.

The outbreak of violence immediately following the October 1993 coup attempt cost more than 50,000 lives. The current civil war has shed an additional 10,000–15,000 lives during the last year alone, and in 1996, about 1,000 individuals were currently being killed each month. Heavily armed Burundian Hutu militias striking from Zaire and Tanzania have conducted cross-border raids into nearly every province and have attacked Burundi military and Tutsi internally displaced persons (IDPs) on a regular basis. In often disproportionate retaliation, Burundi's military has lashed out against densely populated Hutu populations where they assume militias have sought refuge. Countless civilians have been killed indiscriminately while being caught in the cross-fire. Those Burundians fortunate enough to survive, as well as Rwandan Hutu refugees in nearby camps, have fled en masse.

The Humanitarian and Political Challenge

The dynamic state of affairs in Burundi since 1993 makes it one of the most multi-faceted humanitarian challenges that the international community has ever encountered. It is a refugee-producing state, in that thousands of Hutu residents from Bujumbura have fled to Zaire (twenty kilometers away); equal numbers have fled to Tanzania from the northeastern provinces, and to Zaire from the northwestern provinces, following military and militia assaults. Burundi is also a refugee-receiving state. In 1994, thousands of Rwandan Hutu refugees fled to Burundi from their IDP camps in southern Rwanda (ostensibly protected by UN peacekeepers) after military advances by the Rwandan Patriotic Army.[7] Burundi has a sizable population of displaced Tutsi within its own borders as well as dispersed Hutu throughout the northern half of the country and in the capital. In addition, Zairians and a handful of other African nationals with individually determined refugee status have sought asylum in Burundi. The pace at which small and large groups of frightened individuals pour across Burundi's borders, and the constant ebb and flow of population displacements within the country vex even the most senior UN officials in the region.

To meet these challenges, the UN, and to a lesser extent the OAU, have led the international community's response to the events unfolding in Burundi. Whereas OAU initiatives have mainly concerned regional summits and conferences, the UN has initiated a two-pronged approach to the crisis. On the one hand, the UN has attended to the humanitarian crisis that spilled over into Burundi with the influx of tens of thousands of refugees fleeing civil war in neighboring Rwanda. On the other hand, the UN has begun to deal with the political crisis in Burundi to attenuate the possibility of another Rwanda-like scenario occurring there. The extent to which humanitarian action affects Burundi's political crisis is great. The converse also holds true.

NGOs have worked hand-in-hand with the UN to attend to the humanitarian challenges in Burundi. UNHCR sub-contracts to NGOs like CARE and Oxfam to administer the refugee camps, transport and distribute food, maintain potable water supplies, run orphanages, teach elementary school classes, train adults in a particular trade or craft, and staff hospitals. In short, without humanitarian NGOs, the UNHCR would be impotent. Partly in recognition of this reality, the UNHCR office in Bujumbura has held weekly meetings with the large humanitarian NGOs to whom it contracts in order to exchange general information and raise security concerns. Because of frequent information blackouts in the country, many other NGOs who have not contracted with UNHCR attend the meetings as well. UNHCR-Bujumbura also allows both its contracting and non-contracting NGOs to use UNHCR radio channels for communication.

The sine qua non of non-governmental humanitarian organizations is their neutrality and apolitical countenance vis-à-vis civil-war combatants. NGOs in Burundi have striven to be disinterested benefactors providing succor to victims on either side of the ethnopolitical divide. But NGOs now operate in a very politicized arena where their humanitarian relief assistance often ends up being traded on the open market—proceeds from which buy munitions that fuel the ongoing civil war.

Nonetheless, humanitarian agencies have residually contributed to conflict prevention in Burundi by alleviating potential crises that would assuredly erupt if the relief that they provide were not forthcoming.[8] The absence or even insufficiency of basic life-sustaining necessities such as food, shelter, and water would create fierce competition among refugees themselves and with host-country nationals. Indeed, NGOs were the first to realize in 1994 that providing relief assistance to incoming Rwandan refugees and not to similarly disadvantaged, displaced Burundian Tutsi populations living in proximity to the refugees would produce adverse consequences: Non-beneficiaries (for example, displaced Tutsi) would consider NGO field staff as being biased, and would begin attacking such staff. Potentially more destabilizing, non-beneficiaries would begin pillaging refugee camps where "foreigners" were receiving assistance. A scarcity of life-sustaining necessities engenders conflict between the haves and have-nots, and it behooves NGOs to assist both groups in need. Although beneficiaries of such aid often consider benevolence as a "right," this misconception does not obviate the positive effect that providing humanitarian relief has on preventing conflict.

Like humanitarian agencies, human rights organizations also have increasingly been asked to formulate strategies for conflict prevention in Burundi. The leading local indigenous human rights NGO, Ligue des droits de l'homme (ITEKA), has courageously monitored and reported on the worsening human rights situation in Burundi for some time. These reliable, balanced reports from Burundians of both ethnic groups contributed to the early warning of impending conflict in Burundi. At critical times, ITEKA helped prevent conflagrations from spiraling out of control by advocating calm among all political parties, militias, and civilian groups.

Although not an NGO per se, the UN Center for Human Rights maintains a small staff in Bujumbura. While the Center's limited mandate precludes investigation of reported violations, it has been able to educate Burundians about human rights. It has also coordinated school sporting events in which students from both ethnic groups participate. The Center's presence is more symbolic than substantive, but contributes in a small way to conflict prevention. More significantly, at the initiative and with the funding of the United States, additional human rights monitors were designated for Burundi in April 1996.

Projects and organizations which aim to foster conflict resolution among Burundians at large, or among specific segments of the population, have increased steadily since 1993. The Community of St. Egidio, International Alert, the National Democratic Institute, Parliamentarians for Global Action, and a number of churches have all run conferences, workshops, and reconciliation meetings within Burundi and outside the country (to which participants were shuttled) for Burundian parliamentarians, key government and opposition figures, and even leaders of resistance movements. The African-American Institute held conferences in Bujumbura on the role of a military in a democracy. Refugees International, while monitoring the displaced and refugee populations in Burundi, has focused on repatriation issues in Burundi and Rwanda, and assisted traditional Burundian peacemakers (the *abashingantahe*) in their mediation efforts among returnees, the displaced, and those remaining in the villages. Search for Common Ground has initiated a number of innovative projects, such as radio programming that promotes reconciliation, and conflict resolution training for journalists, clergy, and political leaders. It has also helped the Burundian NGO, Collectif des associations feminines, establish a women's movement for peace in Burundi.

Humanitarian Coordination and Conflict Prevention

Although individual initiatives abound on the part of NGOs and international agencies to promote conflict prevention and resolution within Burundi, cooperation on the ground has been limited. Beyond simple information exchanges, concerted efforts within Burundi to persuade NGOs to work strategically with the United Nations (UNHCR, the SRSG's office, and other UN agencies) on conflict prevention issues have largely been unsuccessful. The United Nations does not regularly avail itself of the vast resources and knowledge that humanitarian NGOs contain.[9]

The efforts of those NGOs already go well beyond relief assistance. NGO personnel work in the field and have daily contact with refugees, IDPs, and Burundian nationals. They are thus able to offer valuable information to UN staff who, because of their limited numbers, are not often the first to receive word of human rights violations, population displacements, military incursions, or even signs of imminent poor harvests. NGOs often provide UN officials with reliable data on such events that serve as an informal early warning mechanism. Sharing such valuable information, however, is conducted on an ad hoc basis, often as a result of personal relationships that UN officials maintain with NGO staff in the field.

Partnering with the United Nations can also be unpredictable at best for NGOs, or, at worst, counterproductive. True to its character, the UN often speaks with as many voices in the field as it does in the General Assembly in New York. Although the UNHCR office in Bujumbura cooperated with NGOs, at least in terms of information sharing and communication services, the agency's office in Uvira, Zaire, was unsympathetic to NGOs, if not perceived as under the influence of Zairian officials. Even UNHCR-Bujumbura is kept at a distance by many NGOs, as UNHCR's decision in late 1995, under pressure from Zaire and Tanzania to encourage refugee repatriation to Burundi and Rwanda, made every UNHCR field staff a "repatriation officer." UNHCR's relationship soured quickly with groups that viewed this move simply as *refoulement* (forced repatriation) with the High Commissioner's blessing.

Ould Abdallah's resistance to the stationing of UN human rights monitors; the WFP's phasing out of assistance to displaced Burundian Tutsi while the UNHCR maintained food levels for neighboring Rwandan Hutu refugees; the mixed signals from the Secretary-General on preparing troops to intervene in Burundi; and other actions by the UN all gave NGOs pause to view warily the possibility of any of the world body's agencies being a close partner.

Yet, even if the United Nations were more open to coordination and a more reliable partner, it is not clear that the NGOs themselves would agree to such arrangements. Beyond the weekly meetings under UNHCR auspices in Bujumbura, these organizations have resisted efforts—initiated both by UN staff and individual NGO field operatives—to develop a more coherent, cooperative strategy with targeted objectives. A frequent reason cited by NGOs in Burundi for avoiding coordination has been a fear for the security of their personnel. The deeply polarized climate of Burundi has made the maintenance of even a semblance of NGO neutrality extremely difficult, and association with other organizations could easily lead to accusations of favoritism toward Hutu or Tutsi, thus making an NGO a target of extremists from either side. A united front of NGOs would also attract greater Burundian public attention, which would again make it a more appealing target, especially to the Tutsi militias who want an end to the international presence in their country. Several aid workers have already been killed at the hands of militias from both sides.

Security concerns, however, are not the only source of NGO reluctance to submit to coordination efforts. Ould Abdallah even organized a meeting between many of the NGOs and the Burundian government to address security concerns, and a Burundian general was assigned to assist those organizations. The NGOs in question rejected the offer, citing concerns about perceptions of their neutrality. Certainly, association with the Tutsi-dominated army would have hampered NGO effectiveness in Hutu villages, but these organizations have not sought other alternatives. Some individual members of organizations have attempted to improve coordination, and after two months of negotiations, Médecins du Monde and several other groups were able to establish an NGO security committee in Bujumbura in mid-1995, although its intent to move beyond information exchange to more concerted planning remained elusive. These and similar collaboration attempts received little encouragement from NGOs.

The constitutions of most NGOs often work against strategic partnerships that involve goals beyond the limited scope of their functional mandates. They tend to be fiercely protective of their independence— often with good reason—and their problem-solving orientation naturally makes them focus on immediate demands. Humanitarian workers, for instance, work long, dangerous hours providing food and services to target populations. Planning ambitious strategies for preventing further escalation of the conflict and addressing questions of human rights monitoring can fall low on an overtaxed priority list. In addition, NGOs must demonstrate accomplishments to their donors. This pressure to maximize their performance and service output, when combined with their concern that decisions made in one country influence perceptions of projects elsewhere in the world, increases the reluctance of NGOs to engage in processes like conflict prevention at the local level.

Further, even if NGOs were more willing to cooperate in the field with each other, they do not have a clear sense of what such an overarching conflict prevention and resolution strategy should entail. Field guidance from traditional agenda-setters has been sporadic; NGO links with key international players in Burundi have been tenuous, or at odds with coordination, leaving NGOs to fend for themselves.

Although Ould Abdallah's willingness to work with NGOs was exceptional, and UNHCR-Bujumbura was helpful, the rest of the UN system has been generally inaccessible to NGOs. Even the UN Human Rights Commission's Special Rapporteur on Burundi and the UN-sponsored International Commission of Inquiry have avoided strong partnerships with NGOs, even human rights and conflict prevention groups that are clearly working toward similar goals. UN personnel tend to restrict contact with NGOs to information sharing, and sustained advocacy on each other's behalf has been sporadic and difficult to maintain. Similarly, embassies of major foreign governments in Bujumbura have generally remained aloof from NGO field operatives. The French and Belgian embassies refused to meet with humanitarian organizations of any nationality, and the largest meeting with NGOs that the U.S. embassy arranged in 1995 discussed drug smuggling. In short, NGOs in the field are not entirely certain of how they collectively can foster conflict prevention and resolution in Burundi. They also receive few leads from governments, the UN, or the OAU.

International Cooperation

In contrast to the situation within Burundi, collaboration efforts at the international level increased after 1994 in quality and extent. President

Ndadaye's assassination and the bloody massacres that followed
received limited press attention, and reactions by governments, NGOs,
and international organizations were subdued compared to the preceding
year's response to Somalia. Humanitarian NGOs were operational
quickly in Burundi; indeed, some were already present when violence
erupted. Human rights organizations also tracked the situation closely. In
addition, the UNHCR, WFP, and the office of Ould Abdallah all became
actively involved, but Ould Abdallah's was the only major initiative
addressing the broader concerns for peace in Burundi. The attention of
foreign governments was confined to providing humanitarian assistance
directly, or through UN, European, or non-governmental agencies.

The genocide in Rwanda from April through July 1994 had as profound an effect on international actors' attitudes toward Burundi as it had
on Burundians. Most of the key governments, international agencies, and
NGOs were complicit in the general failure to try to stop the genocide.
As they scrambled to manage the humanitarian nightmare that followed,
many of these organizations began to realize that, miraculously, Burundi
had managed to stay relatively calm throughout the Rwandan crisis even
though President Ntayamira had perished with Rwandan President Habyarimana in the April 1994 plane crash. Attention soon focused on the
work of Ould Abdallah, who played a catalytic role in brokering the Convention of Government and in negotiating compromise after Minani was
appointed speaker of the National Assembly. His influence during these
and other political crises won him the confidence of political leaders on
both sides of the ethnic divide. Motivated by a mixture of guilt and
outrage over events in Rwanda, governments and non-governmental
actors alike began to step up conflict prevention operations in Burundi,
and came to view Ould Abdallah as the focal point for peace negotiations
and strategic thinking.

Two fora for strategic collaboration at the international level on pre-
venting further bloodshed in Burundi were established in January 1995.
The African-American Institute, the Center for Preventive Action of the
Council on Foreign Relations, Refugees International, and Search for
Common Ground jointly sponsored the Burundi Policy Forum (BPF) for
North American efforts targeting the conflict in Burundi; International
Alert gathered a similar assemblage of European organizations. The BPF
has met nearly every month since its founding, and has been well attended
by representatives from U.S. government and UN agencies, the Burundian
and French embassies, InterAction (the umbrella advocacy organization

for most of the major U.S.-based humanitarian organizations), Human Rights Watch, Amnesty International, the Carter Center, Parliamentarians for Global Action, and as many as thirty other organizations.

International Alert's efforts have featured smaller-scale meetings, choosing instead to cooperate with Scandinavian, Dutch, German, Belgian, French, and other European NGOs to advocate specific policy actions on Burundi by the UN, EU, its member governments, and, to a lesser extent, the OAU and African governments. International Alert also organizes trans-Atlantic conference calls and occasionally hosts meetings with its European partners and members of the BPF to coordinate strategies in Europe and North America toward Burundi.

Early BPF meetings served primarily an information-sharing function, but also demonstrated to Burundians (who, from the government down to refugees in the camps, seemed to be well informed of the proceedings) that the international community was watching, and would not allow either genocide or a repeat of the October 1993 massacres to occur in Burundi. Most organizations in attendance agreed that the greatest priority was supporting and assisting the efforts of Ould Abdallah. He sent general advice and "to do" requests through BPF sponsoring organizations. BPF attendees made recommendations to him through the same channels.

Within months the Forum entered a second phase, as attendees began to advocate specific policy options. Human Rights Watch presented to the BPF evidence of arms flows to leaders and militia of the genocidal former Rwandan government exiled in refugee camps in Zaire. Subsequent pressure from many of the Forum organizations created pressure that resulted in the creation of a UN commission to investigate the matter. Over thirty BPF organizations also signed a statement written by the Center for Preventive Action and released by InterAction in July 1995. It called on the U.S. government to appoint a special envoy to Burundi, to deploy UN military observers at the refugee camps in Zaire and Tanzania, and to address the issue of accountability. Alternatives continue to be advocated on a regular basis, such as the deployment of a U.S. military attaché to the embassy in Bujumbura, and support for the Burundian judiciary.

The BPF has entered a third phase of development, moving beyond advocating that governments and international organizations adopt policies, actually to making such policies themselves. Nearly every two weeks, several BPF organizations and U.S. administration officials meet informally to discuss security issues in Burundi; they deliberate on policy options open to the United States, the UN, and NGOs, and BPF groups help to pressure initiatives through the bureaucracies in question. U.S. National Security Advisor Anthony Lake met with a number of these BPF groups in July and December of 1995, discussing policies proposed by Forum members, and asking for creative ideas on how to address the crisis.

NGO policy-making has also been evident in independent actions, like the Carter Center's regional summits in Cairo and Tunis. The UN Secretary-General had assigned an envoy to lay the groundwork for a UN-sponsored regional summit on security issues, but after hearing from the envoy that little support could be found in the region for such an event, President Carter and his Center managed to arrange it within a few months. Similar perceived dawdling on the part of the UN, key Security Council members, and the OAU provoked International Alert and other European NGOs to organize a civilian contingent of human rights observers for Burundi; preparations began in April 1996 to implement this plan.

Perhaps the most striking example of NGO assertiveness in making policy at the international level has been the way in which Burundians, governments, international organizations, and NGOs have supported the mediation of former Tanzanian President Nyerere. Should the situation in Burundi continue to deteriorate and Nyerere's mission fail to rectify it, however, one can expect further assertiveness on the part of NGOs globally. Humanitarian organizations, and other members of the BPF in particular, can be expected to undertake a number of independent initiatives, especially if the U.S. government does not follow through on its commitment to take strong measures to stave off civil war.

Conclusion

International organizations and NGOs still operate to a large extent under theoretical models shaped during a time when governments held overwhelming sway over the political realm. Humanitarian organizations still see themselves primarily as apolitical service providers. Human rights groups target their advocacy efforts primarily on governments, although humanitarian missions and international organizations are now increasingly being held responsible for contributing to a rights-respecting environment.[10] Conflict resolution projects often assume that they can promote local reconciliation, even though they might not fully understand the ways in which those efforts affect overall peace negotiations. International organizations assert that they are the sum of their parts, the member states, and that, because macro-decision-making power belongs to those states, micro-planning at the project level is similarly circumscribed. All of these organizations are now questioning their assumptions, and new models of action are being pieced together.

Most of these new conceptions are built on the understanding that governments will not be playing the pervasive role that they did in the past. Although a nuanced understanding of the politics of a crisis has certainly developed among many of these organizations, most still do not recognize themselves as political actors whose decisions affect the governance of the region in question. NGOs, in particular, have not come to a clear understanding of their own elevated political stature and the subsequent power and responsibilities this change reflects.

The first such responsibility that NGOs must develop further is that of accountability. Since most of these organizations are dependent on governments, philanthropic organizations, businesses, or membership contributions for the funding of their operations, they are inherently accountable to their financial sponsors. Their relationships with their target populations, however, are not as well defined. Certainly, these organizations are responsive to the concerns of the people who benefit from their services. Nonetheless, to what extent do and should these beneficiaries have a say in how those services are provided?

Refugees and displaced persons on both sides of the ethnic divide in Burundi have claimed a right to the relief that they receive, and have also made their displeasure clear when they have felt that NGOs favored one side or the other. Refugee leaders have also used food and other international assistance as tradeable commodities. What can be seen by NGOs as abuses of their services may be perceived by the recipients as acceptable within the parameters of the relationship. In balancing their obligations to donors and recipients, NGOs often give their target populations great voice in local logistics, but little in terms of the internal functioning of the organization or the broader strategic decisions, such as whether to undertake the mission and the duration of engagement. These broad decisions can have great impact on the governance of the target populations involved.

Similarly, NGOs must rethink the sources of the legitimacy of their actions. International human rights covenants, laws concerning refugees, and a growing body of precedents clearly provide a strong justification for the involvement of humanitarian and human rights NGOs to some degree in a country in crisis. But do these sources support organizations making inherently political decisions on the part of the country's population? This question is particularly difficult for conflict resolution NGOs, which do not have a body of international legal documents upon which to rely. Some of these groups cite religious doctrine to legitimize their efforts, while others echo a less explicit common morality of peacemaking and saving lives.

So as not to detract from the precarious trust with which they are endowed, NGOs that independently choose to mediate among government officials, opposition, extremists, and other sectors of society need to make a more defensible case for their actions. Such mediations have occurred on a regular basis in Burundi—at times to the detriment of peace efforts on the part of the United Nations and foreign governments.

Without some agreed upon means of determining the scope of legitimate NGO action, efforts to promote the rule of law can be expected to be undermined by NGOs not observing rules recognized by all people involved. Current calls for the review of humanitarian and other organizations' mandates reflect these doubts over the legitimacy of NGO action within the realm of governance.

International organizations generally have much clearer parameters of accountability and legitimacy in terms of involvement in conflict prevention and resolution. They are creatures of their member states, and as such draw their legitimacy from the mandates and rules decided by those members. International organizations are also held strictly accountable by those members, who call for a mission and write its terms of involvement. The concerns of the target populations are presumed to be voiced by their home governments, or from the Security Council in cases where the home government is irresponsible or non-existent. In practice, however, the UN often finds its disparate personnel having to make a range of governing decisions, both in the field and at headquarters, that are well beyond the vague mandate from its member states. While member states have been quick to blame the United Nations when it runs into difficulties stemming from such decisions, they have been slow to clarify parameters of UN authority at the operational or strategic levels.

Even more ambiguous for both NGOs and international organizations has been the relationship among them, governments, and parties to a conflict. The foremost issue has been coordination, a question that has been ubiquitous in Burundi. The litany of different initiatives is staggering: The UNHCR, UNDP, WFP, and SRSG offices (each having its own policies and rarely consulting with the others); the OAU; U.S. Special Envoy Richard Bogosian; EU Special Envoy Aldo Aiello; the European Community Humanitarian Organization; the Swedish government delegation; President Nyerere's mission; International Alert; the Carter Center; the Community of St. Egidio; Parliamentarians for Global Action; the BPF partners; over thirty humanitarian organizations; church-based initiatives; and so on. Just prior to the involvement of President Nyerere, a number of organizations were beginning to work toward objectives in several different directions, often at cross-purposes. Not surprisingly, parties to the Burundian conflict learned quickly to use the disorganization among the international actors to undermine the positions of their opponents.

The more that these organizations play a role in the governance of the populations that they serve, the greater the obligation must be that they coordinate their agendas. As detailed above, coordination in the field in Burundi has been minimal, while international cooperation has seen increasing success. After eight months of arranging the event, Médecins Sans Frontières was finally able to organize an NGO forum (CLIO) in Bujumbura in March 1996. This meeting, combined with the support for Nyerere at the international level, indicates progress in coordination, at least in the case of Burundi. Overall, however, no formal obligation exists to ensure that policies of different organizations work toward common goals. In some cases, such cooperation is even discouraged. Ould Abdallah, who went to great lengths to work with NGOs, was criticized within the UN system for doing so.

Limits and delineation of areas of authority and responsibility must be developed among governments, NGOs, international organizations, and others in governing roles during a crisis. Those with the power to impose agendas need to understand the extent to which they should consult with other actors. If conflict prevention and resolution in cases like Burundi are to have a single model for international action, then partnership must be the guide. A flexible, accountable process is needed, in which responsibilities are divided among key actors, and through which organizations can recognize their own place in the politics of the region. The forum model used with respect to Burundi in the United States and Europe, and now by organizations in Bujumbura, offers a prototype for such a process, even if a loose one. A new layer of institutionalization is not so important as are agreements among organizations on common objectives, and collaborative efforts towards achieving those goals.

States still have leading roles to play in preventing and resolving conflicts. The heightened attention that the United States has paid to Burundi since 1995 has been pivotal in convincing important Burundian forces, primarily the army, to avoid waging a full-scale war. The United States has also taken a leading role in the UN Security Council in promoting UN initiatives regarding Burundi, although most of these proposals have required modification. At the same time, however, it is clear that if NGOs had not taken an activist role to provoke U.S. action, many other global demands could easily have overtaken the claims of Burundi.

Before widespread killing takes place, NGOs may be able to take the lead in preventing conflicts, provided that important foreign interests are not present. NGOs, in partnership with each other and with the UN, may be able to work with leading factions within a country to foster early resolution of disputes. As in Burundi, however, once conditions of war have broken out, these organizations clearly need to act in tandem with governments. At the same time, all of these actors must recognize the increased roles of international organizations and NGOs in decisions and activities that are governmental in nature. Development of a partnership that utilizes the comparative advantage of each, while minimizing the negative effects of their separate natures, would be a great step forward in improving the international community's ability to prevent and resolve the devastating conflicts witnessed in Burundi and elsewhere.

Notes

1. See UN Doc. S/1995/190 or A/50/94 (8 March 1995) for the text of the Convention on Government, which remains in force until 9 June 1998.

2. The UN Commission on Human Rights appointed a Special Rapporteur for Human Rights on Burundi in April 1995. UN Doc. E/1995/54 (25 April 1995).

3. The International Commission of Inquiry for Burundi submitted its first interim report to the UN Security Council on 20 December 1995. UN Doc. S/1996/8 (5 January 1996).

4. UN Doc. S/1996/116 (15 February 1996).

5. The UN Security Council also rejected the Secretary-General's proposal. UN Doc. S/RES/1049 (5 March 1996).

6. Economist Intelligence Unit, *Country Report*, Uganda, Rwanda, Burundi (March 1996), 35.

7. The UN Security Council extended the United Nations Assistance Mission for Rwanda (UNAMIR) mandate on 12 December 1995, but voted to withdraw all of the peacekeepers by 8 March 1996. The UN resolution reduced the number of troops to 1,200 and military observers to 200. The civilian police component was completely withdrawn. UN Doc. S/RES/1029 (12 December 1995).

8. Approximately thirty humanitarian organizations operate in Burundi, including Action Aid, CARE (Canada), Catholic Relief Services, Concern, the ICRC, International action contra la faim, the International Rescue Committee, Médecins Sans Frontières (France, Belgium, and Holland), Oxfam, and World Vision.

9. The United Nations tapped into this wealth of information when the Secretary-General requested NGOs in the Great Lakes region to collate information at their disposal relating to the mandate of the International Commission of Inquiry for Rwanda, which investigated reports on arming Hutu militia in eastern Zaire, and make that information available to the UN Commission as soon as possible. UN Doc. S/RES/1013 (7 September 1995). See UN Doc. S/1996/67 (29 January 1996) for the report on the Commission's findings.

10. See, for example, Rakiya Omaar and Alex de Waal, "Humanitarianism Unbound? Current Dilemmas Facing Multi-Mandate Relief Operations in Political Emergencies" (unpublished paper, African Rights Project, London, 1994).

NGOs, EARLY ACTION, AND PREVENTIVE DIPLOMACY

CHAPTER ELEVEN

Conclusions: NGOs, Early Warning, Early Action, and Preventive Diplomacy

Robert I. Rotberg

EARLY WARNING is not as easy and as obvious as it sounds. Nor is preventive diplomacy straightforward. Preventive action, preferably early, is essential, but is more easily described than achieved. The role of NGOs in sounding the tocsin of alarm in situations of incipient intrastate conflict, especially in ethnically divided societies, is generally problematic, contextually specific and determined, and fraught with unanticipated obstacles and tactical traps.

Those are among the most salient conclusions of this multi-authored study of preventive diplomacy and early warning across a four-continent set of bitterly divided states. This study pays particular attention to how and under what circumstances NGOs have attempted to forestall the onset of hostilities or contained conflicts after they have erupted. How effectively have NGOs managed to intervene for peace? Have their efforts been heeded? Have they made a difference, and where and why?

Not all NGOs are created equal. International and local NGOs obviously operate differently and with different constraints. Some are well-funded, some are funded hardly at all. Human rights NGOs, refugee NGOs, relief NGOs, developmental NGOs, religious NGOs, and more specialized NGOs overlap in their activities (and usually fit more than one of the categories listed) and in their operations. They hardly think as one regarding the efficacy, much less the wisdom, of early warning. For some, preventive diplomacy has little meaning; for others intervening to prevent conflict is natural and fundamental. For all of these obvious reasons, a first conclusion is that generalizing about the role of NGOs in ethnically divided societies is dangerous and difficult. Moreover, because each conflict is by definition unique, responses to the tensions and troubles inherent in intrastate antagonisms are bound to be specific. That is a caveat, and not just for heuristic purposes.

We generalize about and make recommendations regarding the future performance of NGOs, and about early warning and preventive diplomacy, conscious only of the disarray of the available data. The cases in this book are representative in their complexity, and emblematic of the problems posed for both scholarship and action by all that differentiates them, more than what unites them.

Preventive diplomacy is excellent and essential in theory, but nearly always the preventers are too late, especially when (as is common) there are no international or supranational mechanisms available to compel contending parties to separate or (particularly) to mandate governments to desist from persecuting ethnic groups who are disadvantaged or weak. That is why early warning is such a complex concept, and so hard to practice. If those who become aware of impending eruptions have nowhere certain to turn—if they seek to sound an alarm but are unsure that it will be heard—then efforts capable of initiating preventive diplomacy may too often be stillborn. They will surely be difficult to sustain.

This lack of a direct channel for the transmission of early warnings leads to the use of any and all available alternatives: international and local media, diplomatic missions, UN and regional bodies, and ad hoc informal networks of international NGOs. It is clear that the cries of local NGOs need to be amplified by NGOs with international constituencies, that collaboration by NGOs across national borders is helpful, and that mass-based organizations can yell louder and with greater effect than more narrowly focused groups, however worthy.

Arousing the consciousness of the world community may sometimes result from press and television reporting or the public presentations of NGOs; often, however, as the cases in this book demonstrate, the episodic quality of the alarms, the indirect (and sometimes suspect) nature of the resulting flows of communication, and the easily questioned legitimacy of the ringers of alarms have too often muted the tocsin or retarded its timeliness.

A new network specifically devoted to early warnings, and linking local and international NGOs to a central facility, could in theory enhance the timely quality of those signals, legitimate them, and enable the outcries of smaller as well as larger NGOs to be heard in the head-quarters of the UN and in Washington, London, Bonn, Paris, and Tokyo. The central facility could evaluate incoming bells of alarm; faint noises would be amplified and transmitted with greater assurances that they would be heard, if not acted upon, down the world's dominant corridors of power.

Had a recognizable channel existed in 1994, the Rwandan genocide might have been forestalled. The fears of local NGO leaders might then have been articulated more determinedly and forcefully; the world com-munity might have responded; the UN mandate might have been broad-ened and preventive diplomacy and preventive interposition might have been possible. But the details of the Rwandan experience, the continuing crisis of Burundi, and the experiences of both Guatemala and Macedonia imply that such a network would be almost impossible to deploy, and that using it would have been and might be much too dangerous for NGOs, especially local ones.

The dangers to NGOs in situations of state-sponsored repression are obvious, as the cases of Guatemala and Nigeria show and is apparent in Macedonia. Being perceived as partial is a continuing issue for NGOs. It is unavoidable in intrastate conflicts like that of the Sudan and Sri Lanka. In all of the cases discussed in this book, NGOs have been com-pelled to seek attention—to sound alarms and illumine gross human rights violations—in opposition to men with guns and, almost every-where, without the backing of a sovereign state.

No one is prepared to listen before a crisis. When the shootings or the massacres begin, it is too late for warnings, if not too late for contain-ment and prevention, whether diplomatic or otherwise.

The need for a method of amplifying warnings is apparent. During the Cold War the superpowers used a large array of listening devices to dis-cover what their opponents were saying and communicating. The pre-vention of bloodshed across divided societies demands analogous methods and mechanisms, and they can surely be created. Given the will and modest funds, NGOs can devise a network for early warning, and employ it effectively (despite the caveats of Fraenkel).

Journalists and television correspondents already provide warnings of crises. But editors, readers, and policy-makers—even the reporters them-selves—do not always understand or respond effectively to those warn-ings (as they failed to respond to warnings of famine in the early 1980s).

The UN has its own system of gathering intelligence about future trouble spots. The world's powers pay diplomats to report on anything which would roil the internal waters. No superpower wants to be caught (as so many are) unaware of smoldering fires soon to ignite into conflagrations. The headquarters of international NGOs cannot afford to be poorly informed about intrastate antagonisms. For all of the actors, evacuation and relief is always more costly than prevention, and warnings are thus integral to their operations.

Yet, in Rwanda, before the genocide of 1994 began, UN officials on the ground and diplomatic representatives of the major powers in Kigali knew a massacre was likely; they were more certain than the most acute NGO leaders. And nothing was done. Early action was definitely an option, and nothing was done. Paradoxically, NGOs in Rwanda need not have warned; their most useful role would have been to exert a powerful pressure on the world community to be prepared to act early, and, in the event, to stanch bloodshed from the days of the first killings.

The problem is often not the availability of alarms, or the fact that not all alarms are heard. The problem is what to do with the alarms, and how to mobilize effectively when an alarm is deemed credible. Indeed, in Guatemala, intrastate conflict was endemic; there was a pattern of injustice and a climate of intolerance that altered the role of NGOs from simple warning to raising the incessant hue and cry of compassionate alarm. Crow and Nwankwo suggest that NGOs should investigate and document the role of government agents in fomenting communal violence, as NGOs did so well in Guatemala.

The critical missing ingredient of preventive diplomacy is early action. NGOs can warn all they want; who is to act? How can the world community mobilize itself to act in 1996 and 1997 in Rwanda and Burundi to prevent genocide? How can continuing battles in the Sudan or Sri Lanka be avoided? When long-festering antagonisms in Nigeria boil over, as the chapter in this book warns, who will act, and who will act in a timely manner?

Several of the co-authors of this book argue that there always is a sufficiency of alarm, much of it loud enough to be heard and early enough to make a difference. But action is nearly always belated. Neither the UN system nor the world's powers are capable, given the politics of world order and domestic political realities, of reacting rapidly enough to make a difference. Nor are there accepted ways to interfere within a sovereign jurisdiction. UN Charter Chapter VI and VII decisions are always after the fact. What is needed, obviously, is an effective way of mobilizing world order diplomacy and world order coercion to investigate threats to intrastate as well as interstate order, and then to prevent them.

Burundi, because of its own history and the genocide in neighboring Rwanda, is about the only case where there is a sense of urgency, active NGO involvement with the encouragement of the larger powers and the UN, and an awareness that prevention is essential. Yet even with all of the attention being paid to a situation which has been fired up for decades and, in its current phase, has been hot since 1993, the effectiveness of early action is hindered by the obduracy of Burundi's army and its government.

In Macedonia, the basing there of contingents of foreign troops has helped to prevent the spread of war from neighboring Bosnia. But other early action to diminish Slav-Albanian tensions will probably be influenced little by renewed or additional early warning arrangements. In retrospect, it is clear that in Guatemala and the Sudan, too, warnings were ample; early action or action by way of interposition of any meaningful kind was never possible. It is still practicably difficult.

There is a continuing role for NGOs in conflict prevention, but it is not necessarily a conventional one. NGOs remain the most dispersed and thus often the best placed reporters of rural as well as urban attacks on minorities. Individual NGOs are often the first outsiders to become aware of groups readying revenge, of disappearances, and of covert military incursions and government-sponsored massacres. Verifying and sharing this information is usually dangerous and difficult, which is why cooperation and information sharing by NGOs within an endangered state and beyond is so critical and so obvious, and so rarely accomplished. NGOs compete for attention and respect within nations at risk and, in the mother countries, for renown and financial wherewithal. Any arrangements which, as in Macedonia, can ally NGOs, local and international, for peace will be a crucial and fundamental advance capable of sounding meaningful alarms and encouraging the early preventive action of the world community.

Creating a clearinghouse for situational reporting from the field by NGOs and national groups of NGOs would also help. Despite the insufficiency of such a device, and despite the fact that early warnings are not the entire answer—that how to deter intrastate conflicts, not how to warn about them, is the critical question—an international focal point capable of magnifying the knowledge of NGOs would be helpful. The existence of such a center could make it easier to highlight impending catastrophes. It could publicize otherwise easy to ignore crises and help put pressure upon the world community to act early or to act at all.

Dedicated and impassioned individual NGO spokespersons finally persuaded the UN and national governments to recognize genocide in Rwanda. Persons like them, and individual diplomats and UN personnel, have done and are doing the same in Burundi. Creating a center for the peaceful resolution and forceful prevention or containment of intrastate ethnic, religious, or intercommunal conflict could enlarge and help to channel the continuing efforts of similar individuals, local NGOs, and international NGOs.

The troubled world at the end of this century and the beginning of the next will know no end of antagonism between groups that once lived peacefully side by side, intermarried, shared common languages and cultures, and were ruled by a classically colonial or a Cold War power. The demise of Soviet imperialism has replaced hegemonic competition across states with competition for resources within states. That striving for power and resources within new, largely artificial, states will continue to motivate disappearances, brutalities, ethnic cleansings, massacres of innocent civilians, and genocide.

It will inevitably continue to be the role of NGOs to sound the bells of alarm, to discomfort blood-stained local governments, to plead with world powers and the UN for help and action, and to expose and publicize the gory details of human rights abuses and all too frequent killing fields. That their voices need to continue to be heard is an obvious conclusion. That their voices can be heard best, and early action by governments and the international community enhanced if and when their outcries can be recognized, focused, and converted into public pressure, is also obvious but important. The sooner NGOs can create that center of concern, the sooner innocent and endangered lives around the globe will be spared.

About the Authors

Martha A. Chen is a Research Associate at the Harvard Institute for International Development, a lecturer at the Kennedy School of Government, and program director of the Program on Non-Governmental Organizations at the Harvard Institute for International Development. She received her Ph.D. from the University of Pennsylvania.

Melissa E. Crow was the Sophie Silberberg Fellow at Human Rights Watch/Africa, 1994–1995. Crow previously worked for the Constitutional Rights Project in Lagos, Nigeria, as well as the United Nations High Commissioner for Refugees and the Lawyers Committee for Human Rights. She is a member of the investigative team of the International Tribunal for Rwanda. Her publications include Human Rights Watch/Africa, "The Ogoni Crisis: A Case-Study of Military Repression in Southeastern Nigeria," *A Human Rights Watch Short Report* (July 1995) and *Guide to Human Rights Litigation in Nigeria* (New York, 1994), which she co-authored with Clement Nwankwo. Crow graduated from Brown University.

Francis M. Deng is a Senior Fellow and head of the Africa Project in the Brookings Institution's Foreign Policy Studies Program. He is also the Special Representative of the United Nations Secretary-General on Internally Displaced Persons. He served as Human Rights Officer in the

UN Secretariat in New York. He then joined the Sudan's foreign service, where he served as Ambassador to Canada, Scandinavian countries, and the United States, and for five years as Minister of State for Foreign Affairs. After leaving the foreign service in 1983, Deng joined the Woodrow Wilson International Center for Scholars, first as Guest Scholar and later as Senior Research Associate. He was the first Rockefeller Brothers Fund Distinguished Fellow and one of the first Jennings Randolph Distinguished Fellows of the United States Institute of Peace. Deng has taught at New York University and Columbia Law School and was a visiting lecturer at Yale Law School. He has authored or edited twenty books; his latest Brookings publications include *War of Visions: Conflict of Identities in the Sudan* (Washington, D.C., 1995); *Protecting the Dispossessed: A Challenge for the International Community* (Washington, D.C., 1993); *Challenges of Famine Relief: Emergency Operations in the Sudan*, with Larry Minear (Washington, D.C., 1992); *Conflict Resolution in Africa*, co-edited with I. William Zartman (Washington, D.C., 1991); and *Human Rights in Africa: Cross-Cultural Perspectives*, co-edited with Abdullahi Ahmed An-Na'im (Washington, D.C., 1990). Deng received his LL.B. from Khartoum University, and his J.S.D. from Yale Law School.

Alison L. Des Forges is a historian specializing in the lacustrine region of east central Africa. A founding member of Africa Watch (later Human Rights Watch/Africa), she has served as its research specialist on Rwanda and Burundi since 1991. In that capacity, she has undertaken fifteen investigative missions in the region. Des Forges was co-chair of the International Commission of Investigation into Human Rights Abuse in Rwanda and chair of the similar commission for Burundi. She has published extensively about the history and current situation in that part of Africa. She has an A.B. from Harvard University and earned her Ph.D. at Yale University.

Eran Fraenkel has been Executive Director of Search for Common Ground in Macedonia since 1994. Fraenkel has been a student and scholar of the Balkans since 1970, and has spent more than five years living, working, and conducting historical and ethnographical research in Macedonia. Prior to assuming the directorship of Search's projects in Skopje, Fraenkel worked as an independent scholar and editor. Fraenkel earned his B.A. and M.A. from Indiana University, and his Ph.D. in history from the University of Pennsylvania.

Darren Kew is Program Associate, Center for Preventive Action, Council on Foreign Relations, where he helps manage the Center. He is developing a project to foster preventive action regarding Nigeria, and managed the Center's participation in the Burundi Policy Forum. Previously, Kew was a researcher for the Reebok Human Rights Award and a research associate for the Constitutional Rights Project in Lagos, Nigeria. He also was an editorial assistant for *Foreign Policy*. Kew has published articles on Nigeria in the *Muslim Politics Report* and the *Constitutional Rights Journal*, and is currently finishing a longer work on the Western Sahara and the international self-determination regime. Kew has a B.A. from the University of Notre Dame, and an M.A.L.D. from the Fletcher School of Law and Diplomacy, Tufts University.

Tom Lent is Resident Representative, Guatemala and Honduras, for Redd Barna (the Norwegian division of Save the Children). He has worked in Guatemala for ten years, from 1976–1984, and since 1993. Lent has also worked as International Training Director for Save the Children/US, and as International Training Coordinator for Redd Barna covering Asia and Africa, from a base in Zimbabwe. He served in the Peace Corps in Afghanistan from 1972–1975. He earned both his B.A. and M.A. in International Relations from the School of International Service at American University.

Emily MacFarquhar writes about Asian politics as a contributing editor of *U.S. News and World Report.* She was formerly International Editor and Asia Editor of the *Economist.* She graduated from Wellesley College and earned her M.A. from Harvard in East Asian Studies.

Rachel M. McCleary teaches in the Department of Government at Georgetown University. She is completing a book on the 1993 coup of Guatemalan President Jorge Serrano Elías and the role of the private business sector in restoring constitutional rule. In 1995, on a Fulbright research grant, McCleary lived in Guatemala for six months conducting research on contemporary politics. Prior to that, McCleary was Program Officer at the United States Institute of Peace. She taught at Princeton University and has contributed articles, chapters, and case studies to a variety of scholarly and general interest publications. She edited *Seeking Justice: Ethics and International Affairs* (Boulder, CO, 1992) and holds a Ph.D. from the University of Chicago.

Kalypso Nicolaïdis is Assistant Professor of Public Policy at the Kennedy School of Government, Harvard University, where she teaches courses on negotiation, international institutions after the Cold War, and the European Community. She also taught at the École Nationale d'Administration in Paris. She has published on the EC, Eastern Europe, and GATT, and is the editor of *Strategic Trends in Services: An Enquiry Into the World Services Economy* (New York, 1989). She has worked for or with the OECD, GATT, UNCTAD, IIASA, and the EC, and is currently Chairman of the Services World Forum. Nicolaïdis graduated from the Institut d'Études Politiques and holds an M.P.A. from Harvard's Kennedy School of Government and a Ph.D. in Political Economy and Government from Harvard University.

Clement Nwankwo is Executive Director of the Constitutional Rights Project, Nigeria. He is active in human rights issues in Nigeria and is the recipient of several awards and distinctions in that area, including the Human Rights Monitor's Award from Human Rights Watch. He is a fellow of Ashoka Innovators for the Public and a member of the Nigerian Bar Association. Nwankwo has written numerous articles on human rights and democracy, and is co-author of *The Bail Process and Human Rights in Nigeria* (Lagos, 1992) and *The Crisis of Press Freedom in Nigeria* (Lagos, 1993). He is Editor-in-Chief of the *Constitutional Rights Journal*. Nwankwo received his LL.B. at the University of Nigeria and graduated as a Barrister at Law from Nigerian Law School.

Violeta Petroska Beška is an Associate Professor of Psychology at the University of Skopje, Republic of Macedonia, and Director of the Ethnic Conflict Resolution Project, which is dedicated to training and mobilizing Macedonian citizens to assume an active role in the resolution of seemingly intractable ethnic conflicts. She is the author of several conflict resolution manuals and the author of the only conflict-resolution primer prepared by a Macedonian professional for a domestic audience: *Conflicts: Their Nature and Ways of Resolving Them.* Her work has been done in collaboration with Search for Common Ground, Washington, D.C.; International Center for Cooperation and Conflict Resolution, Columbia University; Centre for Applied Studies in International Negotiations, Geneva; and the Balkan Peace Project, Cambridge, Massachusetts.

Robert I. Rotberg is President of the World Peace Foundation and Coordinator of the Southern African program of the Harvard Institute for International Development. He also teaches at Harvard's Kennedy School of Government. He was Professor of Political Science and History at M.I.T. (1968–87), and then became Academic Vice President of Tufts University and President of Lafayette College before returning to Cambridge. He is the author of more than two dozen books and numerous articles on the politics and history of Africa and Haiti. He holds an A.B. from Oberlin College, an M.P.A. from Princeton University, and a D.Phil. from the University of Oxford.

Richard A. Sollom was Associate Protection Officer for the United Nations High Commissioner for Refugees in Burundi, 1994–1995, where he advocated for Rwandan and Burundian refugees. He was Resettlement Officer for the United Nations operation in Somalia, 1994, overseeing the resettlement of internally displaced persons. Sollom also worked in the Organization of American States in Haiti, in 1993 as a Human Rights Observer and in 1995 as an Election Observer. Sollom received his B.A. from Macalester College and his M.A.L.D. from the Fletcher School of Law and Diplomacy, Tufts University.

Neelan Tiruchelvam is a member of Parliament in Sri Lanka. He is also Director of the International Centre for Ethnic Studies, and Director of the Law and Society Trust. Tiruchelvam is a member of the Select Committee on Constitutional Reform. His LL.D. is from the Harvard Law School.

The World Peace Foundation

THE WORLD PEACE FOUNDATION was created in 1910 by the imagination and fortune of Edwin Ginn, the Boston publisher, to encourage international peace and cooperation. The Foundation seeks to advance the cause of world peace through study, analysis, and the advocacy of wise action. As an operating, not a grant-giving foundation, it provides financial support only for projects which it has initiated itself.

Edwin Ginn shared the hope of many of his contemporaries that permanent peace could be achieved. That dream was denied by the outbreak of World War I, but the Foundation has continued to attempt to overcome obstacles to international peace and cooperation, drawing for its funding on the endowment bequeathed by the founder. In its early years, the Foundation focused its attention on building the peacekeeping capacity of the League of Nations, and then on the development of world order through the United Nations. The Foundation established and nurtured the premier scholarly journal in its field, *International Organization*, now in its forty-ninth year.

From the 1950s to the early 1990s, mostly a period of bipolar conflict when universal collective security remained unattainable, the Foundation concentrated its activities on improving the working of world order mechanisms, regional security, transnational relations, and the impact of public opinion on American foreign policy. From 1980 to 1993 the Foundation published nineteen books and seven reports on Third World security; on South Africa and other states of southern Africa; on Latin America, the Caribbean, and Puerto Rico; on migration; and on the international aspects of traffic in narcotics. In 1994 and 1995, the Foundation published books on Europe after the Cold War; on the United States, southern Europe, and the countries of the Mediterranean basin; and on reducing the world traffic in conventional arms.

The Foundation is now focusing its energies and resources on a series of interrelated projects entitled Preventing Intercommunal Conflict and Humanitarian Crises. These projects proceed from the assumption that large-scale human suffering, wherever it occurs, is a serious and continuing threat to the peace of the world, both engendering and resulting from ethnic, religious, and other intrastate and cross-border conflicts. The Foundation is examining how the forces of world order may most effectively engage in preventive diplomacy, create early warning systems leading to early preventive action, achieve regional conflict avoidance, and eradicate the underlying causes of intergroup enmity and warfare.

Index

277